LAND CONTROL AND SOCIAL STRUCTURE IN INDIAN HISTORY

# LAND CONTROL AND SOCIAL STRUCTURE IN INDIAN HISTORY

*Edited by* ROBERT ERIC FRYKENBERG

*Madison, Milwaukee, and London, 1969*

THE UNIVERSITY OF WISCONSIN PRESS

Published by
The University of Wisconsin Press
Box 1379, Madison, Wisconsin 53701
The University of Wisconsin Press, Ltd.
27–29 Whitfield Street, London, W.1

# List of
# Contributors

BERNARD S. COHN
> Professor of Anthropology and History, University of Chicago, Chicago, Illinois

AINSLIE T. EMBREE
> Professor of History, Duke University, Durham, North Carolina

ROBERT ERIC FRYKENBERG
> Associate Professor of History, University of Wisconsin, Madison, Wisconsin

S. NURUL HASAN
> Professor of History, Aligarh Muslim University, Aligarh, India

THOMAS R. METCALF
> Associate Professor of History, University of California, Berkeley, California

NILMANI MUKHERJEE
> Lecturer in History, University of Calcutta, Calcutta, India

WALTER C. NEALE
> Professor of Economics, University of Tennessee, Knoxville, Tennessee

TAPAN RAYCHAUDHURI
> Director, Delhi School of Economics, University of Delhi, Delhi, India

BURTON STEIN
> Professor of History, University of Hawaii, Honolulu, Hawaii

# Preface

Returning from meetings of the American Historical Association in 1963, Professor Burton Stein and I discussed issues on the nature of land control in India which had been raised during a panel session. We concluded that, unless important conceptual problems about social structure and land control within Indian history were dealt with, increasingly large numbers of studies, based upon legal and administrative terminology and weighed down with Western preconceptions, would have less and less to say. Stein put it succinctly later: "We have reached a point of diminishing returns on our terminological capital. However excellent our data . . . and however diligent our effort, our intellectual output, measured in better general understanding and useful research hypotheses, is poor and becoming poorer."[1]

These failings, we agreed, were not due to any apparent shortage of good source materials, nor to any lack of analytical capacity. Absence of adequate categories and concepts for analysis, inadvertent confusion of data relating to ideal rather than real conditions, and failure to perceive developmental and causal elements and to distinguish between static and dynamic factors of movement and process seemed to us to be the shortcomings. If not faced, they would continually bring the validity of future studies into question.

We next discussed different ways by which the problems of our discipline might be approached. Obviously there could be no substitute for further hard thinking by individuals. Indeed, one might hope that some one person would find a key to unlock the doors to a closet full of

---

1. "Some Comments on the Notes of the Discussions at the Indian Land Tenure Symposium," mimeographed for participants of the symposium held at the University of California, Berkeley, 1964.

new conceptual, categorical, functional, and structural blueprints. One might even hope, moreover, that such a person would be able to provide us with an analytical formula to explain the rich deposits of data available to us with a comprehensiveness and symmetry hitherto unknown.

Since we could see no such genius on the horizon, we considered the possible benefits of joint endeavor—a session of "brainstorming" by those colleagues who shared our concern. In hopes that some meetings might serve to stimulate new intellectual insights and inspire new efforts, if not also to focus wider attention on the problems, two initial proposals were set forth. First, a colloquium might be held at the University of Wisconsin, to which a series of specialists would be invited to present papers concerning their own particular studies on social structure and land control in India. Second, a summer workshop might be conducted in which, after carefully examining each other's papers, we could engage in rigorously critical and, we hoped, fruitful discussions.

A colloquium on The Influence of Social Structure on Land Control in Indian History was held at the University of Wisconsin in the spring semester of 1964. Interested faculty and graduate students attended sessions at which papers were presented by Professors John Broomfield, Bernard S. Cohn, Ainslie Embree, John R. McLane, Thomas R. Metcalf, Morris D. Morris, Walter C. Neale, Tapan Raychaudhuri, and Burton Stein. In addition, papers were requested from Professors B. G. Grover, S. Nurul Hasan, Walter Hauser, Dharma Kumar, Nilmani Mukherjee, and Peter Reeves.

In April of the same year, a panel on the subject was held at the annual meetings of the Association for Asian Studies in Washington, D.C. With Stein as chairman, papers were presented by Cohn, Frykenberg, Metcalf, and Neale, and critical comment and discussion by Raychaudhuri. At an informal meeting held immediately thereafter, all agreed on the need for further discussion. Since a strong program in South Asian studies was scheduled for the summer of 1964 at the University of California, Metcalf extended an invitation on behalf of that institution's Center for South Asia Studies. Accordingly, a symposium on Indian Land Tenure and Social Structure met in Berkeley from June 29 to July 10, 1964. Each day a separate paper became the focal point of vigorous discussion. Around the table were Metcalf (chairman), Frykenberg, McLane, Morris, Raychaudhuri, and Stein. A circle of interested colleagues and graduate students also participated. Exchanges of views were blunt, often exciting, and sufficiently stimulating to carry over into hours of later informal discussion.

As a consequence of the exchanges of views which had been going on for eighteen months and which culminated at the symposium, two papers were circulated: "Some Notes on the Discussions at the Indian Land Tenure Symposium, Berkeley, June 29 to July 10, 1964," compiled by Barbara Daly (now Metcalf) and Thomas Metcalf; and "Some Comments on the Notes of the Discussions at the Indian Land Tenure Symposium," by Burton Stein. As a result, papers went back to workbenches.

After the mauling which most papers received during our discussions, some colleagues are still working on their studies; some will publish their work independently; and still others, although far from sure about the validity of all arguments, have decided to join this cooperative venture. Our aim, in committing this volume to print, is to provoke controversy, arouse interest, stimulate new ideas, and inspire further research. We recognize failings which books of this nature usually possess. The cry of "Too many cooks . . . !" is generally not without justification. Nevertheless, we are of one mind in the conviction that the field of investigation, although thorny, is so important to a proper understanding of historical developments within the Indian subcontinent that we cannot procrastinate. The wringing of hands and shrugging of shoulders perhaps can go on indefinitely while we wait for "the answer to arrive" or "the genius to appear." The more impatient of us, however, would rather launch this modest but, we hope, stimulating pilot project and hope that it will start new chain reactions of thought and research. Throughout the volume, we have tried to standardize the many variant Indian spellings for land and revenue terms by relying on the form given in H. H. Wilson's *Glossary of Judicial and Revenue Terms* (London, 1855).

Acknowledgements and gratitude are due to the Departments of History and of Indian Studies, in the University of Wisconsin, Madison, and to the Center for South Asia Studies, in the University of California, Berkeley, for sponsoring the colloquium and the symposium which made possible our intellectual confrontations. To Mr. Thompson Webb of the University of Wisconsin Press, who generously offered to publish the results of our work before ever it had begun and who has patiently suffered all the inevitable delays which accompany the compilation of a volume such as this, I am especially grateful. In this connection, I must add an extra word of gratitude for the painstaking editorial assistance of Mrs. Barbara Harvey. And finally, I wish to express my personal appreciation to colleagues in this endeavor, particularly to those hares who had to wait and to endure with grace the passage of many months while slower tortoises, who faced many legitimate difficulties, toiled their way to the finish line. For any failings and shortcomings of editing and compilation I alone am responsible.

R.E.F.

*Madison, Wisconsin*
*September, 1968*

# Contents

List of Contributors     v

Preface     vii

Introduction     Robert Eric Frykenberg    xiii

I    Land Is To Rule     Walter C. Neale    3

II    Zamindars under the Mughals     S. Nurul Hasan    17

III    Landholding in India and British Institutions

    Ainslie T. Embree    33

IV    Structural Change in Indian Rural Society

    Bernard S. Cohn    53

V    From Raja to Landlord: The Oudh Talukdars, 1850–1870

    Thomas R. Metcalf    123

VI    Social Effects of British Land Policy in Oudh

    Thomas R. Metcalf    143

VII    Permanent Settlement in Operation: Bakarganj District, East Bengal

    Tapan Raychaudhuri    163

VIII    Integration of the Agrarian System of South India

    Burton Stein    175

IX    The Ryotwari System and Social Organization in the Madras Presidency

    Nilmani Mukherjee and Robert Eric Frykenberg    217

X    Village Strength in South India     Robert Eric Frykenberg    227

Index     249

# Introduction

*Robert Eric Frykenberg*

If each piece of land were exactly
the same as every other piece in physical and chemical properties and
in ultimate promise and potential, perhaps land would not provoke such
concern. If each man were exactly equal to every other in his rank and
possessions and, above all, in intrinsic ability, perhaps social standing
would not present so many problems. But historical geography tells us
how the conditions and relations of land and man have varied. One
man counts as almost worthless. His life and labors are less dear than
the labors of a draft animal. Another man exerts great influence and
inspires great deference. At his bidding countless men, animals, ma-
chines, even waters and lands, move. In the same way, some land—
trackless desert, ice-bound plain, or rock-scarped ridge—is devoid of
worth. Over other land hot words and hot deeds recur and recur. Thus
it is that circumstances of ecology and society combine to create traditions of conflict over land.

Perhaps nowhere have the various conditions of man and land been
interlocked for so long as in the subcontinent of India. India has been
and still is an agrarian country. Even today about 80 per cent of its
nearly half billion people live in over 550,000 villages. At least three
out of four persons live by growing crops. In spite of such important
crops as tea, tobacco, and cotton, some four-fifths of what is grown is
food. The Gangetic plain alone, one of the greatest alluvial areas of the
world, should suffice to provide enough food for India's people. The
fact that it does not, that famine and scarcity have recurred with chronic
and dismal frequency for centuries, is not necessarily due to ecological
conditions. If fault must be found, much of it lies with man.

Many of the chains which have shackled India's great agricultural
potential can be broken. Cheaper chemical fertilizers and cooking fuels

can be made available. Better seeds, implements, and storage facilities can also be provided. Fresh attempts to reform and remake rural life can be made. But it is not for lack of scientific methods that previous attempts to remake rural life have failed. The problems which defy solution have been of an altogether different order. Fundamentally, they have been religious, social, and political.

The predominant proportion of all rural people has long struggled under various forms of land bondage and debt. For centuries beyond counting there have been layer upon layer of landholders and tax officials below whom there have been more layers of subholders and revenue collectors. And at the bottom have been the hosts of manual laborers ready to do a day's work in return for a day's food. Lords at the top of this many-tiered system have often demanded a half or more of each crop. Intermediate lords have demanded equivalent shares out of what remained. Each lower level has had to struggle for a smaller and smaller share of the crop, despite the fact that those at the lowest level have contributed most of the toil and sweat.

Debt in its various forms has contributed to this infinite cycle of seemingly perpetual thraldom. Villagers of lower standing have usually been the first to seek help for other than sound economic reasons. Instead of borrowing money for seed, fertilizer, or repair of irrigation works, such villagers have more commonly sought means to support unproductive ceremonials and extravagances. Typically, a man has borrowed more than he could make in ten years to make sure that the marriage of his daughter was in such style that he would not lose standing, if not caste, among his fellows. But the man of such poor position and caste has thereby been the greater credit risk to the moneylender. Borrowing secretly at some fantastic rate of compound interest, he has watched the original sum owed grow so rapidly that he has been caught in the toils of debt bondage in perpetuity. And in many villages, moneylender and landlord have been one and the same.

Put in this most simplistic of forms, what we see is a spectral view of socially structured land control relationships with gradations between two theoretically absolute polarities. At one extreme is the lord over land and labor, absolute in authority so long as there does not sit above him some greater lord. At the other end of the spectrum is the laborer on land, absolute in servility so long as beneath him there is no lower level of subjection. Between the two are innumerable strata of lesser lords and larger laborers. This would seem a simple if depressing picture were it not for the fact that the relationships between land control and social structure are so complex that at some points in the spectrum some lords may be forced to labor and some laborers may have the opportunity to "lord." So complex could land relationships become that one person could be both landlord and tenant to another person. This blurring of distinctions in the relationships of one man to another and of both to the land has remained one of the most perplexing enigmas to students of agrarian India.

Our problems in understanding the very nature of the entities and interacting processes relating to land in India have been compounded many times over by a veritable jungle of overlapping terminologies. Linguistic survivals from untold centuries jostle each other in virtually every locality. By the late eighteenth century when East India Company officials took over a large portion of the country, "they had to choose between several claimants to rights in tenure systems largely unknown to them and described in a multiplicity of terms in Tamil, Telugu, Malayalam, and Canarese. Added to these were Arabic and Persian terms . . . which often were only substitutes for local words. And the British added their own element of confusion in their natural tendency to look at everything from an English law or 'Lord-of-the-Manor' point of view."[1] All sorts of error and misinterpretation was possible from these confusions.

Whatever the terminology, attempts to classify and differentiate between myriad varieties of zamindars, jagirdars, and ryots, whether great or small, become meaningful only if the observer recognizes that all kinds of holdings and rights were intricately linked to definite socio-ceremonial and communal as well as economic and political roles. When seen in this perspective, the tenant and landholder look very much the same, no matter how large and superior the holding or how small and subordinate the tenancy. The same may also be said for the distinction between zamindar and ryot, to say nothing of the innumerable superior, intermediate, and subordinate categories and the innumerable designations for rank and role.

We might take, for example, the largest, poorest, and most depressed segment of the agrarian society, the landless laborers. More than a century and a half ago, Thomas Munro wrote of these people, "a numerous class of slaves have not the free disposal of their own indus-

1. Dharma Kumar, *Land and Caste in South India* (Cambridge, 1965), p. 9.

try, but are in a peculiar state of servitude."[2] The laborer went with the land, which he could no more desert or renounce than he could his own caste. Dharma Kumar has written that indeed it might be argued that such a laborer can also be regarded as a "landholder" for he held a right to work and a right of occupancy whereby "his master had to employ him and his family in sickness and in health."[3] Land control and land bondage were mutually shaded and overlapping conditions. In other words, "All roles were interdependent in an architectonic whole."[4] Each group has had its own privileges and duties. Higher forms of lords over land have certainly enjoyed larger incomes and higher standards than their menial laborers, but no one has had absolute rights of ownership and possession.

It was William Logan, who, in trying to explain the confusions resulting from attempts to describe the nature of land control in Malabar, aptly declared that *the land belonged to no one.*[5] The *janma,* or hereditary land right, was not a legal claim to ownership of the soil so much as it was a customary authority to exercise power over persons who resided thereon. This perhaps explains why attempts to define and classify the many interrelated positions of social status and landed interest have run into a wild babel of confusing tongues. Whatever the locality or period, clamoring voices are raised in conflicting claims to privilege and position in regard to land. What makes matters worse, each claim often turns out to be partially, if not fully, correct.

The task of correctly analyzing the relationships between social structure and control of land has not been simplified by the ready application of Western concepts during the past two or more centuries. Weighted as they have been with the doctrine and philosophical outlook of a culture which has itself been changing, they have often communicated either more or less than was called for by the phenomena being described.

Having recognized this problem, however, we should point out some of the significant works which have appeared, aside from the classic compilations of administrators such as Sir John Kaye's *The Administration of the East India Company: A History of Indian Progress*

2. Revenue letter from the Government of India to Board of Control, 30 December 1825, Madras Dispatches, India Office Records, London.
3. Kumar, *op. cit.,* p. 45.
4. *Ibid.,* p. 33.
5. *The Malabar Manual* (Madras, 1887), I, 491.

(London, 1853) and B. H. Baden-Powell's *Manual of Land Revenue Systems and Land Tenures of British India* (Calcutta, 1882) and *The Land Systems of British India* (Oxford, 1892). Among the contributions of early pioneers, perhaps the most significant was W. H. Moreland's *The Agrarian System of Moslem India* (Cambridge, 1929). Another important study was P. Saran's *The Provincial Government of the Mughals, 1526–1658* (Allahabad, 1941). To these pioneering works may be added some significant studies of recent years. All of these seek to throw more light upon the complex interrelations of social structure and land control. Among prominent recent works have been: Sulekh Chandra Gupta, *Agrarian Relations and Early British Rule in India* (Bombay, 1963); Irfan Habib, *The Agrarian System of Mughal India: 1556–1702* (Bombay, 1963); Dharma Kumar, *Land and Caste in South India* (Cambridge, 1965); Nilmani Mukherjee, *The Ryotwari System in Madras: 1792–1827* (Calcutta, 1962); Walter C. Neale, *Economic Change in Rural India: 1800–1955* (New Haven, 1962); and Daniel Thorner, *The Agrarian Prospects in India* (Delhi, 1956). Also germane to this study is my work, *Guntur District: 1788–1848, A History of Local Influence and Central Authority in South India* (Oxford, 1965).

For the most part, these works are in marked contrast to those studies of policy-making at the highest levels which have followed each other in dreary and repetitive success for generations. Recent contributions can be considered significant for two reasons: First, large amounts of fresh materials, mainly drawn from manuscript records and writings, have brought to light quantities of new descriptive data—statistical facts and figures not only on revenue demands, agricultural production, and commercial activities, but also on local conditions, leadership, and methods. Second, new attempts have been made to organize and analyze this data in such a way as to bring about a much clearer understanding of agrarian processes in India.

Without attempting to provide comprehensive or exhaustive coverage, the present volume has been organized to highlight some of the significant new aspects of and approaches to questions of social structure and land control in India. Walter Neale lays the groundwork for subsequent essays by examining some fundamental questions of definition and by demonstrating important variations in concepts of land and land control. In effect, he has told us to stop looking at land as *land* and to start looking at what people "hold" in relation to it. He emphasizes the need to understand cultural as well as economic elements in this "holding."

Without such efforts, much discussion about land becomes increasingly meaningless, if not useless.

S. Nurul Hasan and Ainslie Embree throw light upon the twin streams of influence which perhaps did most to impose cultural uniformity and give cohesion to agrarian relations in modern India—the Mughal and the British. In his study of the Mughal Empire, Hasan contributes a perceptive view of the crucial intermediaries, the zamindars, whose positions were essential for linking the villages to the empire. His essay gives us a clearer and more refined glimpse of the system of zamindari control, including the processes of acquiring and relinquishing such control. Embree reviews the influence of British institutions, particularly those of the eighteenth and nineteenth centuries, upon landholding in India. His work serves to remind us of the importance of those ideas which were transmitted to India with the British and which influenced the formulation of official policies and legal codes.

Having thus introduced various aspects of the general and theoretical setting of the subject, the volume next turns to detailed studies which examine the actual workings of the agrarian order in North India, giving special attention to what transpired in Banaras, Oudh, and East Bengal and the role of zamindars, talukdars, and the various lower-level leaders and land controllers. The largest single case study is that presented by Bernard Cohn. Much of the data on changes that occurred within the social structure in the Banaras region during the nineteenth century is completely new. Moreover, both from the questions he has asked and the conclusions he has drawn, Cohn has upset some commonly held notions about the character of the rural social order and the way in which changes occurred.

Cohn's findings are reinforced and amplified by the work of Thomas Metcalf and Tapan Raychaudhuri. The pair of essays by Metcalf discuss the origins, development, and changing character of the talukdars of Oudh during the latter half of the nineteenth century. They show how the role, status, and aspirations of the talukdars were affected by the requirements for survival and success under the British. Tapan Raychaudhuri analyzes how the Permanent Settlement operated within one district of East Bengal. His essay contributes to our growing impressions of fantastic complexity in land relationships. He stresses the fact that efforts to bring order out of the chaos and confusions of juxtaposed relationships must necessarily become exercises in abstraction and oversimplification. His reminder is noteworthy, for it applies in some degree to all of the works which have been put together within this volume.

The remaining studies deal with land systems in South India. Burton Stein has attempted to develop a theory for the history of South India, one based on years of painstaking research and reflection, which concentrates upon the social and economic movement of local forces in a broad pattern of social integration. He delineates three important phases of transition, each of which was accompanied if not provoked by major upheavals. A parallel and supplementary view can be obtained in my article "Traditional Processes of Power in South India: An Historical Analysis of Local Influence."[6] The final two studies of the volume are more detailed considerations of the functioning of the agrarian system in South India. The essay by Nilmani Mukherjee and myself describes the workings of the ryotwari system and its relations to social organization within the Madras Presidency between 1792 and 1827. My own essay examines village influence within one district. It is a series of small case studies showing exactly how certain groups of village leaders corrupted the administrative structure of the East India Company and how they combined with district officers to gain common advantages from their operations.

Having briefly described each study and how it might contribute to our knowledge of land control and social structure in India, we might well ask what new lines of inquiry these studies have suggested. First of all, we can see the need for better terms and concepts which more accurately approximate the phenomena and conditions being described. Furthermore, our use of Indian terminology must be refined. In order to explain what, in the final analysis, may be completely different systems of land control at any given time and in any given locality, we need more functional words and categories.Not only must old concepts be redefined with greater rigor and precision, but old closets of English vocabulary must be ransacked. Our discussions and studies serve to show how inadequate and imprecise have been past usages of such words as *peasant, cultivator, landlord,* and tenurial *right.*

Second, we must endeavor to develop new methodological tools and analytical models. While the existing theoretical constructions are grossly

6. *Indian Economic and Social History Review,* I (1963), 1–21; republished in Reinhard Bendix, *State and Society: A Reader in Comparative Political Sociology* (Boston, 1968).

inadequate, such older models have a tenacious persistence which prevents their being easily replaced. Any new working model also runs the risk of being deified instead of being used simply as a practical abstraction, a functional theorem for tentative solutions to problems of social organization within a given set of circumstances. For the formulation of new theoretical models, we might suggest two kinds of ideas or concepts which have been largely lacking in previous studies: (1) ideas of movement, namely, about process and causation; and (2) ideas of "structural relativity," that is, of dynamic relationships of social entities moving within a defined structural whole.

Several dimensions of movement can be suggested. Burton Stein has noted that we might fruitfully examine *growth in organization* and compare this growth from year to year and decade to decade in various localities. As continuities or similarities emerge from comparisons between areas, we might next dissect the social and ecological elements of organization, the ways in which resources have been managed, and the relationships which have produced and harnessed power in and over ever-widening circles of land and people. We might then look for those fixed, virtually static elements of organization, those features of social process which have hardly changed at all over long periods of time. Also, we might compare the details of changing technology as these have applied to specific aspects of agriculture, for example, in the kinds of crops, planting, methods of irrigation, types of labor, and ratios of persons as related to land reclamation. Finally, we might seek to assess and measure the consequences of social and political migration and mobility.

Ideas of structural relativity may be considered intrinsic to the study of process and structure as these have been discussed above. The dynamic relationships of all social entities moving within a defined structural whole can hardly be analyzed without the invention of working models, some simple and some extremely complex. In our search for meaningful analyses of agrarian relations, we might need to begin with models which are almost patently too elementary and then proceed by stages to more complicated forms. Thus, for instance, we might start by defining and then interrelating three basic elements: land, labor, and lord. Having done this, we would proceed by stages in elaborating and relating the functional and then the structural connections between what are obviously increasing numbers of complex forms of the three basic elements. Just as simple mathematical formulas and equations are either discarded or incorporated into more sophisticated formulations, so simple models might be discarded when outmoded or proved useless or else incorporated into newer models. Our object is not to make the study of the obscure and complex realities of rural society in India even more esoteric and technical; rather, we would seek ways to make what is obscure and complex, clear and plain. But before this can be accomplished, we must foresee the possibility that exceedingly complex, varied, and highly sophisticated scaffolds of theory may be needed. With the aid of such constructs, we hope that in the long run our conclusions and theories can be made simple.

LAND CONTROL AND SOCIAL STRUCTURE IN INDIAN HISTORY

Chapter I

# Land
# Is To
# Rule

*Walter C. Neale*

The thesis presented here rests upon the proposition that there is no objective natural world for mankind, and in particular for economic historians viewing the "natural" setting of social institutions. Although we think of the terms by which we denote aspects of nature as objective, they have a whole group of connotations derived from our experience of the world—an experience which occurs within a cultural context and which we learn to interpret in terms of our cultural institutions. Whether "a hole is to dig," "a hole is not empty," or, like Newark, New Jersey, is "just a hole," depends upon whether we are children, linguists, or New Yorkers. Similarly, *land* is not a clear referent about whose meaning we need never worry. There is perhaps an objective land, as opposed to ocean, but this meaning has never been especially interesting to the social scientist, or to the lawyer, or certainly to the historian of Indian tenure systems. The land in which we are interested is farmed, owned, irrigated, and fought over. It is the location of villages and the area of a state.

I am indebted to Paul J. Bohannan of Northwestern University for the realization that land is not clearly *land*. In an essay entitled " 'Land,' 'Tenure,' and 'Land Tenure,' "[1] he has argued that the meanings of both *land* and *tenure* are quite different in African and European societies. In European societies, he says, land is an area whose referent is an immutable grid written upon paper according to rules which correlate the written grid with astral observations. Tenure is some right or rights, partial or whole, to exclude others from the land represented on the grid.

3

For the West African, he argues, land is continuous topography over which the clan roams. The reference points, if they can be called points, are the positions of other clans. Thus, for clan X, directions are "toward clan Y" and "toward clan Z." At one time clan Y may be due north of clan X and at another time northeast. However, the significant direction for clan X is not north or northeast but always the same, that is, "toward Y."

The "fixed" points on the West African clan map are the residential farm sites of neighboring clans. As the directions, in our terms, vary, so do the distances in miles between these points as the clans, moving in their system of shifting agriculture, draw closer together or move farther apart. Nevertheless, the West African will regard that fixed point as closest at which he has his nearest kin; for instance, women who traveled to what Bohannan thought were distant markets told him that they went to these markets because they were "nearer." Whole tribes, such as the Tiv with over half a million souls, can migrate slowly across Africa without moving the fixed points on their maps of the area in which they live. Notice that this does not mean that the clan moves about in an area of the earth's surface which is fixedly its own (although it can); rather, the whole "area" moves with the clans as they move across Africa.

On a European grid map these "fixed" African clan positions would not be fixed. The reference positions on the African "map" could be made to fit the European grid map only if the former were made of rubber so that it could be stretched or compressed to match the changing loci on the European map.

An African example is used to introduce this argument because it is so striking. I shall not argue that the Indian idea is like the African. It is not. However, Bohannan's illustration brings out the difference between the European view of land and the view of another culture. A moment's thought makes it clear that the European view is not itself objectively real, but is a way of relating a piece of the earth's surface to European methods of astral observation and to a technique of plotting observations on a plane surface. The European grid map and the African clan map are each a "unit of thought"; each is a perception of the "natural" world in which people live.

Some scholars have even considered the possibility of dropping the word *tenure* from their vocabulary because, in their view, tenures do not exist. However, they are wrong. Tenures do exist. What does not exist is land. I continue to follow Bohannan, who says that Africans do not have "land tenure" but "farm tenure." This phenomenon is more widely recognized than the existence of an elastic clan map because it is common to the Bantus as well as the West Africans. What Africans have in their system of shifting cultivation is not the right to a piece of land, but a right to have *some* piece of land in the area around the site of the temporary residence of the clan. As African households move across the surface of the earth, each household carries with it a right to a farm, or perhaps one should say a right to farm. It is this right to farm some land that is held by the African and that may be called *tenure*.

While the Indians did not have a counterpart to the elastic African clan map, they did have arrangements similar to the African farm tenure. I have elsewhere called this "fair shares."[2] The British found that in some areas, where the courses and widths of rivers changed, the Indians customarily reapportioned the land to preserve the relative advantages and productivity of the "holders," who in effect held a right to a farm with certain characteristics, not to specified plots. But more important evidence is to be found in Indian systems of measurement. Any beginning student of Indian agricultural matters is confused by the wide variations among the measures of land. He soon learns not to ask "How big is a bigha?" but rather to ask some such question as "How big is a standard bigha?" or "How big is a Bengali bigha?" As he pursues his studies he will find, however, that some bighas in Bengal are bigger and some are smaller than the Bengali bigha. Why? Because Bengalis did not know how big a bigha was? Because the size of a bigha is culturally determined and different Bengalis came from different cultures? Because a bigha is the area covered by a raja's foot and different areas were ruled by rajas with different-sized feet? I do not think so. The clue is found in descriptions of different-sized bighas in the same village. A bigha was not an area of land in our sense, a square the same size at any place on a specific latitude on our grid map, but a piece of land which satisfied the requirement that the *tenure holder* be able to farm some piece of land whose productivity accorded with his status rights; it was a "fair share" as the people of that village or ruling brotherhood defined equity in relation to different families or castes. I might remark that this has something in common with Aristotle's much maligned remark that price should reflect status.[3]

With the premise that in India, as in Africa, there is no *land,* I wish now to discuss land control in India in terms of a phrase I used above—

units of thought. When I speak of units of thought, I have much the same idea in mind as does Paul Bohannan, if I understand him correctly, when he refers to "organizing concepts"—ideas to each of which many other ideas and many activities are related, ideas which serve as primary postulates in the system of thought and cannot be defined outside of the system of thought to which they give essential structure. Because these units of thought have different ranges of meaning (denotations) and different associations with other units of thought (connotations) in different societies, members of different societies perceive differently the objectives of secular life, how the objectives of life fit together, and how they may be achieved.

For my purpose here I am quite willing to reverse the argument and to say that because perceptions are different, the units of thought are different. What I am insisting upon is that perceptions of reality, social institutions, views of what is possible, and organizing concepts or units of thought form more or less integrated wholes and that the analyst cannot portray a particular situation or understand a range of problems such as "land control in India" without constructing the social situations in which particular people reason and act in terms of the units of thought of the people involved.

I want to suggest that one of the difficulties facing Westerners—whether nineteenth-century administrators or twentieth-century economists—when analyzing the Indian village is a number of differences in units of thought and the way the units are associated. Between the people in control of the Indian countryside and the Englishmen who ruled them, there were differences in thought about the objectives of secular life, about how these objectives fitted together, and differences in the situations in which the Indian and the Englishman reasoned. There were also differences in the range of meaning and the association with objectives in life between some of the basic units of thought of Englishman and Indian. Later I shall focus the argument upon the differences between the English idea of the *estate* as a unit of land management and the Indian idea of the *mahal* as a unit of land management—translating mahal very loosely as "village"—but first I want to point out some similarities and differences between European and Indian perceptions of land and then discuss English and Indian perceptions of the relationships among wealth, power, and the achievement of life's rewarding objectives.

In the European tradition there are at least three distinct social meanings of *land*: there is land as *an area to be farmed or owned*; there is land *as the sum total of natural resources,* which is the economists' view of land; and there is land *as the area over which a political sovereign wields power,* as in the word "fatherland." Generally the context makes the meaning clear and we, who know what *we* are talking about, are rarely confused. But to divide up topography to prohibit the entry of others, to exploit nature to produce useful things, and to delimit the outer reaches to which the king's writ runs—these are not the only ways to perceive the place and function of the surface of the earth in man's social behavior. I submit that the differentiation between *land-to-own* and *land-to-rule* may be peculiar to those who take both their natural and legal ideas from the Greco-Roman tradition. Further, it seems likely that over much of the earth's surface the idea of land-to-rule includes the idea of land-to-own.

I often suspect that land-to-rule is an idea anterior to and more all-embracing than land-to-own—in fact, that land-to-own was a late differentiation of a more general concept of land-to-rule,[4] a differentiation that occurred in the history of Roman-European law as it developed the idea of *citizen* as distinct from the idea of a person as a member of a group which in turn was a member of a larger grouping of groups. This view seems to be implied by the whole tenor of Sir Henry Maine's argument in *Ancient Law.*[5] If I am right in so interpreting his argument, then I am willing to go along with Maine's parallelism between Rome and India, as spelled out in *Village Communities in the East and West,*[6] restating it thus:

Land to the early Romans was one of a number of items which made up the family or clan under the authority of the pater familias. The *family* was a sovereignty—later a subsovereignty—defined in sociopolitical terms; that is, interactions of its members with members of other families occurred through the agency of the pater familias, these interactions frequently involving decisions to use or augment power. Our idea of land as *territory-to-rule* is derived from this aspect of early Roman law and became explicitly political as the state superseded the pater familias.

Land in pre-British Indian society was one of the aspects of rulership, whether viewed in the person of a raja, in the body corporate of a *bhaichara* (brotherhood) village, or in the person of the zamindar, the closest approximation to the pater familias. Thus, the Indian view of land was also political, if we may call a view political when it embraces more than does our concept of politics.

Maine's Roman-Hindu parallel is acceptable then as a statement of similarity in the position of land in the units of thought of early Romans and pre-British Indians. Land in both cases was associated with a unit of thought about legitimate authority—family or village-brotherhood–joint family—or, alternatively, land was connoted by such units of thought.

Another way to modernize Maine is to state the same proposition in terms of Bohannan's organizing concepts. *Family* was an organizing concept, since a full explanation of family necessarily involves a statement of how land use was organized in ancient Greco-Roman civilization. The statement of land use would simultaneously describe land as arable, pasture, or waste, and territory. The same can be said of *village* or *brotherhood* in India. One could, however, have a partial explanation of family—a quick but sufficient identification of the institution—without explaining land use. But, one could not have a quick but sufficient explanation of land use without describing the family system. It is in this way that one can speak of an organizing concept.

I submit here that there were indeed differences between what the nineteenth-century Englishman wanted to get and to do and what the nineteenth-century Indian landholder wanted to get and to do and that there were also differences in the views of how land and labor could be used to achieve the desired getting or doing.

Let us take wants first. The Englishman wanted a steady and increasing income, and he wanted to have this income in money. He also wanted to pass on this income, or the capacity to earn it, to his progeny. Further, he wanted to pass it on in such a way that it would increase under the management of his heirs and under the management of his heirs' heirs. Many an Englishman wanted to have power—there can be no doubt of this—and he also wanted to pass this power on to his children and his children's children.

In the broadest and most meaningless sense the Indian also wanted income; but there were two differences in the kind of income he wanted. He did not particularly want to receive his income in money; and the variety of goods he wanted, whether bought with money or provided directly, was narrower. Many an Indian, like many an Englishman, wanted power. In this there was not so much difference between the Englishman and the Indian, except as one might argue that more Englishmen were willing to trade in more power for money while more Indians were willing to trade in more money, or goods, for power.

If these wants were similar, there were important differences in the ways the Englishman and the Indian believed he could acquire goods or acquire power. To the Englishman, the route to power lay in public administration or in parliamentary politics. Money could, of course, be used to acquire power—in the early nineteenth century directly by bribery, in the late nineteenth century by financing an election campaign. The Englishman could get power by entering politics directly and fighting his way up the administrative or parliamentary ladders, or he could go into the business world to earn money and then later enter politics. Beer barons might be politically important, but it was the barony and not the beer that gave them significance. While money could be used to further a political career and, for that matter, political power could be used to help earn money, the connection was indirect and became increasingly indirect as the century progressed. No beer baron could become prime minister, and no prime minister could use his position to become as rich as Mr. Guinness.

The Indian was in a different position. By and large in the eighteenth century he could not have an administrative career under the Mughals, and for a long period under the British the upper ranks of the civil service were closed. Under both Mughal and English there was no parliamentary ladder. There were not many ways for an Indian to earn money and still fewer ways for an Indian who did earn money to turn it into a "beer barony." On the other hand, the Indian who acquired political power almost inevitably acquired control of land, which was the main source of wealth or income. Not only could the Indian turn political power into economic affluence, but he would find it difficult to avoid doing so.

Cut off from administrative and parliamentary careers, yet accustomed to a system of local government based upon prestige and numbers of followers, the Indian employed the resources at hand in a different manner. Since numbers were important to political power, it behooved the Indian interested in acquiring power to increase, or at least to maintain, the number of his allies and followers. In a social system which conceived of position largely in terms of kinship, the group to which the Indian naturally looked was the kin group; and in looking upon the world in terms of kinship the Indian saw its normal or natural extension as going from the nuclear or joint family through relatives and in-laws to the caste. The Indian also had an idea of locality, so that the other group to which he looked for numbers was the village. Since villages were often split by faction fights, the political

Indian needed to increase the unity of and the numbers in his faction. The ideal position for an Indian interested in power was to be a leader of the dominant faction of the dominant caste in a village. It would have been difficult indeed to differentiate between a person in this position and the owner of the village. It was in part, of course, this difficulty that led the British to recognize as "owners" many whom later scholars have decided ought not properly to be called "owners."

An obvious illustration from recent literature is the history of the village of Bisipara, in Orissa, described by F. G. Bailey.[7] When the British came into the area, the rich, landowning, and politically powerful caste was the warrior caste. The wealth and land of this caste came with the conquest of Bisipara; and the conquest immediately became economic affluence. Conversely, under British rule, the new opportunities to earn a money income provided increasing wealth for persons who were not members of the warrior caste, notably the distillers; but while wealth could be earned and turned into landholding, wealth and landholding were not so easily turned into political power. Even after almost a century of British rule the nonwarrior castes in the village were still unable to acquire the necessary ritual prestige to displace the warriors as the politically dominant caste. The nineteenth-century settlement reports and gazetteers for the United Provinces and Punjab cite instance after instance where the wealth of a leading family or clan came from conquest. Another source of wealth was the use, or abuse, of administrative power by the servants of the kings or rajas. Using their position as royal favorites, such servants seized villages, and this amounted to conquest with a minimum of violence.

These historic relationships between wealth and political power were all part of the Indian's perception of land and its meaning. To the Englishman, the word *estate* expressed a primary idea or unit of thought about rural social and economic organization which was very different from the Indian one. From the eighteenth century on, there was much interest in the estate and a voluminous literature on the proper way to manage an estate. There were many efforts to encourage and to reward good estate management; the Board of Agriculture was *the* example. But it was always assumed that most rural land came in units of estates, as labor came in units of people, or businesses came in units of firms. Tangentially, there were other units of thought relevant to the contrast between Britain and India. The church came in units of parishes, while government came in units of constituencies. It will be noted immediately that these units did not correspond with the units of Indian social thought—family, caste, and village.

For British thought at this period, the "improving landlord" assumed the role which, for some economists today, is assumed by Joseph Schumpeter's *entrepreneur*.[8] If his duties were not so broad nor his liabilities to risk so great as those faced by the entrepreneur, nevertheless the improving landlord was the agent which led to general economic development. To qualify as a "good landlord" the owner of an estate was required to lay out the pattern of the fields, to ditch and hedge, to provide drainage, and generally to equip the farms which constituted his estate with up-to-date fixed capital equipment. He was also supposed to use his judgment in selecting from among possible tenants those who would make the most efficient and scientifically oriented farmers. The "very good landlord" was admired for going further. He brought the results of practical experimentation conducted elsewhere in the kingdom to the attention of his tenants, perhaps even conducted experimental work of his own, and by close contact with his tenants saw to it that they practiced the newest techniques. All owners of estates were secure in their position—bar hoof-and-mouth disease or extraordinarily bad management—and the improving landlord was assured of public respect and approbation. The very good landlord could even expect to be known and admired beyond his parish and his county. Proper estate management could thus be a fully rewarding life for the landlord.

Contrast the idea environment of the improving landlord with the idea environment of the Indian zamindar. An *estate-to-be-managed* was not a primary idea in the zamindar's thought pattern, or in the thought patterns of those around him. Information on how to improve the management of his lands was not available, nor were there any Arthur Youngs traveling the countryside. The "improving zamindar" might expect local admiration and respect for so managing his lands that they produced more, and more regularly, than the average of his neighbors; but he would not achieve fame beyond the villages in his neighborhood and might, at worst, get a local reputation for "sharpness." For the Indian owner of land, improvement was a minor worry compared to the problem of security. Prior to the British he could retain his land no matter how badly he managed it, provided he retained his political power. Even after the advent of British rule a bad manager could retain his land if he were a local leader. Even the working of British, market-oriented land law, which *did* deprive numerous landlords of their property, was modified by a contrary current of British land policy, illustrated, for instance, by the Talukdari Settlement of the Oudh Compromise or the Bundelkhand Land Alienation Act, which prohibited all except the local agricultural castes from owning property in the area.

Faction and village were the unit ideas of primary relevance. Security, fame, and respect resulted from effective management of people grouped in families and castes. To manage a village meant to manage people by manipulating the rules of their hierarchy. The farming of land was certainly necessary for the control of people because followers had to be fed or provision made to assure that they could feed themselves. A crucial difference between estate management and village management was that the estate manager maximized the net produce of his lands while the village manager maximized the number of mouths he fed.

The consequence was not that a village manager behaved completely differently from an estate manager, for both maximized, both "economized," in some sense. But one cannot maximize two measures simultaneously unless they measure the same thing or one is so fortunate as to find the two linked in perfect correlation. This means that when one objective had to "give way" if the other was to be maximized, the estate manager would sacrifice a measure of gross output to increase net profit while a village manager would sacrifice net profit to increase gross output, and even sacrifice gross output to add another mouth to the number of his dependents. There need not always have been a conflict between profits and mouths, but there were certainly occasions upon which they conflicted.

The most striking case in which English "economic behavior" differed from Indian "political behavior" was in the matter of investment. The improving landlord as an estate manager built buildings, laid out fields, and installed drainage because it increased the output of his fields and because it saved the use of labor, the most extreme case being enclosures for grazing sheep. The tenant farmer as an estate manager purchased machinery, equipment, and livestock to earn a larger profit, and the main saving from equipment was saving in labor input. In short, a consequence of "maximizing" or estate behavior—which we call economic—tended to be a reduction in the demand for farm hands.

A larger gross output of food was a good way to increase power in the management of the village polity, but obviously not if it reduced the need for farm hands. Irrigation has always been popular in India, and it fits the needs of the village manager for it increases the need for field hands at the same time that it increases the yield per acre. Fertilizers, in great demand today, have the same linked characteristics. Improved plows, better equipment, and special storage facilities do not generally increase the need for labor; many crop rotations actually reduce the need. Economists' solutions to the problem of how to even out the demand for labor over the agricultural season—for instance, by using crop patterns which keep farm hands busy during a longer period— are not worries for the village manager. He may prefer to have the demand for labor bunched at the beginning and the end of the growing season. The hands which help him at these times may not be entirely dependent upon him for their income, yet they will more likely be in his faction if they derive a significant part of their income from part-time work. In fact, the manager of the polity may derive more strength from a large number of part-dependents than from a smaller number of full-dependents.

The improving estate manager employed land, labor, and capital to increase wealth; the village manager employed land, and did not employ capital, to increase the size and unity of his faction. Labor was an input for his farming operations; but his farming operations were also supposed to produce loyal people as an output. The associations of *estate* were productivity, profit, efficiency; an estate was land viewed as an element in economic activity. The associations of *mahal* were faction, village, power, clientele; a mahal was land viewed as an element in village politics.

There is an increasing body of literature on the importance of British misapprehensions about the content of ownership and "rights in land" as these concepts were given operational meaning in Indian society. Actually, the essential intercultural differences were grasped by Englishmen by the middle of the nineteenth century. George Trevelyan, James Thomason, and H. E. Elliott in the United Provinces had the idea by that time, and even earlier Holt Mackenzie was on the track.[9] Henry Maine presented the position in general terms and spelled out implications both for the history of jurisprudence and for a general sociology of history—a sociology which, alas, has been largely overlooked or forgotten. But after B. H. Baden-Powell and W. H. Moreland the line was not pursued, and comparative as well as Indian social and economic history were left with the rather bare ideas that "Indian ownership was not European ownership," and "Some societies are status societies; others are contract societies." Only recently have scholars returned to the theme, and I think the work of many who are pursuing this or similar lines appears in this volume.

The reasoning which I have presented here follows in the spirit of Maine and Baden-Powell, but attempts to apply the comparative method to other ideas, including Indian organizing ideas, and not to the European idea of ownership alone. This approach makes possible changes in the interpretation of the history of Indian tenures. Let me illustrate:

1.  Typically, the zamindari system created by the Permanent Settlement of Bengal has been regarded as an economic failure. It was. It does not follow, however, that the behavior of the Bengal zamindars is to be explained by irresponsible greed alone. They may equally well have been following a pattern of political behavior which they had learned and which made much sense in the society to which they were accustomed. That under Company and imperial rule there was no large political role to be played by Indians was a fact of the future which the early zamindars could not be expected to have appreciated. *Homo politicus* was miscast as *homo economicus,* and one should be kind in criticizing a miscast actor and restrained in criticizing the casting director until one can point to actors more suitable to the role.

2.  Much the same position may be taken in regard to the talukdars of Oudh before, during, and after the Mutiny. In this case, the illustration also provides evidence of the correctness of the hypothesis suggested here. The British, first in expropriating the lands of the talukdars and secondly in giving them a privileged position after the Mutiny, were in effect recognizing and negotiating with political power. It was a case where good politics was bad economics. Before one can argue that other courses were open to the British, one must show that better economics would have been feasible politics.

3.  As keepers of public records the *patwaris* were notoriously unreliable, which is a polite way of saying dishonest. Another view, although it would not absolve them of sin, would put their behavior in a different light. If they were "ward heelers" as well as record keepers, if they were agents to mete out rewards and punishments in the game of politics, then some of their corruption had a positive value in the ongoing system of village management. Robert Frykenberg's *karnams* are an even better example than the *patwaris* of North India, for his description of their behavior in Guntur District indicates that they were

principals and not merely agents in the process of acquiring and using power.[10]

On functional principle, zamindars, talukdars, *patwaris,* and *karnams* must have been fulfilling roles within an ongoing system. What research in Indian economic history fails to show is their functional roles in an economic system. There is no lazy zamindar or corrupt *patwari* role to be filled on an estate. The postulate which makes sense of their behavior, including the survival of the roles themselves, is that *land-village-mahal* was there to be ruled. The failure to treat topography as *land-to-be-improved* was thus not a failure of intellect, but a consequence of a different perception.

I conclude with an illustration of the importance of power, if not of the essentially political character of village life. An early settlement officer in a district of Oudh asked cultivators if they had an occupancy right to the land they tilled.[11] They replied that they definitely did have an hereditary right of occupancy. The officer pursued his inquiries, asking if it were possible for the zamindar to evict a cultivator. The cultivators immediately replied that, of course, it was possible for a zamindar to evict cultvators: "The man in power can do anything."

## NOTES

1   In Daniel Biebuyck (ed.), *African Agrarian Systems* (London, 1963), pp. 101–15.

2   Walter C. Neale, *Economic Change in Rural India: Land Tenure and Reform in Uttar Pradesh, 1800–1955* (New Haven, 1962), pp. 25–27.

3   See Harry W. Pearson, "Aristotle Discovers the Economy," in Karl Polanyi, Conrad Arensberg, and Harry Pearson (eds.), *Trade and Market in the Early Empires* (Glencoe, Ill., 1957), pp. 64–94.

4   Professor Don Kanel of the University of Wisconsin has pointed out to me that this point is made by John R. Commons in his *Legal Foundations of Capitalism* (Madison, 1957), pp. 52–56, where, however, it is viewed as an aspect of English history.

5   New York, 1960, pp. 1–12, 67–100, 216–34.

6   New York, 1876, *passim.*

7   *Caste and the Economic Frontier* (Manchester, 1957), pp. 94–145, 146–64, 228–76.

8   *Capitalism, Socialism, and Democracy* (New York, 1950), pp. 81–86, 131–34.

9   See Neale, *op. cit.,* pp. 316–25, for sources.

10   See "Village Strength in South India," pp. 227–47, in this volume.

11   George Campbell, "Tenure of Land in India," in Cobden Club, *Systems of Land Tenure in Various Countries* (London, 1870), pp. 218–19, discussing Canning's report on tenures in Oudh.

# Chapter II

# Zamindars under the Mughals

*S. Nurul Hasan*

The zamindar class played a vital role in the political, economic, and cultural life of medieval India. During the Mughal period its importance increased, and its position in society became more complex.[1] The surplus of agricultural production, appropriated from the peasants, was shared among the emperor, his nobles, and the zamindars, and the power exercised by the zamindars over the economic life of the country—agricultural production, handicrafts, and trade—was tremendous. In spite of the constant struggle between the imperial government and the zamindars for a greater share of the produce, the two became partners in the process of economic exploitation.

Politically, there was a clash of interests between the Mughal government and the zamindars. Most of the administrative difficulties which the Mughal emperor had to face were the result of the zamindars' activities. At the same time, the administration had to lean heavily on their support. In the cultural sphere, the close links of the zamindars with the imperial court contributed in no small measure to the process of cultural synthesis between the distinctive traditions of the various communities and different regions, and between the urban and rural cultures. At the same time, the separatist, localist, and parochial trends received powerful patronage from the zamindar class. The Mughal Empire achieved its great power largely because it could secure the collaboration of this class; but the inherent contradictions between a centralized empire and the zamindars were too deep to be resolved. These contradictions within the Mughal Empire contributed to its downfall even before the Western powers were established in the country.

The word "zamindar" gained currency during the Mughal period. It was used to denote the various holders of hereditary interests, ranging from powerful, independent, and autonomous chieftains to petty intermediaries at the village level. Before the Mughals, the chieftains were designated as rajas, rais, thakurs, and so on, while the small intermediaries would be termed *chaudhuris, khots, mugaddams,* etc. The Mughal practice of using the same generic term for the holders of widely varying types of landed interests is a reflection of the Mughal desire to reduce the chieftains to the status of intermediaries while compensating them in other ways.

The existence of the various types of landed interests was the result of a long process of evolution spread over several centuries. By the close of the twelfth century, a pyramidal structure had already been established in agrarian relations. Even though there were important regional differences, the nature of land rights in most parts of the country was basically similar. During the sultanate period (1206–1526), significant changes in land rights occurred, but the essential features remained more or less the same. However, the process of change accelerated during the Mughal period.

Zamindars in the Mughal Empire may be classified in three broad categories: (*a*) the autonomous chieftains; (*b*) the intermediary zamindars; and (*c*) the primary zamindars. These categories were by no means exclusive. Within the territory held by the autonomous chieftains were to be found not only vassal semi-autonomous chiefs, but also intermediary as well as primary zamindars. While the intermediary zamindars exercised jurisdiction over groups of primary zamindars, most of the intermediary zamindars were also primary zamindars in their own right. A chieftain might exercise primary rights over some lands and intermediary rights over others, while simultaneously enjoying "sovereign" or "state" powers over his dominions.

It may be noted that the territories held by the zamindars were not separate from the *khalisa* or jagir lands. The distinction between the jagir and the *khalisa* lay only in the distribution of the state's share of the revenue. If the revenue from a particular area were deposited in the imperial treasury, it would be deemed to be *khalisa*; if it were to be assigned to an officer in lieu of salary, it could be considered a jagir. Thus, the *khalisa* as well as the jagir comprised various types of zamin daris. A careful study of the various types reveals that there was hardly a pargana in the Mughal Empire in which there were no zamindars.[2]

## The Chieftains

The chieftains were the hereditary autonomous rulers of their territories and enjoyed practically sovereign powers. Since the establishment of the sultanate the sultans had tried to obtain from these chieftains the recognition of their overlordship and imposed on them the obligation to pay regular tribute and to render military assistance to the sultanate whenever called upon. But there were many cases of resistance or rebellions; and the nature of control exercised by the imperial government depended upon the extent of military pressure which it could bring against the chieftains. On a number of occasions, during the course of struggles against the sultan's authority, the ruling houses of the chieftains were altogether overthrown or their territories substantially reduced. Conversely, taking advantage of the weakness of the imperial authority, the chieftains would on occasion assume independence, or extend their territories. In either case, the rights of the vassals of the chieftains and of the intermediary or primary zamindars were not substantially affected. By the time Akbar (1556–1605) came to the throne, such autonomous chieftains held sway over the major portion of the Mughal Empire; many who had accepted the overlordship of the Surs had by now become independent.

Akbar and his successors not only continued the policy of the sultans of demanding from the chieftains a recognition of their overlordship, the payment of tribute, and the rendering of military assistance, but also introduced the following new elements in their treatment of the chieftains:

1. Akbar was the first emperor who realized the importance of forging powerful links between the empire and the chieftains by absorbing many of them in the imperial hierarchy and the administrative machinery. This policy was continued by his successors; and it is estimated that during the latter half of Aurangzeb's reign (1658–1707), eighty-one persons belonging to the ruling houses of the chieftains held *mansabs* of a thousand horsemen and above, representing almost 15 per cent of the total number of *mansabdars* of a thousand or more horsemen.[3] When a chieftain received a high *mansab* (a military rank regulated by the supposed number of horsemen the holder of the title could bring into the field), he also received a substantial jagir for the support of

his troops. The revenue from this jagir would far exceed that of the chieftain's hereditary dominion; for example, the jagir granted to a *mansabdar* of five thousand *zat,* five thousand *sawar,* was expected to yield a yearly revenue of 8.3 lakhs of rupees which was several times the income of many of the principal Rajput rulers.[4] This policy resolved to an appreciable degree the basic contradiction between the chieftains and the imperial power and made it more fruitful for them to seek promotion in the imperial service than to cast off the imperial yoke and attempt to expand their territory in defiance of imperial authority. The imperial service also provided to the retainers and clansmen of the chieftains lucrative employment as well as a share in the plunder while conducting campaigns on behalf of the empire. Apart from bringing monetary advantages, imperial service was a source of power to the chieftains and enabled them to strengthen their position by recruiting and maintaining large armies.

2. The Mughals asserted the principle which later came to be known as that of "paramountcy." This meant that a chieftain depended for his position on the goodwill of the emperor rather than on his inherent rights. Only such of the chieftains were designated "rajas" as were given the title by the emperor. While generally conforming to the law of primogeniture and hereditary succession, the Mughals asserted the right of "recognizing" a younger son or even a distant relative of a deceased raja as his successor. The emperor Jahangir (1605–27) specifically claimed this right when he rejected the nomination of a younger son by Rai Rai Singh of Bikaner and nominated the elder one instead. Similarly, on the death of Raja Man Singh of Amber, the claims of Maha Singh, the son of Man Singh's eldest son, were overruled, and Bhao Singh, a younger son of Man Singh, "was given the principality of Amber with the lofty title of Mirza Raja."[5] When Raja Sangram, the chieftain of Kharakpur in Bihar, incurred the displeasure of the emperor and action was taken against him, he was killed and his territories were taken over in *khalisa*; but after some time they were restored to his son, Raja Rozafzun. During Shahjahan's reign (1627–58), the claim of Jaswant Singh of Marwar was upheld in preference to that of his elder brother on the grounds that he was the son of the favorite wife of the late raja, a decision the reverse of that made by Jahangir with regard to Bikaner. The assertion of this right of the emperor to decide who would be the ruler of a principality not only strengthened the control of the central government over the chieftains, but also gave the

latter a sense of personal obligation to the emperor. The well-known policy of matrimonial alliances with the houses of the leading chieftains further strengthened the sense of attachment of the chiefs to the emperor. The Mughal insistence that the chiefs should remain in attendance at the court of the emperor or a governor, or should be represented there by one of their close relatives if they themselves held posts elsewhere, helped to consolidate the imperial hold over the chiefs.

3. Although all the sultans had claimed the right to call upon their vassal chiefs to render military assistance to the sultanate whenever required to do so, the Mughals were successful in utilizing systematically the military services of even such chieftains as did not hold *mansabs*. In practically all the major campaigns conducted by the Mughals the contingents of the vassal chiefs played a prominent part. For example, during the reign of Akbar a number of the leading chiefs of South Bihar served under Raja Man Singh in the Orissa campaign of 1592. At about the same time in Gujarat, many vassal chiefs were required to provide contingents of *sawars,* or horsemen, at the call of the governor. The troops supplied by the chieftains contributed appreciably to the military might of the Mughal Empire. How greatly valued was this military obligation of the chiefs may be judged from Jahangir's statement describing the importance of Bengal in terms of the obligations of its chiefs to supply fifty thousand troops rather than in terms of the enormous revenue it provided.[6]

4. The Mughal emperors appear to have pursued the policy of entering into direct relationship with the vassals of some of the more important chieftains, thus reducing the power of these chieftains and creating a new class of allies. The most obvious example of this policy may be seen in the case of Garha Katanga where Akbar established direct relations with the vassals of the Garha chief. Sometimes the vassals of the ruling chiefs were directly offered imperial *mansabs* as in the case of Marwar after Jaswant Singh's death.

5. Of great importance was the Mughal attempt to treat the hereditary dominions of the autonomous chiefs as *watan* jagirs. This meant that theoretically the chiefs were supposed to have the status of jagirdars, and thus were subject to the imperial revenue regulations, but exercised jagirdari rights in hereditary succession over their territories, which were consequently immune from transfer. Even though this theory could be applied mainly to the chiefs who were enrolled as *mansabdars,* the imperial government made attempts to change the character of the

tribute payable by the chiefs into land revenue assessed on the basis of the actual production. It is difficult to estimate the extent to which the Mughals succeeded in this effort as we find that a very large number of chiefs continued to pay tribute on an irregular basis, which was known as *peshkash*.[7] However, even in fixing the amount of the *peshkash,* the Mughal administrators tried to obtain data regarding the area under cultivation, the crop pattern, and the revenue realized by the chiefs from their vassals or subordinate zamindars. The information in the *Ain-i-Akbari* regarding the states of the chieftains and the account of the revenue settlement of Gujarat conducted by Todar Mal in the sixteenth century provide the most obvious evidence of this effort. In spite of the fact that this policy could be enforced only with partial success, it increased the de jure as well as the de facto control of the empire over the chiefs. It also increased the imperial pressure on their economic resources and compelled many of them to seek imperial service as *mansabdars*. Administratively it tended to bring the land-revenue system of the chiefs in line with the Mughal pattern.

6. The Mughal emperors succeeded to a greater extent than their predecessors in compelling the autonomous chiefs to conform to imperial regulations, especially in regard to the maintenance of law and order and the freedom of transit. Not only were the emperors able to make the chiefs take vigorous action against rebels, criminals, and fugitives who happened to enter their territory, but they also claimed the right to dispense justice to those who appealed to the imperial government against their chiefs. For example, when Raj Suraj Singh of Bikaner arrested the retainers of his brother Dalpat, Jahangir ordered that they be released.[8] Several *farmans* are in existence directing the chieftains not to harass traders passing through their territory or to levy taxes on them. Even though several instances are recorded of chiefs disobeying the imperial orders and levying unauthorized taxes on transit goods, there is no reason to doubt that such orders were generally respected.

The existence of a large number of independent principalities in the country and its political fragmentation could hardly have contributed to its progress. Internecine warfare, a logical corollary of such fragmentation, could not have been conducive to material progress. It is difficult to accept François Bernier's statement that the peasantry was better off under the autonomous rajas than in the rest of the empire,[9] not only because the French doctor's prejudice in favor of feudal rights apparently clouded his judgment, but also because the available original records indicate that the rate of assessment on land and other taxes paid by the peasants in the territories of the chiefs were no lower than those in the contiguous areas outside the chiefs' dominions.[10] Furthermore, if there had been no centralized empire subjecting the chiefs to the payment of tribute, which in the last resort was passed on to the peasants, some other powerful chieftain would have established his overlordship and extracted tribute of a similar type and magnitude.

A centralized empire, by establishing comparatively greater peace and security, by enabling trade and commerce to expand, and by increasing and diversifying the purchasing power of the consuming classes which led to the development of industries, brought about conditions favorable to the growth of a money economy. The emergence of a money economy began to affect agricultural production to a considerable extent, especially because revenue was being realized more and more in cash. It also led to the expansion of cash crops and the extension of the cultivated area, partly as a result of the demand for greater revenue.[11] To the extent that the Mughal Empire succeeded in establishing its authority over the numerous chieftains and the considerable measure of success that it achieved in unifying the country politically and administratively, it played a progressive role in the development of Indian society.

There is no doubt that the Mughals were more successful than any of their predecessors in bringing the numerous chieftains within the pale of their empire. As a result of intensive military campaigning they compelled the chieftains in practically the whole country to accept their suzerainty. In accordance with the tenets of their policy enumerated above they succeeded in securing loyalty and willing cooperation from the overwhelming majority of the chieftains and conformity with the broad aspects of their administrative policy. To this extent they were able to place curbs on the powers of the chiefs.

However, the policy of firmness coupled with friendship was able to resolve the contradiction between the chieftains and the imperial government only to a limited extent. Not all chiefs could have been granted high *mansabs* and lucrative jagirs. Furthermore, many of the nobles who were not zamindars envied the security enjoyed by the chiefs in imperial service and brought pressure on the emperor to restrict the grants of *mansabs* and jagirs to this class. As the pressure on jagirs increased, the emperor was no longer in a position to satisfy the aspirations of the chieftains. In such a situation many of the chiefs enjoying

high positions in imperial service attempted to convert the jagirs as-
signed to them outside their ancestral territories into their hereditary
dominions, as in the case of Sir Singh-deo Bundela during the reign of
Jahangir and Jai Singh Sawai of Amber during the reign of Mohammed
Shah. The imperial policy of demanding the payment of land revenue
based on cultivated area could only have reduced the share of the chiefs.
Rebellions were therefore inevitable. The chiefs hardly ever missed the
opportunity of taking advantage of the difficulties facing the empire.
For example, the chieftains of Orissa and Bengal supported Shahjahan
when he rebelled against his father, but they quickly deserted the rebel
prince when he was defeated by the imperial forces. On the other hand,
whenever, because of various difficulties, the imperial government was
unable to maintain its military pressure on the zamindars, the revolts
became more frequent. Such was the case in the seventeenth century
during the reign of Aurangzeb when the chieftains of Maharashtra,
Bundelkhand, Mewat, and Rajputana, all took up arms against the
Mughal Empire and in their struggle drew upon the support of the
lower classes of the zamindars, and also sometimes the peasants, especially when they belonged to the same clan or caste. The widespread
dissatisfaction of the chiefs with the imperial government seriously weakened the military power of the Mughal Empire. The empire depended
too much on the support of the chiefs to have been successful in sup-
pressing their power completely.

The frequent revolts of the chieftains, leading to long-drawn-out
military campaigns and the inability of the imperial government to prevent the chiefs from expanding their dominions, placed a serious drain
on the economy, adversely affected agricultural production in many
cases, and weakened administrative unity. Consequently, by the close
of the seventeenth century, the economic and administrative advantages
of a unified empire had begun to disappear.

### The Intermediary Zamindars

This category comprised the various types of zamindars who collected the revenue from the primary zamindars and paid it to the imperial treasury, or to the jagirdars, or to the chieftains—or in certain
cases kept it themselves. Such intermediaries not only formed the back-
bone of land-revenue administration, but were also responsible for the
maintenance of law and order. In return for their services they enjoyed
various types of perquisites, such as commissions, deductions, revenue-

free lands (*nankar* or *banth*), cesses, etc. Usually their share of the revenue ranged between 2.5 and 10 per cent. Most of the zamindars possessed hereditary rights, though in a few cases they held their position on short-term contracts.[12] Among the intermediaries may be included *chaudhuris, desmukhs, desais, despandes,* certain types of *mugaddams, kanungos* and *ijaradars,* and the class of zamindars who contracted with the state to realize the revenue of a given territory and who began to be known during the second half of the seventeenth century by the generic designation of talukdars. Practically the entire country was under the jurisdiction of one or the other types of intermediary zamindars. The statement in the *Ain-i-Akbari* regarding the caste of zamindars in parganas other than those under the chieftains seems to refer to this class.[13] The fact that in the majority of the parganas the zamindars belonged to a single caste and also that persons of the same caste were the zamindars of many contiguous parganas suggests that certain families or clans held zamindari rights over large tracts.

While the rights of the intermediary zamindars were hereditary, the state reserved to itself the authority to interfere with succession and even to partition the jurisdiction among brothers or relations. In the case of imperial displeasure some of these intermediaries could be dismissed or transferred. An order of Akbar mentions the dismissal of a *chaudhuri* in Ilahabad on the grounds that he had been harassing the pilgrims going to the Triveni for holy baths.[14] A *nishan* (order) of Murad Bakhsh conferred the *desmukhi* of a pargana in *suba* Telingana on one Rama Reddy, rejecting the claim of half the *desmukhi* of the pargana put forward by the adopted son of his elder deceased brother.[15] Aurangzeb issued an order that there could not be more than two *chaudhuris* in a pargana; if there were, they were to be dismissed.[16] In some cases the Mughal emperors conferred zamindari rights on persons appointed to maintain law and order or to facilitate the assessment and collection of land revenue.[17] Akbar's *farman* to Gopaldas conferring on him the rights of *chaudhuri* and *kanungo* in *sarkar* Tirhut formed the basis of the subsequent rise of the Darbhanga raj.[18] To satisfy the desire of the high *mansabdars* and nobles not belonging to the zamindar class to acquire hereditary territorial rights, the Mughal emperors instituted the practice of conferring *watan* and *altamgha* jagirs. In such cases the persons concerned were given permanent jagirdari rights. Usually the territories granted in such jagirs were small, comprising a single village or a small number of villages, though in some

cases they were larger. The holders of these jagirs tried to acquire proprietary rights and in due course were often called upon to pay land
revenue. For instance, the *watan* jagirs granted by Jahangir to Anirai
Singh Dalan developed into large and powerful zamindaris of Anup-
shahr in Bulandshahr District. A similar case was that of the *watan*
jagir granted during the reign of Jahangir to Miran Sadr Jahan at
Pihani in Shahjahanpur District.

Most of the intermediaries were supposed to prepare the details of
revenue assessment for the perusal of the state, help in the realization
of the land revenue, encourage extension of cultivation, assist the imperial officers in the maintenance of law and order, and supply a fixed
number of contingents. However, in actual practice, they were constantly struggling to enhance their rights and to appropriate to themselves a greater share of the revenue if not the whole of it. The extant
records are full of references to the *zamindaran-i-zor-talab,* that is,
those who paid revenue only when it was demanded forcibly. Similarly,
the intermediaries who contracted to collect revenue, either as *ijaradars*
or as talukdars tried to avoid supplying detailed figures of assessment
and only paid the stipulated amount. The Mughal custom of frequent
transfers of jagirs encouraged the practice of revenue farming, or the
letting of contracts to someone else to collect the revenue.

On the one hand, these intermediaries strove to consolidate their
rights at the expense of the state; thus, for example, they often appropriated to themselves the state's right to dispose of the uncultivated
wastelands. On the other hand, they intensified the exploitation of the
rural population and attempted to depress the position of the primary
zamindars under their jurisdiction. Since they had the responsibility to
pay the land revenue, whether the primary zamindars paid it or not,
they were led on occasion to collect the revenue directly from the
peasants, in which case they were supposed to leave the primary zamindars the customary "proprietary" share (*malikana*). But the temptation
in such a situation to step into the place of the primary zamindars and
become proprietors themselves must have been overwhelming.[19]

At the same time, they sought to build up hereditary territorial rights
and, whenever the occasion arose, tried to become chieftains. As the
Mughal Empire became weak and the crisis of the jagirdari system was
intensified, these intermediaries enhanced their powers and frequently
rose in rebellion along with the other intermediary zamindars of their
own clan or joined hands with some of the chieftains who were in re-

volt against the imperial authority. Apart from the political and administrative disturbances which resulted from the tussle between such zamindars and the state, agricultural production and the position of the peasantry also suffered.

While the imperial authorities strove to subjugate the recalcitrant zamindars and attempted to force them to conform to the imperial land-revenue regulations, they could not afford to suppress this class as a whole. Under strong administrators the intermediaries generally performed their duties in accordance with imperial regulations and exercised their rights within specified limits. But under weak administrators the situation frequently got out of hand. The widespread revolt of these zamindars deprived the imperial officers of their income and consequently reduced their military strength. In turn, the officers started demanding transfers from the turbulent areas and even began to claim cash salaries instead of jagirs.[20]

## The Primary Zamindars

The primary zamindars were for all practical purposes the holders of proprietary rights over agricultural as well as habitational lands. In this class may be included not only the peasant-proprietors who carried on cultivation themselves, or with the help of hired labor, but also the proprietors of one or several villages. All agricultural lands in the empire belonged to one or the other type of the primary zamindars. The rights held by the primary zamindars were hereditary and alienable. Numerous sale deeds of such zamindaris dating back to the sixteenth century are still available.[21] The Mughal state considered it its duty to protect the rights of these zamindars and encouraged the registration of transfer deeds at the court of the *kazi* so that a proper record of claims could be maintained.

In addition to those who had been enjoying these rights for generations or had acquired them by purchase, the Mughals conferred such zamindari rights on a large number of persons. In pursuance of their policy of extending the cultivated area, the emperors freely bestowed zamindari rights to those who would bring forest and waste under cultivation. It is also significant that the majority of the *madad maash* grants (revenue-free grants given for charitable purposes) related to uncultivated land. The *madad maash* grants required confirmation at the accession of each monarch, but the hereditary succession was not usually interfered with. In due course the *madad maash* grants also

acquired the character of zamindari, as appears from the sale deeds of
*madad maash* lands in the eighteenth century.

The zamindars, other than the peasant-proprietors, generally gave
their lands in hereditary lease to their tenants, who enjoyed security of
tenure in terms of the patta granted to them, on the condition that they
paid their land revenue regularly. Even in cases of nonpayment the
tenant was not usually deprived of his landholding rights, but the arrears were realized by other means. Considering the fact that there was
not much pressure on land, the rights of the landholding tenants were
generally respected. At the same time, in view of the shortage of cultivators, the zamindars enjoyed the right to restrain the tenants from
leaving their lands and to compel them to cultivate all arable land held
by them.[22] From the evidence it seems that where the primary zamindars did not pay the land revenue, it was collected directly from the
peasants, leaving about 10 per cent as the proprietary share (*malikana*)
of the zamindars.[23] It may be inferred that this percentage represents
the normal share of the zamindars. In addition to their share in land
revenue, the zamindars were also entitled to a large variety of cesses,
though a considerable portion of the income from such cesses had to
be surrendered by the zamindars along with the land revenue.

The zamindars were deemed to be the *malguzars* or those on whom
land revenue was assessed by the state. They were also expected to collect the revenue from the peasants and to deposit the share of the state
with the higher authorities. It was their duty to assist the administration in the maintenance of law and order and in many cases to supply
troops under the orders of their superiors.

Sandwiched as most of these zamindars were between the superior
zamindars and the state on the one hand and the peasantry on the
other, they were constantly struggling to improve their position and
thus frequently came into conflict with both sides. Unless these zamindars were able to withstand pressure from above, they passed on the
burden of revenue demands to the cultivators and so contributed to the
intensification of the economic exploitation of the latter. On such occasions, they played an economically retrogressive role. But on many
occasions they led the revolts of the peasantry against the growing exactions of the state, often utilizing the caste and clan appeal to rally
support. Where revolts were not possible, many of these zamindars refused to pay the revenue until force was employed. As has been mentioned earlier, the intermediary zamindars often tried to depress the

status of the primary zamindars, and where the attempt was successful a fresh category of subproprietary rights emerged. Sometimes the intermediary zamindars created a class of subproprietors, such as the *birtias,* in order to strengthen their position in the countryside.

Thus, there emerged not only a variety of land rights but also a kind of a pyramidical structure in agrarian relations wherein rights of various kinds were superimposed upon each other. The burden of the shares of the different categories of zamindars and also of the imperial revenue demand ultimately fell on the cultivator and placed such a strain on the agrarian economy that much progress was hardly possible. The imperial government tried its best to ensure that the peasant was not called upon to pay more than 50 per cent of the produce. But as imperial authority declined and as the pressure on jagirs increased, the agricultural economy had to face a crisis which began to deepen in the eighteenth century.

Politically and administratively, the zamindar class in general rendered loyal cooperation and assistance to the Mughal Empire. Yet the conflicts of interest between the zamindars and the state, and between the different classes of zamindars, could not be eliminated. The conflicts led to frequent clashes, disturbed law and order, and seriously weakened the administrative and military power of the state. The numerous measures adopted by the Mughal government to resolve these contradictions worked well, but only for a time. By the middle of the seventeenth century, strains began to appear, and after the death of Aurangzeb in 1707 the central government had become too weak to maintain the equilibrium between conflicting interests. In any case, the dependence of the Mughal Empire on the various classes of the zamindars for its revenue resources as well as administration was far too deep for the conflicts of interest between the empire and zamindars to be resolved. Only a class which was not dependent on the zamindars could have attempted to change the pattern of agrarian relations. Such a class had not emerged by the middle of the eighteenth century.

## NOTES

1   The following discussion of the zamindars is aimed at focusing the attention of historians on the urgent need for a detailed study of the working of the zamindari system during the Mughal period. The opinions expressed are tentative and are based on only a small fraction of the evidence available.

2  See Irfan Habib, "The Zamindars in the Ain," *Proceedings of the Indian History Congress* (Allahabad, 1958).
3  M. Athar Ali, *The Mughal Nobility under Aurangzeb* (Bombay and New York, 1966), p. 13.
4  This figure was calculated on the basis of the eight-month scale. The *zat* rank was the personal rank of the officer, while the number of his horsemen was indicated by the *sawar* rank.
5  *Tuzuk-i-Jahangiri* (Aligarh, 1864), p. 130. Also see pages 106 and 145.
6  *Ibid.*, p. 7.
7  Detailed information on the assessment of *peshkash* from the zamindar of Trichnopoly from the years A.H. 1104–1117 (A.D. 1692–1706) may be seen in the Central Records Office, Hyderabad, Reg. No. 83 of Aurangzeb's reign.
8  *Farman* No. 29, dated 9 October 1614, in the *Descriptive List of Farmans, Manshurs and Nishans* (Bikaner, 1962), published by the Government of Rajasthan Directorate of Archives.
9  V. A. Smith (trans.), François Bernier's *Travels in the Mughal Empire, 1656–1667* (London, 1916), p. 205.
10  Comparing the *arsattas* (monthly accounts of receipts and disbursements) of the parganas of Amber and Sawal Jaipur with those of the parganas of Chatsu and Hindaun reveals a general similarity in the rates of assessment (Rajasthan State Archives).
11  For an excellent discussion of the impact of money economy on agricultural production and for the nature of the agrarian relations existing in the Mughal Empire, see Irfan Habib's *Agrarian System of Mughal India* (Bombay, 1963).
12  For a discussion of the various types of land rights, see B. R. Grover, "Nature of Land Rights in Mughal India," *Indian Economic and Social History Review*, I, 1–23.
13  "Account of the Twelve Subas" in H. S. Jarrett (trans.), Abul-Fazl-I'allami's *Ain-i-Akbari* (2nd ed.; Calcutta, 1949), II.
14  Copies of a number of *farmans* issued in this connection by Akbar and Jahangir were made available to the writer by Dr. M. A. Ansari of Allahabad University.
15  Andra Pradesh State Archives, Hyderabad, Shahjahani Register, Vol. 40, No. 608, *nishan* dated 15 Ramazan, twenty-third regnal year of Shahjahan. The *suba* was a division of the empire, like a province.
16  Habib, *Agrarian System*, p. 292.
17  A *farman* of Shahjahan issued during the fifth regnal year promised zamindari rights to anyone who could bring the turbulent zamindars of the parganas of Kant and Gola under control. He was then to found a town named after the emperor in that region. A photostat of the *farman* is in the possession of the writer. See also Grover, *op. cit.*, p. 12.
18  Qeyam Uddin Ahmed, "Origin and Growth of Darbhanga Raj (1574–1666), Based on Some Contemporary and Unpublished Documents," *Proceedings of the Indian Historical Records Commission*, XXXVI, 88–98. The *sarkar* was a government administrative district.
19  For example, in 1703, Raja Ibadullah Kahn of Muhammadi contracted for the whole of the parganas of Barwar-Anjana and Bhurwara in *sarkar* Khairabad, *suba* Awadh, and in course of time acquired proprietary rights over the whole estate.

20 Numerous cases are cited in a number of contemporary documents included in the Durr-ul-Ulum, a collection of papers arranged by Sahib Rai Surdaj in 1688–89, now in the Bodleian Library, Oxford.
21 Numerous transfer deeds are preserved at the Central Records Office, Allahabad.
22 See N. A. Siddiqi, "Dasturul Amal-i-Bekas," *Proceedings of the Indian History Congress* (Aligarh, 1960).
23 Grover, *op. cit.,* p. 15.

Chapter III

# Landholding
# in India
# and
# British
# Institutions

*Ainslie T. Embree*

*The legislature of England has universally promoted the good
ends of civil society, the peace and security of individuals,
by steadily pursuing that wise and orderly maxim, of assigning
to everything capable of ownership, a legal and determinate
owner.*

Sir William Blackstone, COMMENTARIES

The question of the nature and
extent of British influence on India is curiously complicated. To anyone
familar with the literature on India, particularly that written in the nineteenth century, that influence seems so dominant and obvious that it
scarcely needs comment. Yet one is soon aware that these writings
were frequently contradictory and that even observers with similar experience and knowledge have given surprisingly divergent assessments.
It is possible, however, to classify the endless verdicts on India into four
main categories. Many wrote of the great changes wrought in the political and social fabric of Indian life, of values transformed, and of a
higher civilization transplanted to an alien land.[1] Others emphasized the
enormous extent of British influence, but saw it as a malevolent force
that destroyed the moral and social basis of Indian life.[2] A third category of writers had a totally different vision of the extent of British
influence on India. What impressed them was not how much had been
done, for good or ill, but how little. Some of these, like the missionary

Alexander Duff, believed that Britain had been given a divine mandate for instituting social change but had failed to use it; and having "fondled and favoured superstition and idolatry," the Britsh were justly punished in 1857.[3] A fourth group agreed that nothing had been basically changed in India, but they took this as an indication, not of the failure of the British, but of the essential nature of Indian civilization. At the end of the nineteenth century, in his now forgotten but remarkable book on the differences between Asia and Europe, Meredith Townsend declared that if the British "departed or were driven out they would leave behind them, as the Romans did in Britain, splendid roads, many useless buildings, an increased weakness in a subject people, and a memory which in a century of new events would be extinct."[4]

What these contradictory assessments make clear is that in the identification and evaluation of the impact of one culture on another, even when one of the cultures is in the advantageous position of being transmitted by a ruling power, it is difficult to achieve any precise definition either of the forces at work to produce change or of the areas being influenced in the indigenous culture. In trivial and marginal areas of cultural change, the points of contact are often easy to identify, and it is probably safe to say that the less fundamental a cultural trait is in its own environment the more easily is it accepted by another culture. Cricket in India is an example; its origin and role could probably be defined as accurately as one cared to make the effort. But values and attitudes are at the other extreme, and the manner of their transmission, as well as their influence, is difficult to measure. An example that comes to mind is of the attitudes in modern India that are frequently referred to as "puritanical." This labeling is open to question to anyone familiar with the history of the word in Western society; but what is meant will be recognized by all observers of the contemporary Indian scene. Commentators like Mulk Raj Anand, in his books on Indian art, have often found the origin of these attitudes in the mores of Victorian England.[5] Here, it is suggested, one sees a peculiarly unlovely legacy of colonial rule; yet as one ponders on the nature both of the Victorian and the Indian heritage, doubts obtrude themselves as to the validity of this simplistic analysis. As one examines the current phenomena, reflects on the actual kind of contacts that existed in the nineteenth century, and tries to make some correlation of facts and theories, it soon becomes apparent that the equation of modern Indian value systems with the political dominance of Britain at a particular moment of time will not explain very much. The web of social customs and ethical interpretations of Indian society are too complex to permit one to suppose that values were transmitted in the same fashion as cricket.

In tracing the influence of British institutions on landholding in India, one must be aware that the analogy is with the transmission of values, not of cricket. One is confronted with the interaction of a series of infinitely complex and varied factors, and it would probably be possible to show that almost every British institution introduced into India in the nineteenth century had some effect on landholding. There are, however, three closely related ones that call for special attention. The first of these, and the one that will receive emphasis in this paper, is the institution of property as understood in Great Britain in the late eighteenth and early nineteenth century. This time span is emphasized because the crucial impact was made by the 1850's; after that, despite many efforts to effect changes, the patterns that emerge were determined by earlier decisions. The second institution is that of efficient government as it was understood in the nineteenth century. It is often suggested that when the British evaluated Indian society against their own that they did so in terms of religion. It would probably be more accurate to say that the evaluation was on the basis of the ability of a society to provide political order in which commerce might flourish and property be protected. This is the theme, for example, of the correspondence from the British agents in Burma to Calcutta in the early 1850's, and the assumption is always that a government which could not protect property and trade had forfeited its right to rule.[6] The third institution is the legal system, the establishment of which was intimately connected with questions of ownership of property and the extent to which the Company should interfere in the actual process of government.[7] While only cursory reference will be made to these last two institutions, separately and together they worked with the institution of property, as understood by the British, to create modern India.

In answering a question relating to the influence of British institutions in India, one has to show what happened in the nineteenth century; but this always involves two other questions: What did those who controlled the mechanism of power think they were doing? Why did they think it was necessary to act in this way? An illustration of the necessity of asking these questions can be found in one of the most examined actions in the history of modern India, the creation of the Permanent Settlement. What one sees is a confrontation in which at least three main elements are present: assumptions about Indian society, judgments as to what was politically expedient, and the realities of the Indian land situation.

To ask what the British thought they were doing leads to other questions: How did the rulers understand the society they confronted? What did they understand about the nature of property in India? How did Indians think about property? And one even has to ask the most difficult question of all: What was in fact the nature of property arrangements in India? Not all these questions find answers in this paper, but they are the ones that must be asked by the serious student who wants to understand how Indian society reacted to the alien intruder.

We have been speaking of British influence; but one must always be aware that this adjective is constantly misused in relation to India. Whether referring to land systems, foreign affairs, or moral judgments, the use of "British" as a modifier implies a unity in the Britsh impact that never existed. One must say categorically that there was no British policy in any sphere of activity in India, only varieties of policies, of attitudes, and influences. These often worked at cross-purposes, for they arose out of profoundly different interpretations of politics and morals. One misses much of the significance of the process of the making of modern India unless one keeps this variety in mind and realizes that all that one should mean to convey by the word *British* is a shorthand notation for the complexity of the impact of the West. What was important in the intrusion of British political power into India was not the particular national culture that impressed itself upon the ancient civilization, but the way of thinking that had become dominant everywhere in the West in the nineteenth century.

This reservation against assuming that the influences which were operative in India had a unitary character applies with special force to the concept of property that came into the country in the eighteenth and nineteenth centuries as a constituent element of British political power. There is no British concept of property, any more than there is an Indian one, but to make any sense out of a vital area of contact it is necessary to identify some of the ideas and theories that the British took with them to India. This is not to suggest that the men who devised the land settlements were trying to put theories into practice, but only that certain fundamental concepts were part of their mental equipment and that these colored both the decisions that were made as well as the explanations they gave of what they were trying to do, and why they had to do it in a particular way.

The British concept of property, especially as it relates to land, is a jungle into which one does not enter willingly. Furthermore, as Sir Henry Maine remarked in his famous discussion of property, "Any intelligent man who will be at pains to ask himself seriously what he knows about its origin or the laws or mode of its historical growth will find that his knowledge is extraordinarily small."[8] Yet a few generalizations can be made through reference to various historical formulations which have contributed to the way the British have thought about property.

One strand of the Western European way of thinking about property comes from the practices and legal codes of the Roman Empire. While it is true that Roman law did not have the same role in English life as it did on the continent, Roman ideas and Roman words were part of the intellectual inheritance of educated men in the eighteenth and nineteenth centuries, and they played a part in India. The characteristic Roman idea about property that became rooted in the European mind was the concept of unqualified possession. As Noyes has commented, "The absolute quality of *dominium* seemed so primordial, so fundamentally a part of the nature of things, that it was taken for granted . . . . It appeared obvious that an object could not belong to more than one class at a time . . . . Nor did the idea permit two kinds of interest [in a thing] to exist."[9] This understanding of property is so much a part of the Western tradition that it is probably fair to say it is what most men would regard as a commonsense way of looking at things.

While the Roman understanding of property may commend itself to common sense, there were other influences that shaped both British thought about property as well as actual practice. One of these was the amalgam of social customs that emerged in England following the Norman Conquest. A pattern of land ownership and a way of thinking about property grew up after the eleventh century that was different from either of the originating societies, the Norman or the Anglo-Saxon. The transference of lands from the old owners to the followers of the Conqueror made possible a legal theory that the land was the king's and that the people were not only his subjects but also his tenants. "All the subjects of the king, rich or poor, free or bond, were tenants with the exception of the proletariat and outcasts of town and country;

everyone held a tenure of the king or of an intermediary, and, ultimately, everyone held, directly or indirectly, of the king."[10] How some of these tenants, mightier than the rest, struggled with the kings for power is a familiar story, and up to the fifteenth century effective power was in the hands of an hereditary nobility. The power of this class was based on lordship over great estates, and the relationship between political control and land ownership is a dominant feature of British social and political history.

The significance of the social structure of what was already a remote past in the eighteenth century must not be overstressed; but it is difficult to escape the conclusion that at least the echoes of the medieval legacy are found in British attitudes in India. The idea of the king granting lands to tenants who became both territorial powers and, eventually, the supporters of royal power, is surely one of the organizing concepts that the British used for understanding Indian political and social life. I have in mind not only the creation of landlords in Bengal, but even more the conviction that seems to have been widely held, particularly after 1857, that the sources of leadership would be found in the landed classes, rather than in the Western-educated classes of the great port cities. The most concrete example of this is the land settlement with the talukdars of Oudh in 1858. This attitude is all the more curious when one remembers that the policy-makers in nineteenth century India were not, on the whole, from the landowning classes in England. One gets the impression that they looked at India and drew an irresistible analogy with the moment in British history when a strong conqueror, advised by able men, created a new land settlement.

In the century preceding the time when the British became an active political force in India, theories of property had been much debated in England. This was partly a result of the civil war and the revolutions of 1688, partly of the changing basis of economic power in the seventeenth and eighteenth centuries. As already mentioned, to emphasize ideas is not to suggest that the land settlements of the eighteenth and nineteenth centuries are to be understood as exercises in application of theory, but at the same time to ignore the extraordinary examination of the nature of property that went on in England from about the third decade of the seventeenth century until the beginning of the nineteenth century is surely to miss the significance of much that happened in India. For example, James Grant, in his "Political Survey of the Northern Circars" declared that "one of the first, most essential and the best ascertained principles of Eastern legislation" is that "the proprietary right of the soil is constitutional, and solely vested in the sovereign."[11] One is reminded of Thomas Hobbes' argument that "no private man can claim a propriety in any lands, or other goods, from any title from any man but the king, or them that have the sovereign power."[12] Grant may not have actually read Hobbes, but he was drawing upon ideas that were part of the English inheritance. As will be noted later, Grant accepted a common view of Asian society when he spoke of the sovereign as owner of the soil, but the political implications of his understanding of land tenures was that the existing structure could be used to further British power.

While the Hobbesian analysis provided a way of thinking about property that may have helped some of those concerned with land problems in India to organize their ideas, the classic formulation that dominated eighteenth-century British thought about property was found in the writings of John Locke. Locke's interpretation of the nature of property ownership—or at least what was held to be his interpretation—was part of the cultural inheritance by the end of the eighteenth century. His concepts, which admirably expressed the needs of the age, caused the British to look at land ownership in a way that was probably new to Indian experience.

For Locke, private ownership was a law of nature. While the earth was given in common to all men, nevertheless "every man has a Property in his own Person," and no one else had any claim on this property but himself. This private property arose out of the common possession of the earth by all because, in Locke's famous phrase, man had "mixed his Labour with, and joyned to it something that is his own, and thereby makes it his Property."[13] It was labor, he insisted, that put value on land, and when God gave man the commandment to subdue the earth, he gave the "authority to appropriate. And the condition of humane life, which requires Labour and Materials to work on, necessarily introduces Private Possessions." Locke was probably insisting on the right of the individual against the state, but his argument was used to exalt private property as an inalienable human right. One's human rights included, along with liberty, that of owning and disposing of the property that one had gained by mixing one's labor with the land.

The belief that property was a natural right was one of the pieces of mental furniture that the Company's servants took with them into rural Bengal in the 1770's and 1780's as they faced the problem of translating political power into administrative control. The story of those years is so familiar that it does not need retelling, except to emphasize that the picaresque events ought not obscure the interest the period should have for everyone concerned with understanding in detail the process of the creation of a modern administrative state. When the peasants declared that they had worked the land, and therefore had a right to its use, even though they had no deeds, the Company servants were inclined to recognize the validity of their argument. But they also saw that the tax farmer had "mixed his labour," although in a somewhat metaphorical way, in the same land. An example of this kind of discussion is found in the interesting exchange of letters that took place in 1780 between the commercial resident at Malda and the collector at Dinajpur.[14] Both men, the one supporting the peasants, the other the tax farmer, were arguing in terms of the immediate practical need for revenues and cloth for the Company's investment, but the references to property rights suggest that they were not able to avoid appealing to abstract ideas about property that were, strictly speaking, irrelevant to Bengal.

At the very end of the nineteenth century, Locke's concept of property as derived from "mixing one's labour" received influential restatement in India in the works of B. H. Baden-Powell. Baden-Powell was especially concerned to disprove the theory that all land had been owned by the ruler, and he argued that the idea of a right in land derived from original use was accepted throughout India. He admits, however, that the concepts of "possession" and "just title," as known in Western jurisprudence, are not found anywhere articulated in Indian thought.[15]

Locke's understanding of property found its ways into the actual fabric of law in India, as in Great Britain and America, through the immensely influential systemization of law found in Sir William Blackstone's *Commentaries on the Laws of England*. The strong influence of Blackstone on the institutions of Great Britain and the United States is well known, but in India the influence of his great opponent, Jeremy Bentham, is so easily documented that there has been a tendency to overlook the *Commentaries* as a source of ideas. Wherever one looks in nineteenth-century administration, there is plenty of evidence of the fulfillment of Bentham's prediction that after he was dead he would be the despot who ruled India.[16] Macaulay's penal code and the codes of civil and criminal procedure are clearly products of

Benthamite teaching, and as Sir Courtenay Ilbert remarked, they demonstrated the values of codification for "unprofessional judges and magistrates."[17] But even if Blackstone never occupied in India the position he did in Great Britain and America as a legal reference, his interpretation of laws was part of late-eighteenth-century thinking. His demonstration, to the satisfaction of his contemporaries, that the laws of England made property central to the concept of liberty is an integral assumption of the debates in England over the rights of the East India Company and in India over the land settlements.

While Blackstone accepted the general proposition that the institution of property is a natural right, he argued that it was at the same time a product of civil government and its laws. Despite the origin of property in nature, "the method of conserving it in the present owner, and of translating it from man to man, are entirely derived from society."[18] In effect, those attributes of property which make it peculiarly valuable—the right of enjoyment without hindrance and the right of alienation—are dependent upon the state. As Daniel Boorstin said in his study of Blackstone, "The law of nature had made property possible and necessary, but the laws of England had fulfilled the possibility which nature herself had not dreamed of."[19] What emerges is an understanding of property admirably suited to a society dependent upon trade and commerce, where land was scarce, and political stability had been achieved. Ownership meant that neither sovereign nor intermediary landlord could prevent the sale or transfer of property, nor was the use of property hindered by any services to be rendered to them, for, according to Blackstone, "Experience hath shown that property best answers the purposes of civil life, especially in commercial countries, when its transfers are totally free and unfettered."[20] And at the same time that civil government guaranteed these claims of private ownership, property provided a foundation for the state itself, for until the institution of property was recognized there could be no peace, which is "the very end and foundation of civil society." Without private property, and its defense by the state, there would be anarchy.

This particular emphasis on the relationship between private property secured by the civil government and the general peace and prosperity of society is the assumption that underlies much of the discussion in the late 1780's over the Permanent Settlement in Bengal and is especially evident in Cornwallis' minutes. It comes strongly to the fore, for example, when questions of justice are raised. Cornwallis recognized that injustices would be done under the terms of the proposed settlement, but again and again he returned to the position that only when property was defined, and ownership known and respected, could the foundation be laid for a peaceful and prosperous state. The point is also made in discussing rights other than in land claimed by the zamindars. Many of them had the right to collect duties on internal trade, and this privilege was quite as clearly defined as their right to collect rents. Cornwallis agreed that both claims were of equal validity, but the zamindars had their rights confirmed in the land but not in the custom duties. Ownership of the land, he argued, was the basis of prosperity, while ownership of the rights to exact levies on trade was "incompatible with the general prosperity of the country."[21]

We have been speaking of the way the British thought about property, particularly as this thinking was articulated by Locke and Blackstone, and this answers, in a rudimentary fashion at least, the question originally posed as to why the new rulers believed it was necessary to act in the fashion they did when they dealt with questions of land ownership. This leads to the other questions of how they regarded the Indian institution of property and how this understanding corresponded to reality.

One of the first Europeans to describe what seemed to him to be the peculiar features of land ownership in India was the French traveler, François Bernier (1620–88). "The Great Mogol," Bernier declared, "is the proprietor of every acre of land in the kingdom"; there was "no idea of the principle of *meum* and *tuum,* related to land or real possessions . . . ."[22] This view was widely held by servants of the East India Company and was the central argument of James Grant in his voluminous study of the revenue settlements of the Mughal rulers. The same principle was advanced with great skill by James Mill in his *History of British India* (London, 1817). From the facts gathered by travelers and by East India Company officials, Mill thought the only conclusion that could be drawn was that "The property of the soil resided in the sovereign; for if it did not reside in him, it will be impossible to show to whom it belonged."[23] As Eric Stokes has pointed out, this interpretation of Indian conditions had immediate practical importance, for Mill not only believed that in the past the rulers of India had owned the soil, but, from his influential position within the Company, he argued that the British should not, through land settlements, renounce the rights traditionally held by Indian rulers.[24]

Here a question of great fascination for anyone interested in the history of ideas must be asked: What was the reason for the widespread acceptance of the belief that Indian rulers owned all the land and that private property was unknown in India? One answer, of course, might be, "because it was true"; but almost no one would now accept the statement in the way that Bernier or Mill put it forward. There is too much evidence that suggests the picture of ownership was far more complex than the early observers realized.

One explanation of the unanimity of the early European observers is given by Irfan Habib in his careful study of the agrarian system of Mughal India. The European travelers were mistaken, he says, since there is documentary evidence to show that "persons other than the king laid claim to a right upon land that in name was ownership."[25] The reason for the Europeans not realizing this may have simply been ignorance, but the more likely explanation, Habib thinks, is that the Mughal jagirdars appeared to be the same as European landlords. Since the jagirs were transferable at the emperor's will, the Europeans therefore concluded that there was no private property in India.

As for the Utilitarians, it is probably true that the idea of state or royal ownership appealed to them because of tendencies within their general philosophical system. One of the problems they had debated was the means of "setting free of some portion or other of the net produce of the year, and the conversion of this produce into capital."[26] By a single tax on land, that portion of the net produce needed for capital could be obtained. When he looked at India, Mill believed that he saw a system actually in operation that, if properly maintained, could provide for the needs of the government while adjusting the opposition which existed between the landlord and the community.

While these explanations have much to commend them, there is another reason, which I think is the most important one for the curious unanimity of interpretation in regard to the ownership of the soil by the sovereign. All of the European travelers, as well as the Company officials, were drawing upon an ancient and well-articulated view of the nature of Asian society. From the time of Herodotus, Europeans had accepted an image of Asian government as despotic, and an integral feature of this despotism was the ownership of all the land by the sovereign. One finds this view in the Greek writers, and it appears very strongly in the writings of Bodin, Montesquieu, and Diderot. The Utilitarian theorists, as well as travelers like Niccolo Manucci, Jean de Thevenot, François Bernier, Sir Thomas Roe, and Abbé Dubois were conscious of this interpretation, and their reading and observations confirmed the traditional views of India as an Asian despotism. It is true that some writers in the eighteenth century questioned the belief that land was all owned by the sovereign. Notable among these was Anquetil Duperron, who translated the Upanishad into Latin and wrote an interesting account of India. Duperron argued that the whole idea of Asian despotism was false and that in India there were written codes obeyed by the rulers as well as the subjects.[27] This was a minority report, however, and the traditional interpretation remained dominant, especially after it received its restatement in Mill's writing.

The reasons, then, for the continued acceptance of this traditional European view of property in India, even after fairly careful investigations had been carried out, are fairly clear. First of all, it grew out of the understanding of the nature of property that was, as has been suggested above, part of the climate of opinion of the British in the eighteenth and early nineteenth century. Everything, but particularly land, must be owned by someone. Added to this was the deeply rooted belief—confirmed by experience in eighteenth-century India—that political power in Asia was organized in a despotic fashion that permitted no freedom of initiative to the individual. These two assumptions inform James Mill's conclusion that the ruler *must* be the owner, since otherwise it is impossible to show to whom property belonged. Richard Jones, who taught political economy at the East India College at Haileybury, and whose writings on the nature of Indian tenures influenced John Stuart Mill, made this connection between despotism and ownership very explicit in his work on peasant rents. The uniformity of the political systems of Asia was due, he wrote, to the "national habits of submission in the people and the absolute power in the chiefs." Throughout Asia, the sovereign power owned the land, and the peasant must have land to till or starve. "The body of the nation is therefore in every case dependent upon the great sovereign proprietor for the means of livelihood." Like James Mill, Jones found this view of property corroborated through a reading of Colebrooke's translation of Manu.[28]

These two presuppositions—one drawn from the understanding of the nature of property and the other from the understanding of Asian government—ultimately depended upon the actual nature of Indian society. Admitting the overriding importance of the mental attitudes of Europeans and also their ignorance, nevertheless, there must have been something in Indian society that confirmed their prejudices. What this was is surely clear: The idea of ownership as understood either in the Roman inheritance or in the British formulation was lacking in India. This statement must be hedged about with many reservations, since property laws differed from region to region, and with the Muslim conquests entirely new practices entered India. And yet, despite the long centuries of Muslim rule, one can be fairly safe in making the generalization that Islamic concepts of property made very little difference to Indian society. Islamic law and theory recognized private property, and the rules governing it had been influenced by Roman-Byzantine law.[29] In the case of a conquered country, however, there were rules that varied with the different legal schools. According to the Shafii school, all the lands gained by conquest were divided among the soldiers. After the great conquests in Iraq and Iran, this was not done, and the original inhabitants were left in possession, on the condition that they paid the tax known as *kharaj*. In India, further accommodations were made, both at the time of the Arab conquest of Sind and during the sultanate. The teachings of the Hanafi school held that a ruler, once a settlement had been made with a conquered people, could not revoke their ownership of the land (even though they were non-Muslims). This became accepted as a guiding rule of Islamic jurisprudence in India.[30] What this meant in effect was that the rules of custom which had governed inheritance and other claims upon land remained unchanged for most of the people of India. It is, therefore, necessary to ask what Hindu views of property were, even after five centuries of Muslim rule.

What the *practice* was in regard to land ownership has been stated succinctly in Walter Neale's illustration earlier in this volume; as the peasant remarked, "The man in power can do anything."[31] But under this political reality one can always discern attitudes grounded in local customs and sanctioned by religious formulations. What must have been a very common attitude is summed up in a comment of J. H. Nelson, the administrator who was also an acute student of law. Nelson remarked of the villagers he had known in South India that ordinary people had no idea of *meum* and *tuum* and spoke always of "ours," not "mine." A thing of value was regarded as being part of an aggregate, rather than belonging to a single person.[32] So deeply rooted was this idea of group possession, and so absent was the sense of absolute private ownership, that Nelson claimed that the idea of selling an estate never entered the head of a South Indian until British times. This may be far-fetched, but it points to what seems to have been a fairly common attitude towards land. One might have absolute rights of a certain kind in a piece of land, but others might also have rights of another kind, equally absolute, in it. Alienation of these rights was possible, but not alienation of the land itself in a way that excluded the exercise of the rights enjoyed by others. Richard Jones and James Mill quoted Manu to show that the sovereign was owner of the soil, but the same useful text can be quoted to show that different people—notably the cultivator, the Brahman, and the king—all had rights in the land which it would be impossible for anyone else to alienate.[33] These rights were inherent in the functions that each performed, and they could be so stated as to exclude usurpation by other groups. An interesting example is the rule that Brahmans could not sell lands that had been given to them as religious gifts to anyone except another Brahman who had such endowments.[34] This was a very particular kind of interest, but it would probably have applied to all those other groups, which, according to a description quoted by James Mill, made up village life:

> The Potail, or head inhabitant . . . ; the Tallier and Totie . . . ; the Boundryman . . . ; the Superintendent of water courses and tanks . . . ; the Brahmen, who performs the village worship; the calendar Brahmen . . . ; the Smith and Carpenter . . . ; the Potman or potter . . . ; the Washerman; the barber; the Cowkeeper; the Doctor; the Dancing Girl who attends at rejoicings; the Musician, and the Poet.[35]

Overarching all these interests was that of the king. Since the king's rights were so regularly and dramatically asserted through tax collection, it is easy to see, given the European understanding of property, why the ruler was regarded as the owner.

In place of ownership, then, one gets the idea of "interests," of claims made upon the land for reasons quite other than that it had been acquired by some means for personal use. There was no need of the concept of ownership since what the society was concerned to defend were the "interests" the different groups had. The extreme concern of Hindu political theory with the preservation of order in society has often been noted, and while reference is sometimes made to insecurity of property rights as a mark of disorder, the overwhelming emphasis is always on the confusion of classes, and the refusal to recognize just claims, as the mark of a degenerate age.[36]

Lord Cornwallis once remarked that the question of ownership of land, which was debated at such length by the Company's servants, seemed to be "very uninteresting" to Indians and that they were much more concerned with other kinds of claims.[37] This was an acute insight, although Cornwallis did not have any particular understanding of Indian ideas of property. Cornwallis and his advisors were trying to create a system of ownership in land on the assumption that this was the basis of a prosperous state. In their discussions and the results that followed from them one sees most clearly the different assumptions of the two civilizations confronting each other. One might hazard a guess that the change from social relationships based on "interests" to those based on exclusive claims of ownership has been one of the greatest consequences of the period of British rule.

An aspect of Mughal revenue collection of great importance for the interpretation of property in terms of "interests" rather than of "ownership" is the compulsion exercised to make peasants cultivate the land. What was involved here, as Irfan Habib has pointed out, was not that the king owned the land and therefore could compel the peasants as his serfs to work it, but that the king was deprived of his just interest when the land was not worked.[38] Since there was plenty of arable land that had not been brought under cultivation, the peasants' normal reaction to what they considered oppressive taxation was to migrate and establish another village. That this still happened until late in the eighteenth century is clear from Bengal records. A group of peasants in Dinajpur District felt they were overtaxed and tried to give up their lands, but the tax farmer refused to take the lands back and made them continue cultivating.[39]

Given the institution of property as understood by the British and the Indian understanding of "interests" in the land, the changes that took place in relation to landholding were inevitably complex and hard to control. Men like Metcalfe and Malcolm wanted to preserve the indigenous forms of Indian institutions once adjustments were made to the needs of the new ruling power. But because the two forms of property were so different, there could not be any genuine adjustment. Renovation of the existing forms, as John Malcolm wanted in Central India, or their preservation, as Charles Metcalfe wanted in North India, was impossible. Nor could there be a radical transplanting of the British institution of property. The result was not a synthesis of the alien and the indigenous. Instead, distortions took place that, strictly speaking, were not the product of the new institution, but were alterations in the old structure.

The first settlement made in Oudh in 1856 can be used as an illustration of this point. After the annexation of the territory early in 1856, the Chief Commissioner was ordered to make a settlement of the land revenue with "the parties in possession, but without any recognition, either formal or indirect, of their proprietary right."[40] The land officers were especially warned not to make settlements with the talukdars, the great landlords who had gained control over the zamindars, or small proprietors, during the long years of the nawab's weak rule. Apparently an earnest attempt was made to create a settlement that would give a measure of justice to the peasants and the small proprietors, and this meant disregarding the claims of the great talukdars. In theory, the settlement should have been welcomed by everyone except the talukdars who lost land; in fact, it has been among the most criticized of all revenue settlements. During the Mutiny, the talukdars, not very surprisingly, rose against the British; but what was unexpected was that many zamindars, or the small landlords who had profited from the settlement, joined their former masters. The reason for this behavior is probably that the zamindars understood the talukdars, but not the new form of rule that had been imposed on them. The result of the zamindars helping the talukdars was that the British had to promise the talukdars that their grievances would be redressed in order to bring the fighting to an end.

After the Mutiny, the settlement with the village proprietors and zamindars was rescinded, and the talukdars who a few years before were bypassed as parasitic middlemen were now referred to by Lord Canning as an "ancient, indigenous, and cherished" institution of the country.[41] The new settlement made in 1858 contains echoes of many of the ideas and attitudes towards property that have been mentioned. A proclamation issued by the Governor-General declared, "The proprietary right in the soil of the province is confiscated to the British Government, which will dispose of that right in such manner as to it may seem fitting."[42] Here is an assertion of the idea that the ruler is proprietor of the soil joined with the idea, going back to Blackstone, that the civil government was the creator of property rights. When the grants of land were made, the talukdars received nearly two-thirds of the villages of Oudh. Out of the application of British ideas of property to what were understood to be the realities of the Indian situation had come a landed system that bore little relation to anything that had been known either in India or the Western world.

For purposes of analysis, we have abstracted the institution of property from other social developments; but two other institutions were the necessary concomitants of the new ideas of property. One of these was the institution of efficient government; the other, the institution of law. The institution of property, as understood by the British, required a state; and the state, in turn, needed property that was owned by some-one. I think it could be shown that neither of these propositions were necessary to the social organization of Hindu India, or even of Muslim India. The point has frequently been made, and no doubt correctly, that in its concern for land settlements the British Government in India was following a pattern that had been established by the Muslim rulers, and very probably by their predecessors as well. But the particular ideas of the British about property in the eighteenth and nineteenth centuries were fundamentally different from that of the Muslim rulers. Both were interested in land revenue; but the emphasis on property ownership in the eighteenth and nineteenth century settlements led to a very different social result than did those of the Mughals. The fate of the civil govern-ment was bound up with property ownership in a way that was unique in Indian history, and so also was the fate of the property owners with the state.

The legal system is the third of the institutions that affected land-holding. A society that places a high valuation on the rights of personal ownership of property will, of necessity, require a system of law and of courts to safeguard it. There were law courts in ancient India—one thinks of the trial scene in the *Mricchakatika*—but it is likely that questions relating to property were dealt with in caste panchayats or some other form of group organization that was regional and local. The law courts that the British inherited in Bengal did have as one of their functions the settling of disputes between landlords and tenants; but they did not survive for very long. Their eventual breakdown is not to be explained simply in terms of corruption and inexperience. New problems were raised by new concepts and definitions of property, and new courts were required to adjudicate them. Inheritance, marriage, rights of succession, religious endowments, were all included in the personal law that was defined either by Hindu or Muslim religious customs and, in theory, need not have been affected by the changes brought about by the land settlements or the introduction of new con-cepts of property. But in fact all these aspects of personal law were quickly influenced by the new arrangements since they were all con-cerned with property. Such compendiums as John D. Mayne's *A Treatise on Hindu Law and Usage* (London, 1878) bear witness on almost every page to the complexities of trying to adjust a traditional system of customary law to the new system of law courts. The early attempts at codification of Hindu law and the application of precedents had the effect of creating a kind of personal law that had not existed before —a law that was applicable throughout India, and one where change and growth were inhibited. This would have been true even if personal laws had been concerned wholly with religious customs; but since property was almost always an issue, the new property arrangements had an immediate effect. The intention had been to avoid interference in laws that had religious sanction; but the result was a transformation of the nature and spirit of many of these laws. Again, as in the case of the talukdars of Oudh, what emerged was not a synthesis of the old and the new, but frequently a distortion of the old, or something that, while preserving the outward form of the traditional rules, had been inwardly transformed.

One is frequently forced to conclude that in the attempt to identify the influence of British institutions on Indian institutions one is never quite sure that a phenomenon one labels as the product of foreign impact may not actually have been Indian in origin. The intrusive institution, especially when it is backed by political power, may reinforce the indigenous institution at a point where they have something in common, giving this feature a prominence it had not had under the old system. A possible example of this may be found in the ryotwari tenures, where the administrators saw something that seemed to them to correspond to private property in the West and proceeded to create a land settlement that emphasized this feature. The result was the distortion of the old system into a form that bore little resemblance to what had actually existed before. Another kind of reaction took place when its advocates, in an effort to defend the traditional culture, attempted to use mechanisms borrowed from the alien culture. An obvious example is found in the history of religious movements in the late nineteenth century, when the Arya Samaj sought to bring about a return to what was considered to be a pristine past, but made use of the techniques of Western activist religion. The result was the creation of a sect that espouses the virtues of the traditional society, but whose form and spirit is often alien to it. In a somewhat more complicated way, the same thing happened in regard to laws of inheritance. One suspects the anxiety of traditional groups to preserve their social forms led them to seek the sanction of the law courts, but use of precedents drawn from other regions must have often led to decisions at variance with expected patterns. Another kind of distortion occurred when an alien institutional pattern was quite consciously introduced in order to preserve the existing social order, and the new structure developed in a way quite at variance with its purpose. This happened, according to Percival Spear, with the introduction of police into villages in North India in the 1830's. The police restored law and order, but in doing so they "undermined the authority of the village elders and the whole system of village responsibility by providing an alternative system."[43]

All these kinds of probabilities have to be kept in mind as one tries to assess the influence of British institutions on any aspect of Indian life. A careful study of the complete interaction would help in an understanding of the whole process that led to the creation of modern India.

## NOTES

1   Sir Alfred Lyall, *The Rise and Expansion of the British Dominion in India* (London, 1907) is perhaps the most judicious statement of this point of view. An extreme example is Katherine Mayo, *Mother India* (New York, 1927).

2   B. D. Basu, *The Rise of the Christian Power in India* (Calcutta, 1931) and *Ruin of Indian Trade and Industries* (Calcutta, 1935) will provide many illustrations of this argument.

3   *The Indian Rebellion: Its Causes and Results* (London, 1858).

4   *Asia and Europe* (New York, 1904), p. 27.

5   *Kama Kalpa* (Geneva, 1958), p. 8.

6   National Archives, New Delhi, Foreign Department, Secret Consultation, 27 February 1852, Nos. 107–20.

7   See Ainslie T. Embree, *Charles Grant and British Rule in India* (New York, 1962), pp. 87–92.

8   *Village Communities in the East and West* (London, 1890), p. 221.

9   C. Reinhold Noyes, *The Institution of Property* (New York, 1936), p. 282.

10   C. Petit-Dutaillis, *The Feudal Monarchy in France and England* (London, 1949).

11   "Political Survey of the Northern Circars," in W. K. Firminger (ed.), *The Fifth Report from the Select Committee of the House of Commons* (Calcutta, 1918), III, 19.

12   Quoted in Richard Schlatter, *Private Property* (New Brunswick, 1951), p. 140.

13   John Locke, *Two Treatises of Government* (London, 1824), p. 146.

14   W. K. Firminger (ed.), *Dinajpur* (*Bengal District Records*, Vol I [Shillong, 1914]), pp. 9–23.

15   B. H. Baden-Powell, *The Origin and Growth of Village Communities in India* (London, 1899), p. 130, and *The Indian Village Community* (London, 1896), p. 206.

16  In John Bowring (ed.), *Works of Jeremy Bentham* (Edinburgh, 1843), X, 577.
17  *Legislative Methods and Forms* (Oxford, 1901), p. 126.
18  Edward Christian (ed.), Sir William Blackstone's *Commentaries on the Laws of England* (London, 1818), p. 138.
19  *The Mysterious Science of the Law* (Boston, 1958), p. 180.
20  Quoted in Schlatter, *op. cit.,* p. 171.
21  Minute of Lord Cornwallis, 3 February 1790, in Firminger, *The Fifth Report,* II, 527–43.
22  Archibald Constable (trans.), François Bernier's *Travels in the Mogul Empire* (London, 1914), pp. 204–32. For a discussion of the intellectual currents that influenced the Permanent Settlement, see Ranajit Guha, *A Rule of Property for Bengal: An Essay on the Idea of Permanent Settlement* (Paris, 1963).
23  James Mill, *The History of British India* (London, 1824), I, 265.
24  Eric Stokes, *The English Utilitarians in India* (Oxford, 1959), p. 90.
25  Irfan Habib, *The Agricultural System of Mughal India* (Bombay, 1963), p. 112.
26  Elie Halévy, *The Growth of Philosophical Radicalism* (Boston, 1960), p. 360.
27  Abraham Anquetil Duperron, *Législation Orientale* (Amsterdam, 1778).
28  Richard Jones, *Peasant Rents* (New York, 1895), pp. 97–100.
29  Maurice Gaudefroy-Demombynes, *Muslim Institutions* (London, 1950), p. 147.
30  S. M. Ikram, *Muslim Civilization in India* (New York, 1964), pp. 11, 48; and L. S. S. O'Malley, *Modern India and the West* (Oxford, 1941), p. 119.
31  "Land Is To Rule," p. 15.
32  *A Prospectus of the Scientific Study of the Hindu Law* (London, 1881), p. 189.
33  A. C. Burnell (trans.), *The Ordinances of Manu* (London, 1884), VII, 169–72.
34  N. N. Law, *Studies in Ancient Hindu Policy* (New London, 1914), p. 163.
35  Mill, *op. cit.,* I, 267.
36  H. H. Wilson (trans.), *Vishnu Purana* (London, 1840), Bk. VI, Chap. 1.
37  Firminger, *The Fifth Report,* II, 537.
38  Habib, *op. cit.,* pp. 115–16.
39  Firminger, *Dinajpur,* p. 5.
40  H. C. Irwin, *The Garden of India* (London, 1880), p. 179.
41  *Ibid.,* p. 184.
42  *Ibid.,* p. 195.
43  Percival Spear, *Twilight of the Mughals* (Cambridge, 1951), p. 112.

Chapter IV

# Structural Change in Indian Rural Society 1596-1885

*Bernard S. Cohn*

In 1819, Holt MacKenzie, a perceptive and knowledgeable East India Company civil servant who spent a major part of his career in the administration of revenue collection in Upper India, wrote that as a consequence of the Company's rule in India there was "an extensive and melancholy revolution in the landed property of the country."[1] The belief in this revolution, the assessment of its effects on the Indian economy and social structure, and attempts to right the wrongs believed to have taken place have been prominent themes in discussions of India from the early nineteenth century to the present.

In the period immediately following Indian independence, most provincial governments wrote and implemented land reform acts whose rationale included the acceptance of the idea of the social revolution wrought by the early years of British rule. For example, in 1948, the Uttar Pradesh Zamindari Abolition Committee, in speaking of the effect of British revenue policy, stated:

> Millions of people were, by these settlements, deprived of rights that they had enjoyed for well over two thousand years; hereditary cultivating proprietors of land were turned into rack-rented tenants at will, and conditions were thus created that led to continuous social discord and economic deterioration and the decay of agriculture.[2]

The discussion of the revolution in the land-holding structure rests on a series of assumptions about the nature of the economic and social

53

structure of pre-modern India. The first of these assumptions concerns the stability of traditional structures. This stability is implied in the above statement when it refers to rights "enjoyed for well over two thousand years." The most extreme form of this type of assumption is the idea of the unchanging "village republic" which was articulated in its fullest form by Sir Charles Metcalfe in his description of villages in the early-nineteenth-century Delhi territory.

> The Village communities are little Republics, having nearly everything they want within themselves, and almost independent of any foreign relations. They seem to last where nothing else lasts. Dynasty after dynasty tumbles down; revolution succeeds to revolution; Hindus, Pathan, Mughal, Mahratta, Sikh, English are masters in turn, but the village communities remain the same.[3]

Another set of assumptions involves the internal social composition of the village republics and the relations between the village republics and the state, particularly in the assessment and collection of revenue. It is widely held that land was not a commodity that could be sold or transferred in the market; rather, the system centered on the product of the land and rights to shares of this product. Immediately prior to the eighteenth century in Eastern and Northern India, three distinct groups shared the product of the land. They were the cultivators who actually tilled the soil, the controllers of cultivators (usually labeled zamindars or intermediaries), and the state. The three were in constant conflict and negotiation over rightful claim to the product of the soil and the results of the labor of the cultivator. In this system, legal title over the land itself was irrelevant.

A third set of assumptions relates to what happened in the eighteenth and early nineteenth centuries. It is believed that with the decline of the centralized military and political control which the Mughal emperors had been able to exercise and the rise of regional powers, circulation at the level of the controllers of cultivators (intermediaries) increased markedly. The leaders of the successor states tried to wipe out some of the controllers of cultivators in order to replace them with their own officers and relatives. At the same time, the growing number of tax farmers squeezed the cultivators in order to meet their obligations to the regional leaders. Warfare seems to have increased during the eighteenth century, and Europeans of that period believed that the wars and a disastrous famine in Bengal caused a great deal of productive agricultural land to be abandoned.[4]

It is assumed by most writers on this period that even though many cultivators died or migrated, and traditional intermediaries were reduced to cultivators, died, or were driven off, the system did not essentially change; it was still the produce from the land, not the land itself, which was important. It is assumed that it was the British who destroyed the old land control system by establishing an absolute, heritable, and salable right in land on the part of that person or corporate group deemed responsible for full and prompt payment of land revenue to the Government.

Under the British, men who had been tax farmers, petty revenue collectors, bankers, moneylenders, and traders obtained control of the land, first at auctions of the rights of delinquent revenue payers and later through moneylending activities. With the emergence of this new class of landlords, the cultivators and smaller intermediaries became economically and politically less significant. Many cultivators lost their hereditary rights to cultivate particular lands, and the number of tenants-at-will increased. In addition, craftsmen, like weavers, potters, blacksmiths, and carpenters, who supplied the limited nonagricultural products needed in the village community were impoverished because of the increased supply of British manufactured goods. Village "servants," such as water carriers, Chamars, barbers, and priests, lost their clientele. All of these supposedly linked changes are assumed to have turned the village community into a headless, disorganized body in which most of the population was poor, degraded, and helpless.

This paper will be devoted to an examination of data on what actually happened to land control and social structure in a limited region in Upper India, the major portion of the old Banaras Province, which today is divided into Ballia, Ghazipur, Jaunpur, Banaras, and parts of Mirzapur in Eastern Uttar Pradesh.[5] In particular, the central question I have asked is: What happened to the controllers and cultivators of land dispossessed by the new groups who obtained absolute proprietary rights in the land in the early years of British rule? In answering this question, the first step is to determine who actually controlled and cultivated land in the region before the arrival of the British.

### LAND CONTROL: 1596–1795

One of the early sources of land information is the *Ain-i-Akbari,* of which Abul Fazl is usually considered the author. In reality, it is a com-

pilation of a number of sources and writers.[6] A description and handbook of Akbar's kingdom in the late sixteenth century, it contains an
account of the revenue demand, the parganas (revenue subdivisions of
a *sarkar* district), and a list of the caste groups from which revenue was
obtained.[7] From the statistics presented in the *Ain-i-Akbari*, a picture of
the distribution of revenue payment can be obtained.[8] Table I is based
on revenue demand, in dams (a fortieth of a rupee) given in the *Ain-i-
Akbari* for the parganas which can be identified as being part of the
districts of Jaunpur, Ghazipur-Ballia, and Banaras. The caste given as
responsible for payment of revenue probably was numerically the most
important and other castes who also paid revenue in the pargana were
probably omitted.[9]

TABLE I

CASTES PAYING LAND REVENUE ACCORDING TO THE *Ain-i-Akbari, ca.* 1596

| CASTE | JAUNPUR | | GHAZIPUR-BALLIA | | BANARAS | | ALL DISTRICTS | |
|---|---|---|---|---|---|---|---|---|
| | Revenue | Per Cent | Revenue | Per Cent | Revenue | Per Cent | Revenue | Per Cent |
| Rajput ............ | 445,000 | 64 | 112,000 | 39 | 30,000 | 16 | 587,000 | 50 |
| Brahman-Bhumihar.. | 43,000 | 6 | 170,000 | 59 | 151,000 | 79 | 364,000 | 30 |
| Brahman-Rajput .... | 122,000 | 18 | ...... | .. | 11,000 | 5 | 133,000 | 11 |
| Muslim ........... | 35,000 | 5 | ...... | .. | ...... | .. | 35,000 | 3 |
| Muslim-Rajput ..... | 43,000 | 6 | ...... | .. | ...... | .. | 43,000 | 4 |
| Other ............. | 6,000 | 1 | ...... | .. | ...... | .. | 6,000 | 1 |
| Unknown .......... | ...... | .. | 7,000 | 2 | ...... | .. | 7,000 | 1 |

Some explanation of the castes involved is necessary. Rajputs are
usually listed by their clan name, such as Bisen or Bachgoti, for a particular pargana. In most instances, I would infer that these were lineages
of particular Rajput clans who were responsible for payment of the
revenue and who had the linked obligation of providing troops and
cavalry for the Mughal armies. Their position as land controllers and
revenue payers was usually based on conquests of semi-aboriginal tribes
—Soeris, Bhars, and Cherus—in the fourteenth to sixteenth centuries
and of other Rajput clans or of Muslim jagirdars from pre-Mughal
times.[10] It would appear that there were also territories held by lineages in which a particular individual was recognized as a raja and made
responsible for the payment of the revenue. The Harbans Rajput raja in
Ballia and the Chandel Rajput raja in Agori Barhar in Mirzapur are
examples of such chiefs. Rajputs were responsible for payment of 50
per cent of the total revenue demand and shared responsibility with

Brahmans or Muslims for an additional 15 per cent. The 30 per cent of the land revenue paid by Brahmans and Bhumihar's requires some explanation. In the *Ain-i-Akbari,* Bhumihars, as such, are not listed. Bhumihars are a caste, found in Western Bihar and Eastern Uttar Pradesh, who claim Brahman status, but who are essentially landed classes, do not carry out priestly functions, and are distinct in tradition and culture from Brahmans and Rajputs.[11] Elliot mentions that Abul Fazl, whom he considered the compiler of the *Ain-i-Akbari,* did not appear to know the difference between Brahmans and Bhumihars.[12] From what is known of the distribution of land-controlling groups in the late eighteenth and early nineteenth centuries, it may be conjectured that those groups listed in Table I as Brahman-Bhumihar in Ghazipur are primarily Bhumihar. In Banaras District, many of those listed as Brahman-Bhumihar are Brahman.

The relative paucity of Muslim revenue payers, 3 per cent for those parganas which they controlled in entirety and 4 per cent for those which they shared with Rajputs, indicates how quickly the land rights some Muslims had enjoyed in pre-Mughal times had been lost.

As for the concrete details of land control, the *Ain-i-Akbari* tells us very little. However, the relatively low holdings of the Rajputs, from 50 to 65 per cent, refute the assumptions of late-eighteenth-century observers that Rajputs had always controlled almost all the land.

In discussions of India in general, and on agrarian structure in particular, it is often assumed that for large areas and over long periods of time one model or form of land control and revenue administration was followed. It will be seen in what follows, that particularly in the eighteenth century, for at least fifty years before the British began to exercise even indirect influence over the revenue system of the Banaras Province, the system was undergoing rapid change. The principles of revenue administration under the rajas of Banaras (1738–75) and during the period of indirect rule by the British (1775–95) and their effects on the structure of land control within the province must be understood before we can determine what happened from 1795 to 1885 when the province was under the direct administration of British officials.

## Land Control under the Rajas of Banaras: 1740–88

Under the rajas of Banaras, a wide variety of individuals and groups with widely different claims of legitimacy controlled the land. There were petty rajas, jagirdars with imperial *sanads* (grants), and groups such as Rajput lineages who were in a position to control both the land and those who directly produced crops from the land. Each of these had differing legal, political, social, and economic rights to the land and obligations to the imperial or regional rulers. Similarly, their ties to the agricultural producers differed.

If the emperor or the regional ruler granted a jagir to an officer, this sometimes meant that the individual or corporate body previously responsible for payment of revenue to the ruler paid it instead to the jagirdar. This transition could be peaceful, or the jagirdar might have to eliminate the previous revenue payers by force. One lineage of Rajputs might subjugate another, so that the former zamindars were reduced to the status of cultivators and left with only the income from their home farm (*sir* land) which they cultivated with their servants or tenants-at-will. In general, Rajputs were replacing Muslim families as zamindars during the sixteenth and seventeenth centuries. However, it is my impression that before 1738 the changes taking place in land control simply involved different actors playing the same roles, rather than structural changes in which the roles and associated social relationships of superiors to subordinates were changed.

From 1738 to 1795, structural change in the system of land control did take place. This period can be divided into three phases. The first phase was from 1738 to 1775 during which time Mansa Ram and his relatives established themselves first as *amils* (tax officials), then as superior zamindars (land controllers), and finally were recognized by the emperor, the Nawab of Oudh, and the East India Company as rajas of Banaras. The second phase, 1775–87, began with the treaty concluded by Asaf-ud-daula ceding the Banaras province to the Company. After Chait Singh, a descendant of Mansa Ram, paid the Company two million rupees and agreed to provide troops, he was allowed to run the province as his own kingdom. In 1781, after Chait Singh's rebellion against the Company, Warren Hastings instituted some changes in the government of the raja, but basically allowed Mahip Narayan Singh, a collateral relative of Chait Singh, to continue to rule much as did his predecessor. The final phase started with the appointment of Jonathan Duncan as resident in 1787, with authority from the Council in Calcutta to run the revenue system on behalf of the raja. Theoretically, his appointment did not affect the raja's sovereignty over his domain. During

Duncan's time as resident, a revenue settlement was carried out which, although based on the principles of revenue settlement then practiced in Banaras, had a fixity and regularity of type not known in the area for fifty years. The period ends with the declaration of the permanent settlement of land revenue in 1795, the extension of all the Bengal Regulations of 1793 to Banaras, and the complete loss of sovereignty of the Raja of Banaras over the region. From 1795, the Banaras province was administered as part of British India, first as part of Bengal, then as part of the North-Western Provinces.

In general, the goal of the rajas of Banaras—Mansa Ram (*ca.* 1732–40), Balwant Singh (*ca.* 1740–70), Chait Singh (1770–81), and Mahip Narayan Singh (1781–95)—was to establish a dynasty and to make themselves sole zamindars in the region. The founder of the family, Mansa Ram, had been made *amil* or superintendent of revenue collection for the present districts of Jaunpur, Banaras, and part of Mirzapur by the Nawab of Oudh in 1738. After Mansa Ram's death in 1740, this right was confirmed by the emperor in Delhi and the Nawab of Oudh on behalf of his son, Balwant Singh. In 1758, his charge was extended to the present districts of Ballia and Ghazipur.[13]

Between 1738 and 1775, the rajas of Banaras carried out extensive military operations against all other rajas in their territories, as well as against some of the Rajput, Brahman, and Bhumihar corporate bodies which controlled land. A British officer, D. B. Morrison, in reviewing the history of the rajas in 1842 commented:

> [Balwant Singh] proceeded to great lengths in ousting the old Zamindars and forcing them to give up tenures which they had from former governments. So perseveringly was this system followed up, that it became dangerous for any one under his rule to assert a right to be called Zamindar. The records and offices of the Canoongoes were destroyed and every means taken to render the substantiation of Zamindar's claims as difficult as possible.[14]

Among those who were attacked and defeated by the rajas were: the Goatam Bhumihars in Banaras, before 1728; Rajput chiefs of Murreahu in Jaunpur, 1739; the Mans Rajputs of Bhadhoi in Mirzapur, 1748; the Chandel Rajput of Bijaighar, Mirzapur, 1752; the Mohammedan zamindars of Bhagwat, Mirzapur, *ca.* 1753–54; the Latifpur zamindars of Mirzapur, *ca.* 1753–54; and the Chandel Rajputs of Burhar, Mirzapur, 1753–54. From 1755 to 1758, the raja was engaged in subduing lineages of Rajputs in Jaunpur District; after 1758, Balwant Singh turned to Ghazipur and defeated the Hurbans and Ujjaini Rajputs of Ballia.[15]

Apparently some rajas, like the rajas of Raja Bazaar, Singramau, and Badlapur on the boundary between Oudh and Banaras, and some lineages of Rajputs, like the Sengar Rajputs of Lakhnessar, were successful in preventing the raja from dispossessing them. The raja had to settle for a lump sum paid to him directly and not through the intermediary revenue officers (*amils*). This payment was more in the nature of a tribute than revenue.

In terms of the area of land controlled and amount of revenue paid in the eighteenth century, the lineage territory was the predominant type of landholding. The members of the lineages lived in mud forts, either in the center of the territory they controlled, or on a river or stream so that they could control river traffic. In their fort, there would also be a bazaar which they controlled and taxed, as well as artisans producing tools and some articles of consumption, such as cloth and ornaments. The surrounding villages would be occupied by cultivators, usually of low caste, and there would be an occasional Brahman village established on *krishnarpan* (land granted to Brahmans for payment of ritual service). In some areas, there were also resident Rajputs in the villages. These Rajputs were sometimes of a different clan than the fort-dwelling, dominant Rajputs and had been subjugated by the dominant lineage, or else were cadet lines who developed as the parent lineages outgrew their forts and younger sons and their families had to be settled in a village. However, I think there is evidence to support the proposition that throughout the eighteenth century over most of the area, the dominant lineages tended to be based in forts, not villages.

This contention is supported by the manner in which the product of the land was divided. In the eighteenth century there were several ways these lineages divided the land and its product. Following the genealogical charter from the mythical ancestor, every male member of the lineage had a claim to part of the product or the land. As long as a group of agnates lived together, the sharing could be done by sharing the crop and keeping the land undivided. However, this form of division appears to have been rather uncommon. Usually the lineage members would actually divide up the land by village or villages. Sometimes the sons or grandsons of a founder of a lineage took portions of villages so that the lands they controlled were intermixed.

The rajas of Banaras, although they strongly attacked these Rajput landholders, usually recognized the grants of previous rulers of *muaafi* (revenue-free land) to *kazis* (Muslim law officers), and to some "serving" castes, such as Kohars (potters). In some instances, the latter were settled in hamlets near roads and bazaars to provide earthenware to government officials and other travelers. In the villages, lands were granted to Brahmans, Muslim fakirs, and village servants. Lands were also provided for *sarai* (rest houses) and to holy men.[16]

In some regions of their territory, the raja's officers had considerable difficulty in imposing their demands on those who controlled land in villages or groups of villages, particularly in Kantit and Bhadhoi in Mirzapur and in parts of Banaras. Brahmans, who appear to have been local land controllers in these areas, often had displaced Kunbis, an agricultural caste, as cultivators in the early eighteenth century. In actuality, the Brahmans did not cultivate in the sense of plowing and reaping as did their predecessors, the Kunbis, but had their employees and lower-caste dependents do this work.[17] When the raja's *amils* (revenue collectors) tried to have the Brahmans pay the same revenue rate as the Kunbis, the Brahmans insisted on a lower rate because they were Brahmans. Usually Rajputs and Brahmans paid at a lower rate per unit of land they "cultivated" themselves than did other castes. In Jaunpur District in 1788, the general rate of revenue per bigha (two-thirds of an acre) ranged from twelve annas to seven rupees; but Brahmans and Rajputs never paid more than three rupees per bigha.[18] When revenue was paid in kind, Rajputs and Brahmans paid 50 per cent of the crop, and other castes paid 58 per cent. Brahmans went to great lengths to prevent the raja's officials from raising their revenue payments legally or illegally through poisoning themselves, slashing their bodies with knives, and placing female relatives on funeral pyres with the threat of killing them—all to the end of invoking supernatural wrath on the officials who would be responsible for the death or mutilation of a Brahman.[19]

Brahmans and Rajputs appear to have been successful in preventing the rajas from raising revenue rates or interfering in the internal management of their lands.[20] In 1789, John Neave commented that the Rajputs of Jaunpur had:

 . . . a military spirit . . . mixed with a degree of wildness and the idea of *Hoormut* (honor) which makes them prone to resist the native collectors, which they can do by their distinct castes, living many of them together in one or more adjoining villages, so that being this united they of course adopt each other's quarrels.[21]

In addition to the bonds within the lineages, many of the Rajputs had strong control over their low-caste followers and dependents and often would abscond with crops and their agricultural workers to prevent the raja's collection of the revenue.

Under Mahip Narayan Singh, just before the British took direct charge of revenue administration in Banaras, regular assessment and collection of revenue had all but broken down. By this time, the *amils* were mainly tax farmers who bid annually for the right to collect taxes. The revenue they collected was paid into the raja's treasury through the agency of Banaras bankers. The *amils* used every means possible—false weights and measures, overestimation of standing crops, and direct force—to collect as much as possible from the cultivators. In 1788, there were thirty-five *amils* responsible for payment to the raja. Of the thirty-five, eight were Muslims and paid 40 per cent of the revenue; one of these, Kulb Ali Beg, and his relatives, paid over three-quarters of the total amount due. Fifteen Rajputs and Bhumihars paid 37 per cent. Many of the Bhumihar *amils* were dependents or officers of the Raja of Banaras who had been granted mixed *jagiri-amildari rights*; for example, Ausan Singh, Mahip Narayan Singh's *diwan* paid a revenue of approximately fifty thousand rupees on a pargana, Saidpur Bhitri, which produced well over a hundred thousand rupees in revenue. The difference between what Ausan Singh paid and what he collected represented part of his salary. In addition to the eight Muslim and fifteen Rajput and Bhumihar *amils,* three Kayathas, three Brahmans, and six Hindus of trading and banking communities collected 13 per cent of the revenue. I have been unable to find out who was responsible for the collection of the remaining 10 per cent of the revenue demand. The *amils* were partially controlled by the bankers who advanced them money to meet the raja's demands.[22]

Raja Mahip Narayan Singh, in turn, was under pressure from the British, who in 1781 had raised the tribute demanded from the raja from two and a half million rupees to four million, which had led the raja to increase his demands on the revenue officials. The continual raising of the revenue demand "legally" and "illegally" appears to have forced many cultivators to abandon their fields. V. A. Narain summarized the situation as follows:

Since the expulsion of Chait Singh, the revenue had no doubt been maintained but the country declined. Duncan when on tour through the province in the Spring of 1788 saw many of the parganas in a state of decay. Some of the largest and best of them were little better than a waste. The pargana of Kharid was for more than fifteen miles one continued [*sic*] waste covered only with rank grass. The pargana of Balua was also as desolate as Kharid. In the pargana of Sikandarpur, one-fourth of the land was lying fallow, and Duncan could not see more than twenty fields of cultivated grounds. Equally noticeable was the decline of once fertile and productive parganas like Chausa, Zamania and Narwas.[23]

## Jonathan Duncan's Land Settlement: 1788–90

Jonathan Duncan's revenue settlements of 1788–90 were carried out on the basis of the revenue records which had survived the Raja of Banaras' campaigns of destruction and of information supplied by *kanungos,* other local officials, and the panchayats (councils) of locally recognized leaders. Investigations were also carried out by Duncan's British and Indian assistants.[24] Two major questions had to be settled from this information: Who was to pay the revenue, that is, who was to be recognized as holding zamindari rights? How much were those holding zamindari rights to pay?

The person engaging to pay the revenue, if he were recognized by those making the settlement as holding zamindari rights, received a *patta* (deed of lease), setting forth the amount of revenue to be paid and the name of the part of the village or villages over which he held rights.

Duncan knew that the raja's campaigns against the zamindars had effectively destroyed the rights of some groups and individuals to be considered zamindars. He also understood that corporate groups as well as individuals had landed rights. Whenever possible, Duncan tried to restore zamindari rights to the holders of such rights before the Raja of Banaras' campaigns. In practice, the rule became that any person who could prove that he paid the revenue, as de facto zamindar, for any year after 1775 (the year of the grant of de jure sovereignty by Asaf-ud-daula of the Banaras Province to the East India Company) could be recognized as zamindar, as long as he was willing to agree to pay the revenue in the future. Proof of holding zamindari rights included possession of tax receipts, a *patta* from previous tax officials, entry in the *kanungo*'s records if they existed, or the statement of "leading" men in the area. As a last resort in a dispute between several claimants, the case could be referred to the land revenue court established in Banaras.

If no claim was accepted for zamindari rights, or if no one wanted to accept the obligation to pay the revenue, the land was offered on lease to a tax farmer, initially for a period of five years; in Duncan's later settlement the farming arrangements were for ten years. The farmer agreed to pay the revenue demand and, in turn, collected from the cultivators. In a few instances in which neither zamindari *pattas* nor farming *pattas* were granted, the government officials collected directly from the cultivators.

Duncan wanted to collect the revenue from and to grant zamindari rights to what he termed the "village zamindars," by which he meant those men in lineage territories, or taluks, who stood forward as leaders of the corporate body or those individuals who could establish their rights to parts of villages or whole villages, either as grants from previous governments or through tradition. In addition to "village zamindars," some large zamindars, usually former chiefs, the rajas of Badlapur and Ballia for example, were granted zamindari rights over extensive lands on the basis of their former "royal" positions. Approximately 10 per cent of the land revenue was alienated to jagirdars (land grantees), many of whom, like Ausan Singh and Beni Ram Pandit, owed their jagirs to Warren Hastings who granted them as rewards for support of the Company during Chait Singh's rebellion.

Duncan ran into considerable difficulty in trying to identify "village zamindars." Most of the cosharers in the lands of the villages held by corporate bodies, which appears to have been the most common type of holding, did not necessarily recognize leaders in a formal way. Even in lineages where there were formal leadership roles, leadership did not necessarily have anything to do with zamindari rights or with tax-paying functions. Frequently the leader was only *primus inter pares*. In most lineages the land often was divided, following genealogical principles, into smaller divisions (mahals, *pattis, thoks*).

For example, the Raghubansi Rajputs of Dobhi taluk had an ancestor, Ganesh Rai, who had conquered the taluk in the late fifteenth or early sixteenth century. He had two sons, Iswardas and Ramdeo, each of whom inherited half of the taluk. Iswardas had four sons, and Ramdeo had eight sons. Therefore, each of Iswardas' sons inherited a half of their father's estate or an eighth of the original land. Ramdeo's sons inherited an eighth of their father's estate or a sixteenth of the original land. Each of the members of the lineage traced his descent back to one of the twelve grandsons of the founder of the lineage. In the nineteenth century, the living representatives of each of the twelve grandsons formed, for purposes of landholding and internal political organization, a group known as a mahal. Each member of the mahal had a share in the lands of the mahal known as a *patti,* the holder of which was termed a *pattidar.* The size of his holding depended on the number of close agnatic kin he had. Hence, an only son of an only son of an only son would have a relatively large share in the land or its produce, while a man whose father had many brothers, and whose grandfather had many brothers, would have a relatively small share. Often members of a sub-segment of a lineage—let us say all of the male offspring of a great-grandfather—might live jointly and hold their lands jointly; nonetheless, the rule for equal partition for all agnatically related males existed, and any male of the household could calculate his share of the land or its produce.

Even when actual control over the land and its tillers had been divided, the *sair* income from the rental of fishing and timber rights and fruit trees was often held jointly and used to defray corporate expenses. The mahals, *pattis,* and *thoks* frequently did not follow village divisions in a neat fashion; for example, in a taluk of twenty villages with five mahals, each mahal might have a share of the twenty villages, or each mahal might control four distinct villages. The holdings within *pattis* could become very complex indeed because of internal transfer of land within the lineage, and at times of partition efforts were made to make the division equal in type of land as well as amount.

In the settlement made by Duncan, there was confusion and complexity even at the pargana level, as the case of the Mongra pargana in Jaunpur District illustrates. Nineteen *kabuliyats* (revenue agreements) for a total revenue of 84,502 rupees represented individual obligations ranging from 401 to 22,602 rupees. Duncan commented on this pargana:

> It is here to be observed that all the above separate cabooleats have not this year been taken in exact conformity to their natural or family shares as they are involved in much confusion. Naher Sing, for instance, is farming several Mahals which Sheopersand claims as his Zamindari and Sheopersand also holds in farm the Zamindari of others, viz. of Ayn Sing and Singram Sing. Again in Chope Sing's farm there are two claimants to Zamindari rights, viz. Sheo Sing and Assreh Sing, the decision of which has been submitted by the parties to the arbitration of Naher Sing.[25]

In this particular case, Naher Singh apparently was recognized as principal zamindar on behalf of a family who claimed leadership of a corporate body, and he was left to settle the shares of the revenue of the relatives subordinate to him.

In some taluks, the members of the corporate group refused to divide their lands, as in a case in Katihar pargana in Banaras. Duncan reported:

> It was proposed to the Zamindars of this Talookah to take pottahs for their respective shares, but this they declined as they declared such shares or pattees had never been divided, and they are willing and anxious to keep together and did not therefore wish or desire to have separate pottahs.[26]

In some instances, even when it was known who had clear claim to zamindari rights through grant or position, the zamindars were afraid to accept the obligation of revenue paying, because for many years in the past the revenue payers had been subject to considerable pressure and extortion, and they had no reason to expect that the administration of the settlement of Duncan and his assistants were undertaking would proceed any differently. Therefore, younger or less important members of the lineage sometimes received zamindari rights on behalf of their co-proprietors.

In all, 5,735 agreements for revenue payment were entered into in the settlement of 1789–90. Of these, 3,204 were made with zamindars; the rest were made with farmers or were held *amani* (to be collected directly by the Government).[27] In terms of the area of the province, "two-thirds were settled with village Zamindars; one-fourth was left with the revenue farmers, and one-twelfth remained Amani."[28]

In addition to the difficulties of identifying and getting zamindars to accept the revenue obligations, there were grave faults in Duncan's settlement of 1789–90. There was no field by field survey, so that the establishment of the revenue rates was somewhat haphazard. Some estates were underassessed, particularly if the holders or their predecessors were strong in relation to revenue officials and hence could keep the assessment down. Similarly, weak individuals had high assessments. Estates which were poorly cultivated and those with waste land were lower assessed than highly cultivated estates. Duncan and his assistants tried in some instances to take into account the potential as well as the actual agricultural production of an estate, but without close observation of each village and its fields and waste this was very difficult. As a result, some estates were underassessed, some fairly assessed, and others over-assessed.

In the settlement of 1789–90, no boundaries between fields within a mahal or between mahals or between villages were established. This led to a considerable number of disputes among cosharers and neighboring zamindars and proprietory groups, to the detriment of agricultural production and the payment of the revenue. No record of rights of subordinate members of proprietory groups were recorded. Internal division of the revenue obligation was left to be recorded by members themselves. No record of rights of permanent tenants and other tenants was kept, so that subordinate cultivators had no legal protection. Between 1795 and 1840, each of these defects of the settlement of 1789–90 were to have consequences in the transfer of rights to land.

The major sanction for ensuring the full and prompt payment of the land revenue was distraint of crops and other assets of the defaulting payers, or imprisonment. If an estate was consistently in arrears, the revenue was collected by a *sazawal,* a specially appointed officer, who collected payments from the cultivators on behalf of the defaulting revenue payers. There were no sales to realize arrears of revenue during Duncan's time in Banaras (1789–95).

On the basis of records in the India Office Library and the Uttar Pradesh Central Record Office in Allahabad, it is impossible to make any reliable quantitative statement about who became zamindars under Duncan's settlement. Table II gives the numbers by castes for seven of some ninety parganas in Banaras Province about which I was able to find data. Little can be inferred from the table, as the amount of land held or revenue to be paid by the holders is not stated in the records. It would appear that there was one predominant caste or community who were the landholders in each pargana. Rajputs were dominant in Katihar, Kolaslah, Majhwa, and Mongra. Bhumihars were dominant in Zaherabad and Kopah, and Muslims in Haveli Ghazipur. The percentage of other castes is small.

By and large, nineteenth-century local British officials believed that Rajputs were the numerically dominant caste of landlords in the province as a whole, particularly in Jaunpur, Mirzapur, and Ballia, and parts of Ghazipur and Banaras. The Brahmans were significant in Banaras, and Bhumihars were found as landlords in large numbers in Ghazipur, a few parts of Ballia, and scattered through Banaras. There were some Muslim landholding groups scattered through the area, but Jaunpur and Ghazipur were the only two districts where they had any sizeable representation. With the exception of some of the jagirdars, who like Beni Ram Pandit and his family lived in Banaras City, landed groups

*Bernard S. Cohn*

## TABLE II
### Castes of Zamindars on Seven Parganas, 1789–90

| CASTE | KATIHAR | | KOLASLAH | | MAJHWA | | H. GHAZIPUR | | ZAHERABAD | | KOPAH | | MONGRA | | ALL PARGANAS | |
|---|---|---|---|---|---|---|---|---|---|---|---|---|---|---|---|---|
| | No. | Per Cent | No. | Per Cent | No. | Per Cent | No. | Per Cent | No. | Per Cent | No. | Per Cent | No. | Per Cent | No. | Per Cent |
| Rajput ....... | 81 | 76 | 13 | 62 | 18 | 90 | 3 | 3 | 8 | 5 | 10 | 14 | 11 | 55 | 144 | 29 |
| Bhumihar .... | 7 | 6 | 2 | 10 | .. | .. | 17 | 17 | 80 | 55 | 44 | 59 | 2 | 10 | 152 | 31 |
| Brahman ..... | 6 | 6 | 2 | 10 | 1 | 5 | 10 | 10 | 11 | 8 | 12 | 16 | 2 | 10 | 44 | 9 |
| Muslim ...... | .. | .. | 1 | 4 | .. | .. | 59 | 59 | 24 | 16 | 3 | 4 | 1 | 5 | 88 | 18 |
| Kayastha ..... | 2 | 2 | .. | .. | .. | .. | 2 | 2 | .. | .. | .. | .. | 1 | 5 | 5 | 1 |
| Other Hindu .. | 6 | 6 | 3 | 14 | 1 | 5 | 10 | 9 | 24 | 16 | 5 | 7 | 2 | 10 | 51 | 11 |
| Unknown .... | 4 | 4 | .. | .. | .. | .. | .. | .. | .. | .. | .. | .. | 1 | 5 | 5 | 1 |
| Total .. | 106 | 100 | 21 | 100 | 20 | 100 | 101 | 100 | 147 | 100 | 74 | 100 | 20 | 100 | 489 | 100 |

Sources: Katihar (Banaras), A.C.R.O., Banaras Commissioner's Office, Proceedings of the Resident at Banaras, Book 134, *Basta* 47, p. 18–86; Kolaslah (Banaras), *ibid.*, *Basta* 27, Register No. 29, 1 March 1790; Majhwa (Mirzapur), *ibid.*, 17 March 1790; Haveli Ghazipur (Ghazipur), *ibid.*; Zaherabad (Ghazipur), *Basta* 26, Register No. 27; Kopah (Ballia), *ibid.*, *Basta* 27, Register No. 29, 22 January 1790; Mongra (Jaunpur), *ibid.*, *Basta* 23, Register No. 13, 27 January 1789.

lived in or near their lands. Although some Kayastha and merchant castes held land, their holdings were small—a village or a few villages granted for government service.

In 1795, Duncan's imperfect settlement was declared permanent, along the lines laid down in the Bengal Regulations of 1793. In 1795, Duncan's younger brother, Alexander Duncan, who had acted for a time as Jonathan's assistant was made collector, and four district courts were established. The administration of the Banaras region became completely part of Bengal.

## LAND SALES AND THE NEW POSSESSORS: 1795–1885

Under the Bengal Regulations of 1795, estates declared to be in arrears of revenue could be auctioned off to the highest bidder, who thus obtained zamindari rights and the obligation to pay the Government revenue. The first public auction of the land of a zamindar declared a defaulter in payment of public revenue took place in 1796. In a few years' time, by 1800, zamindari rights in lands valued in tens of thousands of rupees were being auctioned annually.[29] In Ghazipur District, on October 7, 1799, ninety mahals, paying a *jama* (land revenue) of 146,470 rupees were put up for public auction, as they were declared in arrears in payment of the Government revenue. Of these, forty-five were recorded by the Collector of Banaras as having been sold, representing land revenue of 53,336 rupees. The purported balances due on these forty-five estates was 17,313 rupees; the amount realized from the sales was 15,531 rupees. One estate was not sold because the balance had been paid; forty-four others were not sold because there were no bidders.[30]

The Home Authorities in 1810 stated that under James Barton, Collector of Banaras from 1801 to 1806, nearly half the property of the province of Banaras had been transferred.[31] In 1815, W. Cracroft, a magistrate in Ghazipur, believed that "nearly all the principal estates had changed proprietors."[32]

Wilton Oldham, who served almost ten years in Ghazipur during the 1860's and early 1870's, and who wrote two excellent studies on the history of Ghazipur (*Historical and Statistical Memoir of the Ghazeepoor and the Province of Benaras,* [Allahabad, 1870] and *Tenant Right and Auction Sales* [Dublin, 1873]), stated:

It is probable that about one-quarter of the whole district of Ghazipur is in possession of representatives of purchasers at auction sales for realization of revenue.[33]

William Irvine, settlement officer for Ghazipur District from 1880 to 1885, reviewed the statistics on land transfers between 1842 and 1882 and concluded:

In forty years [1842–1882] one quarter of the land has changed hands . . . . If we add the immense areas which passed from old Zamindars in the period 1795–1820, when sales for revenue arrears were frequent, it is not too much to assume that three-fourths of the districts have changed hands since the commencement of British rule.[34]

During the first period of rapid transfer of zamindari rights, the sellers of these estates were representatives of lineages, clans, and relatively small holders with whom the land had been settled between 1789 and 1795. During this period the revenue was collected by Indian officials termed *tahsildars*. These officials collected the revenue from the zamindars within the parganas of which they had charge. The *tahsildars* had police power and were responsible for the maintenance of law and order. They received an 11.5 per cent commission on the revenue they collected. In this period there were over ninety parganas, and an average of forty-four *tahsildars* were officially listed on the Government's books. However, three men, the Raja of Banaras, Sheolal Dube, and Devikinundan Singh, controlled two-thirds of the actual collection of revenue. They often had relatives and employees standing for them as *tahsildars*. These men made huge profits from their control of revenue collections, legally through their commissions and illegally through extortion and by raising illegal taxes on the zamindars. In addition, these men knew which estates had become profitable through being underassessed in the settlement of 1789–90, and through their positions they could have such estates brought to the block.[35]

R. O. Wyne, a judge in Jaunpur District from 1809 to 1816, summarized the situation as follows:

Resistance by force or recourse to dharna and kaor however does not appear to have prevented considerable rights as landlords from going to the tahsildars . . . . The tahsildars controlled the Sharistadars and other record keepers so it was simple for them to make it appear in the records, which in the collector's office or the courts were taken as the evidence of arrears of revenue due, that a particular estate had failed to pay its government revenue. The estate revenue was then collected directly by the tahsildar, affording him additional commissions and opportunities for corrupt charges on the cultivators or auctioned-off land purchased by a relative or dependent of the officials.[36]

Although some of the abuses of the *tahsildari* system were eliminated in 1807, sales for arrears of revenue still continued as the major means of land transfer. After 1822, with the increased awareness of influential men like Holt MacKenzie, W. W. Bird, and R. M. Bird of the consequences of the large-scale sale of rights, there was some lessening in the number of auctions. However, as auctions for arrears of revenue decreased, the number of auctions to satisfy decrees of the courts increased. In these auctions, zamindars who had fallen into debt and had used their zamindari rights as securitity lost their estates if they were unable or unwilling to pay their creditors. After the settlement of 1839–42, most auction sales were for debt rather than arrears of revenue.

Tables III, IV, and V summarize data on 283 public auctions.[37] Considerable caution is necessary in the interpretation of these data. The transactions summarized are only a small portion of all lands sold at auction in the period 1795–1850. In the tabular presentation of the data abstracted from these 283 transactions, I have often had to infer caste from the names given in the certificates. By and large, Brahman names, such as Misra, Pande, Dube, and Chaube, are simple to identify in the region. There is some inaccuracy in the distinctions between Rajput or Thakurs and Bhumihar names as both may be identified in the records by the surname "Sing" or "Singh." Bhumihars frequently used the title "Rai" or "Rao" as part of their names, a practice less frequent among Rajputs or Thakurs. In addition, later settlement reports and census material indicate in which parganas of Ballia and Ghazipur there were a large number of Bhumihars, and I inferred that in these parganas the name "Singh" indicated a Bhumihar. Some Baniya names, such as Dos (Das) and Chund, are easy to identify. There is probably some overlap between Kayasthas and Baniya names as some of each group use Lal as a last name. I took the title "Lalla" appearing in the certificates as indicating Kayastha caste status. In some of the certificates, caste names for various castes are used, for instance, Agarwal, a trading caste, and Kalwar, a low caste of distillers and traders.

In general, though the presentation of data in statistical tables seems precise, the reader should be aware of possible errors in identification of caste status. It is my feeling that I may have overstated the number of Rajputs and Kayasthas and understated the number of Bhumihars and Baniyas involved in the transactions summarized below.

## TABLE III
### SELLERS OF LAND AT AUCTION, 1795–1850

| CASTE | BANARAS | | | GHAZIPUR-BALLIA | | | JAUNPUR | | | MIRZAPUR | | | ALL DISTRICTS | | |
|---|---|---|---|---|---|---|---|---|---|---|---|---|---|---|---|
| | No. | Revenue | Per Cent | No. | Revenue | Per Cent | No. | Revenue | Per Cent | No. | Revenue | Per Cent | No. | Revenue | Per Cent |
| Rajput ........ | 71 | 118,818 | 59 | 4 | 4,402 | 12 | 50 | 56,196 | 61 | 9 | 12,474 | 48 | 134 | 191,890 | 54 |
| Muslim ....... | 19 | 25,684 | 13 | 7 | 15,527 | 43 | 8 | 5,356 | 6 | 4 | 3,813 | 15 | 38 | 50,380 | 14 |
| Brahman ...... | 20 | 22,843 | 11 | 1 | 800 | 2 | 4 | 7,019 | 8 | 6 | 4,033 | 16 | 31 | 34,695 | 10 |
| Bhumihar .... | 11 | 9,520 | 5 | 6 | 12,105 | 33 | : | ..... | : | : | ..... | : | 17 | 21,625 | 6 |
| Baniya ........ | 10 | 8,895 | 4 | 1 | 1,005 | 3 | 4 | 12,033 | 13 | 5 | 3,037 | 12 | 20 | 24,970 | 7 |
| Kayastha ...... | 2 | 1,076 | * | : | ..... | : | : | ..... | : | : | ..... | : | 2 | 1,076 | * |
| Low Caste .... | 5 | 2,970 | 1 | 1 | 386 | 1 | 3 | 1,176 | 1 | 1 | 755 | 3 | 10 | 5,287 | 1 |
| Other ......... | 3 | 596 | * | : | ..... | : | 1 | 852 | 1 | : | ..... | : | 4 | 1,448 | * |
| Unknown .... | 21 | 11,959 | 6 | 1 | 2,175 | 6 | 1 | 9,500 | 10 | 4 | 1,565 | 6 | 27 | 25,199 | 7 |
| Total .. | 162 | 202,361 | 100 | 21 | 36,400 | 100 | 71 | 92,132 | 100 | 29 | 25,677 | 100 | 283 | 356,570 | 100 |

*Less than 1 per cent.

TABLE IV

BUYERS OF LAND AT AUCTION, 1795–1850

| CASTE | BANARAS | | | GHAZIPUR-BALLIA | | | JAUNPUR | | | MIRZAPUR | | | ALL DISTRICTS | | |
|---|---|---|---|---|---|---|---|---|---|---|---|---|---|---|---|
| | No. | Revenue | Per Cent | No. | Revenue | Per Cent | No. | Revenue | Per Cent | No. | Revenue | Per Cent | No. | Revenue | Per Cent |
| Rajput ........ | 27 | 22,532 | 11 | 7 | 14,275 | 39 | 10 | 16,825 | 18 | 4 | 2,207 | 9 | 48 | 55,839 | 16 |
| Muslim ....... | 17 | 13,026 | 6 | 8 | 14,613 | 40 | 8 | 10,664 | 12 | 2 | 550 | 2 | 35 | 38,853 | 11 |
| Brahman ...... | 13 | 11,553 | 6 | 1 | 851 | 3 | 5 | 3,685 | 4 | 11 | 11,430 | 45 | 30 | 27,519 | 8 |
| Bhumihar ..... | 20 | 52,480 | 26 | 2 | 1,852 | 5 | 17 | 31,083 | 34 | 1 | 2,956 | 11 | 40 | 88,371 | 25 |
| Baniya ........ | 56 | 77,235 | 38 | 1 | 3,610 | 10 | 10 | 9,605 | 10 | 7 | 7,060 | 27 | 74 | 97,510 | 27 |
| Kayastha ...... | 24 | 22,221 | 11 | 2 | 1,199 | 3 | 16 | 17,782 | 19 | .. | ..... | .. | 42 | 41,202 | 11 |
| Low Caste .... | 1 | 2,081 | 1 | .. | ..... | .. | 5 | 2,488 | 3 | 1 | 997 | 4 | 7 | 5,566 | 1 |
| Other ........ | .. | ..... | .. | .. | ..... | .. | .. | ..... | .. | 3 | 477 | 2 | 3 | 477 | * |
| Unknown ..... | 4 | 1,233 | 1 | .. | ..... | .. | .. | ..... | .. | .. | ..... | .. | 4 | 1,233 | * |
| Total .. | 162 | 202,361 | 100 | 21 | 36,400 | 100 | 71 | 92,132 | 100 | 29 | 25,677 | 100 | 283 | 356,570 | 100 |

*Less than 1 per cent.

## TABLE V
### OCCUPATION OF BUYERS OF LAND AT AUCTION, 1795–1850

| OCCUPATION | BANARAS | | | GHAZIPUR | | | JAUNPUR | | | MIRZAPUR | | | ALL DISTRICTS | | |
|---|---|---|---|---|---|---|---|---|---|---|---|---|---|---|---|
| | No. | Revenue | Per Cent | No. | Revenue | Per Cent | No. | Revenue | Per Cent | No. | Revenue | Per Cent | No. | Revenue | Per Cent |
| Zamindari ......... | 23 | 23,435 | 12 | 5 | 8,694 | 24 | 19 | 30,957 | 34 | 14 | 10,256 | 40 | 61 | 73,342 | 21 |
| Raja of Banaras .. | 20 | 52,470 | 26 | .. | ..... | .. | 14 | 27,921 | 30 | .. | ..... | .. | 34 | 80,391 | 22 |
| Commerce and money-lending ......... | 53 | 70,993 | 35 | 1 | 3,610 | 10 | 3 | 6,598 | 7 | 9 | 10,327 | 40 | 66 | 91,528 | 26 |
| Service ............. | 14 | 12,256 | 6 | 1 | 813 | 2 | 29 | 17,121 | 19 | 2 | 550 | 2 | 46 | 30,740 | 9 |
| Law ............... | 27 | 21,193 | 10 | .. | ..... | .. | .. | ..... | .. | .. | ..... | .. | 27 | 21,193 | 6 |
| Unknown ........... | 25 | 22,014 | 11 | 14 | 23,283 | 64 | 6 | 9,535 | 10 | 4 | 4,544 | 18 | 49 | 59,376 | 16 |
| Total ........ | 162 | 202,361 | 100 | 21 | 36,400 | 100 | 71 | 92,132 | 100 | 29 | 25,677 | 100 | 283 | 356,570 | 100 |

The category "Occupation" in Table V is derived directly from the data recorded by the collector at the time of sale. It would appear difficult to draw the line between *mahajans* (bankers and traders) and zamindars as to occupation, as many bankers and traders were land-holders and some zamindars engaged in trade and money lending. "Service" appears to have been a residual category at the time for the collectors. It encompasses clerks, lower government officials, employees of large zamindars, or almost anyone not self-employed.

A general point must also be borne in mind about these data. There is no way of knowing what was the origin of the rights being auctioned. The seller himself may have been an auction purchaser at some earlier date. Some of the sales of 1795–1830 were themselves fraudulent means of establishing title to land, and the buyer and seller may have been the same person. It is also possible that some estates were frequently sold and resold; this would be true of estates overassessed at the original settlement.

I do not know of any way by which any inference can be made about the relationship between the sales on which I have information and the total number of sales which took place in the region from 1795 to 1850. Although I tried to make my survey of existing available records as complete as possible, it is probable some pertinent data were overlooked in the almost one thousand volumes examined. In addition to my errors of omission, Dewar states:

> The records appertaining to the United Provinces [the present Uttar Pradesh] have suffered in various places from one or other of the following causes of destruction:
> 1) Ravages of the mutineers in 1857
> 2) Accidental fires in record rooms
> 3) Indiscriminate weeding of records
> 4) Careless preservation of records, which has resulted in the destruction of many documents by white-ants, fish, insects, etc.[38]

Dewar wrote this in the early twenties of this century, and although the rate of destruction has greatly diminished since then, some weeding and some continued destruction by insects has occurred.

Therefore, the tables summarizing the data found do not illustrate anything about the universe of all sales for arrears and decrees of court which took place. They are not a representative sample. The only thing that can be said for the 283 transactions summarized is that there is no basis I can see, except accident, which preserved them or which enabled me to find and record them. The data are much fuller for the period 1830–50.

The heaviest sellers at the auction sales were Rajputs, who sold or "lost" land paying 191,890 rupees. This represents almost 54 per cent of the total land sales covered; of the amount, Rajputs bought lands paying 55,839 rupees in revenue, so their absolute loss was 136,051 rupees or 40 per cent of the land transferred. Of the three groups, Rajputs, Brahmans, and Muslims, who were forced to sell more than they bought, Rajputs accounted for most of the total lands "lost." By any measure, the conclusion that the Rajputs, who were controllers of corporate land holdings in the pre-1795 period, were the heavy sellers of land is inescapable. The conclusion drawn from the statistical material agrees with the judgments made on the nonstatistical records as well. In short, the Rajput corporate bodies (largely lineages and segments of lineages) became the "dispossessed."

The gainers of land were Bhumihars (mainly the Raja of Banaras) who bought lands paying 88,371 rupees in revenue out of the total of 356,570 rupees, or about 25 per cent of the lands bought. Their land-buying activities were confined largely to Banaras and Jaunpur districts, and since a large portion of transactions summarized in Tables III–V were from these districts, their role in land purchasing is over-stated in these tables. Tables IV shows that two groups, Kayasthas and Baniyas, who had not been important landholders, were, relatively speaking, heavy purchasers. These groups were transferring income gained through public service, business, and legal practice into land. Table V illustrates this process. Subtracting the total of 80,391 rupees of revenue on lands purchased by the rajas of Banaras, and the lands transferred on which there is no data on the occupation of the buyer (59,376 rupees), approximately 41 per cent of the lands transferred went to families whose principal occupations were money lending, service, and law. In addition, residence of the majority of the buyers was urban, principally in Banaras City, as shown in Table VI. Other land buyers lived in Jaunpur, Mirzapur, and Ghazipur.

Of the 183 purchasers defined as urban, 147 who bought lands paying 197,686 rupees lived in Banaras City. A list of 280 estates bought at public auction, compiled by the Collector of Ghazipur district *ca.* 1851–52, confirms the urban character of purchasers of estates at public auction, as shown in Table VII.

Sociologically, economically, and politically, the place of residence of

TABLE VI
RESIDENCE OF BUYERS OF LAND AT AUCTION, 1795–1850

| Residence | No. | Revenue | Per Cent of Revenue |
|---|---|---|---|
| Urban .............. | 183 | 250,675 | 70 |
| Rural .............. | 56 | 64,233 | 18 |
| Unknown .......... | 44 | 41,662 | 12 |
| Total ......... | 283 | 356,570 | 100 |

TABLE VII
RESIDENCE OF BUYERS OF LAND IN GHAZIPUR-BALLIA, 1795–1850

| Residence | No. | Revenue | Per Cent of Revenue |
|---|---|---|---|
| Urban .............. | 139 | 176,000 | 56 |
| Rural .............. | 132 | 134,000 | 43 |
| Unknown .......... | 9 | 4,000 | 1 |
| Total ......... | 280 | 314,000 | 100 |

Source: A.C.R.O., Banaras Commissioner's Office, Miscellaneous Revenue Files, Vol. 3, File 103, List of Estates Obtained at Public Auctions, 1 September 1852.

the purchaser of land was of great significance to the family or group selling or forced to sell the land because of its effect on the internal structure of the village or local area in which the land auctioned was located. Over half of the purchasers in the Ghazipur-Ballia list were urban, and 70 per cent of the purchasers of land in the 283 transactions in the area as a whole were urban. Table VIII summarizes the distance from the land purchased of the residence of the buyer in the Ghazipur-Ballia District List of 1851–52.

Over two-thirds of the revenue came from estates whose purchasers lived over ten miles away. The inference drawn from Tables VI, VII,

TABLE VIII
DISTANCE OF RESIDENCE OF BUYER FROM LAND BOUGHT IN
GHAZIPUR-BALLIA, 1795–1850

| Distance in Miles | No. | Av. No. of Acres | Revenue | Per Cent of Revenue |
|---|---|---|---|---|
| 0–4 ................ | 69 | 611 | 42,207 | 13 |
| 5–10 ................ | 32 | 798 | 25,553 | 8 |
| 11–20 .............. | 55 | 1,004 | 55,256 | 18 |
| 20+ ................ | 118 | 1,586 | 187,161 | 60 |
| Unknown .......... | 6 | 705 | 4,232 | 1 |
| Total ......... | 280 | 1,122 | 314,409 | 100 |

Source: See note to Table VII.

and VIII is that the new purchasers were overwhelmingly nonresident. Typically, they were urban and usually engaged in nonagricultural activities. For many of the new land-owning groups there was little direct contact with their estates, the cultivators, and former zamindars, except through agents. The concern of the landlord was with prompt and full payment of the rent due from his tenants, many of whom were the former zamindars, and little else.

### Social Origins of the New Possessors: 1885

Some information on the social origins of the new owners can be obtained from the data available in the reports on the revision of rights and settlements in the Banaras region from 1878 to 1885.

The 134 revenue payers classified as paying over a thousand rupees per year in land revenue paid a little less than one-third of the revenue collected in the districts of Banaras, Ballia, Ghazipur, and Jaunpur around 1885. Well over one hundred thousand others paid the remaining two-thirds of the revenue levied in the four districts.

The question of the social origins of these large payers is a complicated one, and the classification developed in Table IX is imprecise. However, within the limitations of the data, Table IX does provide a preliminary picture of the large revenue payers at the end of the nineteenth century.

In some sense, most of the large revenue payers in the Banaras region in 1885 were "new men." Most owed their wealth and position to

TABLE IX

SOCIAL ORIGINS OF REVENUE PAYERS PAYING MORE THAN ONE THOUSAND
RUPEES LAND REVENUE YEARLY, 1885

| Origin | No. | Revenue | Per Cent of Revenue |
|---|---|---|---|
| "New men" ...................... | 39 | 397,900 | 31 |
| Commercial ...................... | 36 | 168,400 | 13 |
| Eighteenth-century aristocrats ......... | 8 | 314,600 | 25 |
| Traditional aristocrats .............. | 23 | 243,400 | 21 |
| Religious institutions .............. | 4 | 8,200 | 1 |
| Unknown ...................... | 24 | 129,100 | 9 |
| Total ..................... | 134 | 1,261,600 | 100 |

Sources: Records for Jaunpur were found in P. C. Wheeler, *Report on the Revision of Records of the Settlement Operations in the District of Jaunpur, 1877–1886* (Allahabad, 1886), p. 54; for Ghazipur, in William Irvine, *Report on the Revision of Records on the Settlement Operations in the Ghazipur District, 1880–1895* (Allahabad, 1896), p. 19; for Ballia, in D. T. Roberts, *Report on the Revision of Records of Part of Ballia District, 1882–1885* (Allahabad, 1887), pp. 26–27. Mirzapur was omitted from the table because no statistics were available on the distribution of revenue payers.

the conditions established by British rule. A few could trace or develop connections to older dominant families in the region or outside. However, the majority directly derived their landed wealth by capitalizing on their positions as under civil servants employed by the British. They exploited the commercial opportunities attendant on British rule or were from families who established their status as "aristocrats" in the eighteenth century and had this status fixed and supported by the British.

## The "New Men"

As can be seen from Table IX, the thirty-nine "new men" paid 31 per cent of the total amount paid by those paying over a thousand rupees in land revenue annually. The origin of the wealth of these new men largely derived from occupations or activities associated with the establishment of British rule in the Banaras region.

Most of these men or their forefathers held administrative positions under the British, such as *tahsildars, sarrishtadars* (head clerks), deputy collectors, and *amins* and *sadar amins* (lower court judges). The two largest payers were the descendants of Sheolal Dube and Devikanundan Singh, who profited greatly from the *tahsildari* systems of 1795–1808. Twenty-eight of the founders of these families had been in government service. Of the eleven others, five appear to owe their financial beginnings to positions as agents of large landholders who bought up estates between 1795 and 1840; four were lawyers; and two were in the East India Company's military service.

The caste and community ascriptions of these men is interesting; of the twenty-eight whose origins derive from government service, fifteen out of twenty-eight were Muslim, six Brahman, three Kayastha, two Bhumihar, one Baniya, and one Eurasian. With the exceptions of the descendants of Mahlvi Abdulla Majzi of Jaunpur, who had been a *sarrishtadar* and who was rewarded for loyalty to the British in 1857–58, none of the Muslim new men were particularly large revenue payers. The large number of Muslims who owed the establishment of their family fortunes to government services reflects the British policy of continuing Persian as the language of administration until 1835 and of continuing the pre-British pattern of drawing civil servants from families of Persian origin who made their living as administrators and scribes.[39] Out of the thirty-nine new men, only three are Rajput by caste; two of these had served or had ancestors who had served in the

Company's armies, and one was an agent of a large zamindar. This is another indication that until the end of the nineteenth century, new opportunities of gaining wealth were not taken by the Rajputs, whose position was based on landholding in the pre-British era and whose economic position, we may assume, was most likely to be declining in relation to other groups.

### Commercial Families

The thirty-six men who owed their rise to commerce are heterogeneous in family occupation. The category includes families engaged in banking, moneylending, grain trading, sugar manufacturing and shopkeeping. These occupations were, of course, not mutually exclusive, and the commercial families tended to engage in a wide range of activities, including government service, law, management of landed estates, as well as commercial pursuits.

Of the thirty-six commercial families, fifteen were primarily active in banking. Most of the banking families in Banaras date from the eighteenth century, and most were not indigenous to Banaras. Some, like the family of Sataram Naik, were Marathas from Nagpur. The Das family, Babu Brij Mohan Das and his cousins, who collectively paid almost twenty thousand rupees a year in government revenue on their estates, originally came from Ghind in the Punjab and came to Banaras in the late eighteenth century with members of the Mughal royal family.[40]

The Mitters were another wealthy banking family who illustrate the conversion of income from government service into banking, commerce, and land. The family came from Bengal, where an ancestor, Gobindram Mitter, was made naib-zamindar of Calcutta in 1720. This post included collection of the ground rents in the city, as well as management of the other revenue-producing activities.[41] His son, Raghunath Mitter, dissipated much of the wealth his father had amassed. The biographer of the family commented:

> He was more fond of ease and indolence than business or any active duties. He was always addicted to pleasure and amusements. Music and singing were his constant enjoyments. He had a regular set of salaried dancing girls . . . . He was a great patron of religion and the arts, but ran into debt because of his indolence.[42]

Krishna Churn, second son of Raghunath, and Abhoy Churn, son of Radha Churn, Raghunath's eldest son, restored part of the family fortune through employment under the British. Through the patronage of Sir

Edward and Henry Colebrooke, Krishna Churn was appointed *diwan* to the Collector of Dacca. His nephew, Abhoy Churn, became *diwan* to the collector of the twenty-four parganas in Bengal, and "being naturally shrewd, intelligent, and industrious, Abhoy Churn became a favorite of the then Collector, and thus began to make hay when the sun shone above him."[43]

After helping reestablish the family's fortune in Bengal, Krishna Churn ran into financial difficulties through a series of lawsuits and moved to Banaras. Here he was joined by Annand Moy Mitter, who established a banking business which prospered greatly. His son, Rajendra Mitter, was one of the wealthiest men in Banaras.[44] A significant number of bankers resided in Ghazipur City as well. The descendants of Jassi Lal were the largest merchants, bankers, and landholders in the city.

Both in English and in the vernacular used in the records of the period, there is no clear distinction made between bankers, moneylenders, and money changers. The most frequent words used are *mahajans* (bankers and merchants) and *sarrafs* (bankers and money changers). In the seventeenth century, according to Irfan Habib, *sarraf*, an Arabic word, came closest "to the Indian equivalent of the English 'banker.' "[45] The term *sarraf* "was also applied to the bankers or money-changers . . . . But it seems that the *Sarrafs* concentrated chiefly on commercial credit."[46] B. B. Misra, in his discussion of Mughal economic structure, seems to use *sarraf* and *mahajan* interchangeably.[47] It is my impression that in the Banaras area in the late eighteenth and early nineteenth century the word *mahajan* was more widely used to cover banking and moneylending functions and *sarraf* had a more restricted use in describing a money changer and evaluator of coin.[48] Of the thirty-six commercial families paying over a thousand rupees as land revenue in 1885, five are listed as moneylenders and zamindars. Unlike those described as bankers, who all resided in Banaras or Ghazipur City, the "moneylenders" were residents of villages or small bazaars, for example, Dip Narain Singh of Kaithi in Banaras.

In the material in the settlement reports there is also a caste difference between those described as bankers and those described as moneylenders. Of the fifteen banking families, ten are Agarwal by caste, one Maratha, one Rora, one Brahman, one Khatri, and one of unknown caste. Of the six families paying over a thousand rupees in land revenue included in this category, three are described as sugar manufacturers, two as grain dealers, and one as in the indigo business. The others are described loosely as merchants, traders, or bankers. The castes of these fifteen are much more varied and include a Koeri and Kandu, both in the sugar business, three Muslims described as traders, two Brahmans, three Rajputs, four Agarwals or Baranwals, and one Kalwar.

Although many of the commercial and banking families date from the eighteenth century or earlier in the Banaras region, their zamindar activities all began in the early nineteenth century. Two assumptions are generally advanced to account for the fact that the vigorous and numerous class of bankers and traders in the eighteenth century eschewed investment in land.

It is usually assumed that land was not marketable in the sense that it was in the nineteenth century under the establishment of British administration and courts. There is evidence that land was sold and seized in the eighteenth century, but one needed military force to support a claim to land and had to be willing to fight for it. With the establishment of British rule, land became a commodity. Clear title could be established. Land could be sold freely, and great quantities appear to have been brought to auction in the Bengal Presidency to realize assumed arrears of revenue.

The second reason advanced for the buying of land in the Bengal Presidency by commercial groups is that it was a better investment than alternatives available to bankers and merchants. I have tried to demonstrate the unevenness of assessment of land revenue in the Permanent Settlement of Banaras in 1795, and I assume the same was true in Bengal and Bihar in 1793. A low assessment, combined with rising agricultural production and prices, would lead to a high return on the money invested compared to other alternatives. The alternatives for investment in the eighteenth century appear to have been internal and overseas trade,[49] handicraft industries for internal and overseas production,[50] loans to Indian states and chiefs,[51] and loans to tax collectors and farmers.[52] In addition, the bankers in this period seem to have made a considerable amount of money as money changers, as there were a large number of different coins of different value circulating in India.[53]

In the nineteenth century, the opportunity and need for moneylending to agriculturalists large and small probably increased, if there was, as I will try to demonstrate, an expansion in the growing of sugar cane and indigo, which were somewhat more expensive crops to grow, an increase in the monetization of the rural economy because of more cash crops, and a refusal on the part of the British government, unlike its predecessors, to accept payment of revenue in kind. I would hypothesize that bankers lent money more readily to large landholders in the nineteenth century than they did previously, as they could take over and collect the revenues from estates if the borrower defaulted on the loan or mortgage.

The rajas of Kantit in Mirzapur provide an example of large-scale borrowing and the profits which bankers and moneylenders could make. The usual rate of interest on long-term mortgages in the 1840's and 1850's appears to have been 12 per cent per year.[54] The raja's estate produced a gross rental of 159,498 rupees annually, of which 61,799 rupees had to be paid to the government as revenue, and 20,382 rupees were the cost of running the estate; thus, there was an assumed profit of 77,317 rupees annually.[55] The Kantit raja's family in 1850 owed to creditors 462,351 rupees, of which the sum 334,540 rupees was principal and the rest represented unpaid interest charges. In addition, 225,000 rupees were still owed to mortagagees, who had the benefit of collecting income from the raja's land.[56]

The raja appears to have become indebted to pay necessary expenses, such as government revenue, in years in which there were poor crops; but he also appears to have been encouraged by bankers and moneylenders to live well. Some of the more unscrupulous moneylenders appear to have taken over management of some estates on the raja's behalf and systematically defrauded him. In commenting on the relation between the raja and his creditors, Collector E. A. Reade stated:

> It seems to be a common delusion with extensive landholders to regard debt as a reputable incident of their position, [as] their creditors keep up a show of deference, and are often most accommodating when most extortionate.[57]

The raja was in debt to several large bankers, the most important of all being Mohant Parsram Gir, a Gosain banker of Mirzapur to whom he owed 288,000 rupees. In addition, he owed considerable amounts to the Raja of Dumraon, a large landholder in a number of districts in Bihar, Ballia, and Ghazipur.[58]

Small-scale moneylending appears to have been profitable as well. Moore, an assistant collector who had been deputized to investigate conditions in southern Mirzapur, found that Soho and Company had a large number of the *asamis* (permanent tenants) in debt to them. For example, Suraj Dosadh borrowed 19 rupees, 8 annas, to buy three heads of cattle in 1845. Twelve years later, Suraj Dosadh claimed to have paid 71 rupees against the debt, and Soho and Company claimed he still owed 100 rupees.[59]

An argument could be made that in the first half of the nineteenth century the older alternatives for investment on the part of bankers and moneylenders were progressively declining. With the end of the Maratha wars in 1818, the demands for financing short-term military operations in North India ceased. With the elimination of the *tahsildari* system in 1808, bankers lost their function in financing tax collection and remittance. In 1835, with the establishment of a uniform currency, profit from money changing declined considerably. After 1813, with the end of the Company's trade monopoly and the establishment of joint stock banks in the Presidency town, there was little role for indigenous capital in directly financing overseas trade. In the North-Western Provinces the spread of joint stock banks did not occur until the 1840's, when in addition to Agra and the United Service Bank, which had been established in 1833, five more European banks were established in Meerut, Delhi, Simla, Kanpur, and Banaras.[60] The Banaras and United Service Bank had forty-one shareholders; however, only three of these were Indians.[61]

I would also argue that investment in land on the part of commercial families was important symbolically. The life style and consumption patterns of wealthy families in Banaras continued in the first half of the nineteenth century. The ideal of the "nawab" which developed around the Mughal courts of the sixteenth through eighteenth centuries and set the standards for upper-class manners and customs continued well into the nineteenth century.[62] Part of the "nawabi" life style was control of land, since control of land meant control of followers, a necessary facet of the nawabi style. I believe that the potential of good profits, lack of alternatives, and a cultural ideal of being landed, all led to commercial groups investing in land as they had not done in the eighteenth century.

*Eighteenth-century Aristocrats*

First and foremost among those I have termed eighteenth-century aristocrats was the Raja of Banaras, the single largest revenue payer in the area, who paid 243,000 rupees in land revenue in 1884, or a little over 5 per cent of the total revenue demand of the region. The raja paid 20 per cent of the total revenue paid by the large revenue payers.[63]

Macaulay's rhetoric in his famous essay on Warren Hastings notwithstanding, the rajas of Banaras were not ancient Hindu lords, but newly arisen chiefs. In the space of a generation's time in the early eighteenth century, Mansa Ram had risen from being a petty land controller with a few hundred bighas in a village in the Banaras District into the principal official of the Nawab of Oudh in the Banaras Province. In the next generation, Balwant Singh was recognized as a raja by the Nawab of Oudh, the emperor in Delhi, and the East India Company. The story of Mansa Ram and Balwant Singh is a typical "success story" of eighteenth century India, when, with skill, cunning, intelligence, perseverance, and luck, one could parlay a position as the *vakil* (agent) of a pargana *amil* (local tax collector) into that of the most powerful officer in the province.

Mansa Ram, Balwant Singh's father, advanced by the device of undercutting the position of his employer with his employer's supervisor. First, Mansa Ram convinced Rustam Ali, who was responsible for the province of Banaras under the nawabs of Oudh, that he could do a better job than the *amil* Mansa Ram worked for. Then Mansa Ram was able to replace Rustam Ali as tax collector for the present districts of Jaunpur, Banaras, and Mirzapur. While Mansa Ram was busy intriguing at the courts, he also built a strong hold in his native area of Banaras by fortifying his home village and raising an army. In 1738, Mansa Ram obtained for his son, Balwant Singh, the title of Raja of Banaras from the Mughal emperor in Delhi. For ten years, 1738–48, Balwant Singh obeyed and faithfully collected taxes on behalf of his superior, the Nawab of Oudh. In 1748, at the time of the Afghan invasions, while his supervisors were engaged in Delhi, he made his first overt move to consolidate his position by successfully attacking a lineage of Rajputs, the Monas, who were under the protection of the Nizam of Allahabad. Over the next five years, he subjugated several rajas and lineages in Banaras and Mirzapur and, most important of all, captured Bijaigrah in the hills of Mirzapur and turned it into his main fort. At the time, Bijaigrah was thought to be impregnable. After 1755, when he eliminated most potential military opposition in Banaras and Mirzapur, Balwant Singh extended his program of conquest by force and subversion into Jaunpur and in 1758 began his expansion into Ghazipur. Through this period he successfully fended off his revenue obligations to his nominal superior, the Nawab of Oudh, who because of his concerns in Delhi was never able to mount a full scale military operation against him. In 1764, he came to terms with the British after the Battle of Buxar, and the expansion of British influence had little effect on the province until Chait Singh's rebellion in 1781, when the latter, the illegitimate son of Balwant Singh, was replaced by Mahip Narayan Singh.

Wilton Oldham summarized Balwant Singh's success aptly:

> The success of Balwant Singh in his ambitious projects, is, I think, to be attributed to the adaptation of his character to the circumstances in which he was placed, and to the state of India at the time . . . . [He was] treacherous, unscrupulous, skilled in allaying the suspicions of others, [but] his own cautious vigilance never slept. Brave and willing to fight when fighting was politic, he preferred to use gold rather than steel, and rarely attempted an enterprise in which success was doubtful. Cruel and vindictive towards fallen foes, he was ever willing to forgive the injuries of the powerful, and in cases where he could not destroy his enemies, he accepted them without hesitation as friends and allies.[64]

In addition to the Raja of Banaras, the category of eighteenth-century aristocracy includes the descendants of Ausan Singh, one of the raja's principal servants, his *diwan* in the 1770's, who materially aided Warren Hastings at the time of Chait Singh's rebellion in 1781. He was rewarded by the confirmation of the jagir of a pargana, Saidpur Bhitri, and his descendants prospered in the nineteenth century through clever management. In addition to the Raja of Banaras and the descendants of Ausan Singh, three of those families I have termed eighteenth-century aristocrats were direct or collateral descendants of the Mughal emperor in Delhi, who had been "exiled" to Banaras in the late eighteenth century. A family descended from the nawabs of Oudh and two families of important early-eighteenth-century Muslim noblemen in Ghazipur also held land in the Banaras Province at the end of the nineteenth century.

*Traditional Aristocrats*

Eleven per cent of the land revenue paid by the large revenue payers was paid by two rajas, those of Dumraon and Vizianagram, who, although long established in their home areas, bought extensive "new" lands in Banaras. The Raja of Dumraon's ancestral home was in Western Bihar, and his land acquisition was heaviest in Ballia and Ghazipur. The Raja of Vizianagram's home was in what is now Andhra Pradesh, but he built a large palace in Banaras and settled there in the 1840's. He was responsible for the development of the municipal gardens in 1866, and the construction of Alfred Hall, the town hall of Banaras, in 1873–75.[65]

Of the twenty-one families holding their ancestral estates, fourteen were Rajputs, only two of whom were rajas in the eighteenth century. The other twelve were representatives of lineages, such as the Rajputs in Kopachit and Saidpur Bhitri, who received or controlled larger shares of the corporate holdings than did their agnatic kin. The most important of the pre-eighteenth century rajas holding parts of ancestral estates are descendants of the Raja of Raja Bazaar in Jaunpur. Also in this category were three Muslims in Jaunpur, two Bhumihars, one in Banaras and one in Ballia, and two Kayasthas whose ancestors had received lands as compensation for their duties as *kanungos* in the seventeenth century and who were able to maintain their estates.

## Religious Establishments

Two Gosains paid five thousand rupees in land revenue in Ghazipur on lands which were old religious endowments, and which careful management had maintained. Two Brahman families in Ghazipur owned several villages which had been *muaafi* (revenue-free grants for religious purposes) and which, although they were taxed after the settlement of 1839–42, when most *muaafi* lost their revenue-free status, continued in the hands of the original Brahman families.

## Caste Distribution of Landholders

Table X shows the distribution of landholders by caste in the Banaras region in the late nineteenth century. In commenting on these statistics, W. C. Bennett, Commissioner of the Banaras Division in 1889, stated, "The proprietary classes are still, in the main, the same as they were when the country was first annexed."[66] It is difficult to agree with Bennett, as there is no indication of what he based his assumption on or of what the distribution of landholdings by caste was in the late eighteenth century. As was discussed above, subjective accounts in the early nineteenth century and my impression of the records suggest that Rajputs had lost land and Muslims and banking and trading castes had gained land. In addition, there had been a polarization of landholding, with 7 families holding large estates, 127 holding medium-sized estates, and 110,000 holding the rest. In the late eighteenth century, some rajas, like those of Badlapur, Singramav, Raja Bazaar, and Haldi, had large estates; but by the middle of the nineteenth century they had lost their lands. The largest Rajput landholder in the region in 1885 was the Raja of Dumraon, all of whose holdings were obtained after British annexation.

TABLE X

DISTRIBUTION OF PROPRIETORS BY CASTE, 1885

| DISTRICT | TOTAL ACREAGE | RAJPUT | | BRAHMANS AND BHUMIHARS | | MUSLIMS | | BANIYA | | OTHER | |
|---|---|---|---|---|---|---|---|---|---|---|---|
| | | Acres | Per Cent | Acres | Per Cent | Acres | Per Cent | Acres | Per Cent | Acres | Per Cent |
| Ballia ........ | 461,000 | 340,000 | 74 | 69,000 | 15 | 8,000 | 2 | 12,000 | 2 | 32,000 | 7 |
| Banaras ....... | 567,000 | 206,000 | 36 | 191,000 | 34 | 47,000 | 8 | 72,000 | 13 | 52,000 | 9 |
| Ghazipur ...... | 935,000 | 245,000 | 26 | 353,000 | 38 | 191,000 | 20 | 28,000 | 3 | 117,000 | 13 |
| Jaunpur ....... | 970,000 | 403,000 | 42 | 145,000 | 15 | 274,000 | 29 | 39,000 | 4 | 99,000 | 10 |
| Total .. | 2,933,000 | 1,194,000 | 41 | 758,000 | 26 | 520,000 | 18 | 151,000 | 5 | 300,000 | 10 |

Source: See note to Table IX.

Bhumihars' holdings decreased as well. The total amount of Bhumihar holdings may have been the same in 1885 as it was in 1795; but in 1885 the Raja of Banaras' holdings accounted for at least one-third of the Bhumihar total holdings in the region, and most of his land was acquired after 1795.

By the end of the nineteenth century, a new group of landholders had emerged in Banaras. Some of them may have been of the same caste, in a cultural sense, as landholders in pre-British times, but they were not necessarily from the locality nor did they have the kin ties that previous holders had.

### THE "DISPOSSESSED": 1795–1885

It is much easier to identify those who obtained rights to land between 1795 and 1885 than it is to identify those who lost rights to land, or to determine the subsequent fate of the "dispossessed" economically, socially, and politically. One can describe the decline and pitiful state of a few of the dispossessed, such as the Raja of Haldi, in Ballia. In 1850, P. C. French, Collector of Ghazipur, called the attention of the Government to the situation of this raja.

> The Rajahs of Haldi have held, in former times, large landed possessions and have been reputed wealthy. The estates of the family have, one by one, passed out of their hands and there remains but one now . . . . Improvidence, extravagance, and, apparently a total want of business habits . . . have resulted, as is always the case, in pecuniary embarrassment . . . . He [the raja] is reduced . . . to a state of very deplorable destitution. . . . an old, ragged, red-striped tent, and a half-starved elephant are all his establishment when he has met me in the district, and the efforts he makes to cling to the "externals" of his class and station in the midst of the grinding poverty are sad enough to see.[67]

The family was so poor that the raja would not allow his two grown daughters to marry because he could not pay the established dowry.[68]

Were the tens of thousands of other families, particularly rajas who had lost rights in land, similarly reduced financially and left in a state as depressed as that of the Raja of Haldi? My argument is that they probably were not. In fact, my conclusion is that the majority of individuals, families, and lineages who "lost" land between 1795 and 1885 retained their positions, economically, politically, and socially *within* the local areas in which they had held rights as zamindars. This conclusion is based on tentative answers to a series of interlocked questions. What did sale or loss of landlord zamindari rights mean socially to those who lost them and to others in their native villages and local regions? What was happening to the agricultural production during this period? If agricultural production and income were increasing, who received the benefits of the increase? What forms of control over land groups, dispossessed or otherwise, were the new men who gained zamindari rights able to utilize?

When a new man bought zamindari rights to an estate at a public auction, what was he legally obtaining? He obtained the right to collect the landlord's share of the produce of the land from cultivators who tilled the soil. This was a right which he could bequeath, sell, or mortgage. He had the obligation to pay a fixed and unchanging revenue to the Government. His success depended on his ability to collect his share of the produce of the land. To do this, he had to persuade or force three kinds of cultivators to pay him the customary and legally demandable share of the produce.

The first type of cultivators which auction purchasers confronted were permanent tenants, usually Ahir, Koeri, Kurmi, Rajput, Brahman, and Bhumihar, who had cultivated the land for generations and who paid a fixed rate of roughly half the crop to those who held zamindari rights. They frequently viewed themselves as dependents or clients of the previous zamindars. If the previous zamindars were Rajputs, and the permanent tenants were Rajputs, they were of a different clan. The Brahmans, as well as the Ahirs, Kurmis, and Koeris, were descendants of groups brought to serve the Rajput landlords. The higher caste Rajput, Brahman, and Bhumihar permanent tenants did not actually till the soil themselves, but had permanent employees of lower castes farming for them for a share of the crop. The second group of cultivators were the tenants-at-will, often of low caste, particularly the Chamars and Bhars, who had no customary or fixed rights to the land.

The third group who held land, and from whom the new zamindar had to collect, were the former holders of zamindari rights. Their position depended upon their continued possession of their *sir* land. *Sir* is the "name applied to the lands in a village which are cultivated by the hereditary proprietors or village zamindars themselves, as their special share, either by their own laborers and at their own cost, or by tenants-at-will, not being let in lease or farm; these lands were sometimes allowed to be held at a favorable assessment."[69]

When an estate was sold, the previous zamindar was allowed to keep, at a low revenue rate, that land which he had cultivated for his own use as his home farm. In some estates, the *sir* land of the zamindars and the *pattidars* amounted to as much as 75 per cent of all cultivated land. *Pattidars* were agnates of zamindars in what had been, before British control, a corporately held estate. They were recorded as *pattidars* in British records, although their rights were much like those of the zamindars.

The social, legal, and economic issues involved in the general question of what happened to the "dispossessed" are complicated, and answers to the question do not lend themselves to easy general answers; hence, the answers will be suggested in a number of case studies.

## Case Study I: Ghamar and the Kausik Rajputs

Ghamar was a taluk of thirty-two villages, covering 13,036 acres in Ghazipur District, the zamindars of which were Kausik Rajputs. In 1795, under Jonathan Duncan, a revenue settlement was concluded in which the Kausiks who wished to hold their lands corporately were forced to divide their taluk into eighteen parts (*pattis*). Eighteen of the Kausiks were designated lambardars and were made responsible for the collection of the revenue from their lineage mates. The total Government demand was 7,775 rupees or a little more than eight annas per acre, in a district in which the average revenue rate was three times that amount.

The Government auctioned the zamindari rights of the *pattis* several times for failure to pay the Government revenue. In 1799, no one would bid on the taluk and the eighteen *lambardars* were imprisoned. In 1801, troops were sent to support a creditor with a court order, attaching the product of the land. In 1808, one of the eighteen *lambardars,* Abdhut Rae, agreed to be responsible for total payment of the revenue, but this led to internal fighting among the Kausik Rajputs, some of whom refused to recognize his right to collect from them. By 1829, many of the descendants of the original eighteen *lambardars* had obtained civil court decrees, invalidating the right of Abdhut Rae and his son to collect revenue from them. In 1844, there was a partition of the lands of the thirty-two villages, and 601 families were recognized as holding zamindari rights. The largest single payer paid a little over 125 rupees and held approximately 250 acres.[70]

It was difficult for any outsider to take over the Ghamar taluk, because a high portion of *sir* land remained in the hands of the former zamindars. Even if they could have been prevailed upon to pay the revenue demand to the new purchaser, the taluk would have yielded little profit, since the purchaser could only have raised the rent rate on 25 per cent of the land which was not *sir* land of the ex-zamindars.

In Ghamar, as in many other parts of the region, the non-*sir* land available to the outside purchaser was inferior to the *sir* land. The former zamindars invariably appropriated to themselves the best land as their *sir*. In addition, in the case of Ghamar the outside purchaser faced 1,500 to 2,000 Rajput ex-zamindars (figuring three adult males to a household) who, despite fights among themselves, could combine against an outsider when they felt themselves threatened. The new proprietor would have to maintain a large establishment of agents and private police in each village merely to collect the revenue, and he would need Government troops in order to dispossess the former zamindars and replace them with more amenable tenants even if he could legally manipulate the situation to do so.

### Case Study II: Maniar *Tappa* and the Barwar Rajputs

The history of the Maniar *tappa* in Ballia illustrates what happened when an auction purchaser, well supported by the Government, tried to collect an enhanced demand from the *sir* land of the former proprietors. The *tappa* contained twelve thousand acres and sixty villages and was held in three uneven portions, or taluks, by three different segments of a Barwar Rajput lineage, who were to pay revenue of about 13,500 rupees, or a little more than a rupee an acre.

Jonathan Duncan had erred initially in the settlement of 1789–90 in combining the three taluks of the *tappa* and having the members of these three quite distinct units enter into an agreement to pay the revenue of the whole *tappa*.[71] This led to a situation in which there were no internal means, through "public opinion," direct ties of kinship obligation, or established leadership to force a member of a taluk to pay his share of the revenue.[72] Hence, as in 1814, when there was a shortage of a thousand rupees out of the three thousand rupees of the revenue demand, the land was put up for public auction. One of the cosharers of the estate, Jag Deo Singh, offered 99,000 rupees for the estate, but his bid was refused by the collector on the grounds that Singh, as cosharer, could not bid on the estate. This provision of the sale law was later amended to encourage cosharers to bid on estates, and, in fact, the principle became one in which relatives, lineage mates, and other cosharers had first priority in bidding on estates put up at public auction.

The estate was then sold to Devi Sahai, who was, in fact, the agent of Shivanarayan Singh, a powerful jagirdar.[73] This Bhumihar jagirdar was the son of Ausan Singh, who had been granted a jagir worth fifty thousand rupees a year, by Warren Hastings for assistance in 1781 when Raja Chait Singh had "rebelled." According to Oldham, Shivanarayan "pursued a steady and relentless policy of taxation, extortion and expulsion of the owners of the soil from their lands."[74]

The former proprietors, the Barwar Rajputs, sought relief in the courts. The Banaras Court of Appeal gave a decree in their favor which invalidated the sale on the grounds that the amount of arrears did not warrant the sale, and that the collector should only have sold a portion of the estate large enough to pay the arrears. The Banaras Court of Appeals found that the collector also had refused to stop the sale except on payment of more than the advertised balance. It turned out that on the day of the sale the Barwars had been prepared to pay the arrears, but had not been told that the arrears included interest on a thousand rupees of overdue revenue, and this they refused to pay. The sale was declared illegal because it was also *benami,* that is, the purchaser, Devi Sahai, was not the real purchaser, but merely had loaned his name as the agent of the real purchaser, Shivanarayan Singh.

The decision of the Banaras Court of Appeal was overturned by the Sadar Divani Adalat on September 12, 1820, and the sale was confirmed.[75] The head judge of the Sadar Divani Adalat had been the commissioner of revenue in the Banaras Province at the time of the sale and was, in fact, supporting the decision he had previously made.[76]

The *tappa* was basically very valuable, since, when the original settlement was made in 1789–90, there was a great deal of land not under cultivation which was subsequently brought under cultivation. After the revenue was permanently fixed in 1795, the profit of the estate was considerable. Much land brought under cultivation was considered the *sir* land of the families of the Barwar Rajputs. However, its distribution among the three taluks and within the taluks among the actual zamindars was uneven. Hence, although the estate as a whole increased in value, it was unequally divided among the zamindars. Therefore, a few zamindars found themselves unable to expand their *sir* land, while the majority of the zamindars became richer due to more land brought under cultivation as their *sir*. It was this *sir* which was the most profitable, for it was carried at a much reduced rate on the *jamabandi* (revenue role) of the *tappa. Sir* land, in most parganas, was assessed at least eight annas an acre less than pargana rates. In situations where land was brought under cultivation after the Permanent Settlement, it was permanently assessed at the rate for waste land. Hence, a zamindar paid a few annas of revenue on such land, the profits from which could be ten or twenty rupees or more an acre, depending on the crop.

It is my impression from a study of the documents that zamindars usually grew valuable cash crops such as sugar cane, poppy for opium, or indigo, on their *sir* land. It was clearly the intention of the auction purchaser to raise the "rent" which he received from the former zamindars on their *sir,* or even, if possible, to eject the former zamindars.[77] There were, therefore, two simultaneous conflicts in the *tappa*; one was between those who had less *sir* and thought the revenue roll should be adjusted to account for the uneven distribution of the profits of newly cultivated *sir* land and those who had large quantities of the new *sir* and who wanted to keep the rate as it had been in 1795. The other dispute was between the auction purchaser, Shivanarayan Singh, and the former zamindars, over the attempt to get the *sir* land into his hands or raise the rents. Within a year, the auction purchaser, seeking ejection or rent enhancement, had brought 6,068 separate civil suits in the courts. He claimed he had invested over 110,000 rupees in court and lawyers' fees, payment to clerks, and the like, to bring these suits. In addition, through his agents and private police, the auction purchaser was dunning and pressing individual ex-zamindars.[78] As Oldham suggested, Shivanarayan, was an effective operator and was able to increase the amount collected from tenants in his jagir of Saidpur Bhitri by two and one-half times, in the space of one generation.[79]

In 1821, a year after the Sadar Divani Adalat had confirmed the sale of the *tappa* of Maniar to the auction purchaser, the Government appears to have felt that it had been too harsh in its actions and sought a plan by which the *tappa* could be returned to the original Barwar Rajput zamindars. After negotiation, the auction purchaser, Shivanarayan Singh, agreed to sell the estate to the Government for almost two hundred thousand rupees, or four times what he had paid for it at auction. He demanded and received this price on the grounds that he had spent a great amount of money in addition to his purchase price in court and administrative expenses. The Government bought the estate, then planned to sell it back to the Barwars, by allowing them to pay off the price the Government had paid over a fifteen-year period by each year paying an enhanced revenue. For a number of years, the estate was held *kham* (managed by the Government). There was a Government official, a *sazawal*, delegated to collect the revenue plus the amounts due to pay off the Government's cost of repurchasing the estate, from the former zamindars.[80]

While the estate was held *kham* (1822–36), some of the former zamindars continued to refuse to pay the Government demand and simply hid their harvested crops.[81] Not only did the cultivators refuse to pay or were unable to pay revenue, but also the Noniyas (caste of saltmakers) ran off, thereby stopping the supply of salt in the *tappa*, another source of income to the former zamindars.[82]

From 1822 to 1836, the Government, through the *sazawal* and Collector Robert Barlow and his successors, tried with varying success to collect the revenue from the principal payers. The former zamindars, who numbered roughly a hundred, claimed that their 2,500 brethren who were underholders were refusing to pay them.

The hundred former zamindars and their 2,500 underholders claimed that there had never been an adequate division of rights and responsibilities. Barlow tried to induce those involved to settle an equitable division among themselves, but the attempt led to serious fighting. Barlow reported:

> Certain individuals composing the Taluka of Doda Ray, on the occasion of my last visit, within a few yards from my tent, burst forth in a furious manner, quarrelling amongst themselves and beating each other . . . . I am informed that they again quarrelled lately and three or four individuals were wounded by swords.[83]

Some of the more important former zamindars maintained three-hundred armed retainers.[84] In addition to their physical power, some of the Barwars availed themselves of the courts to fight the auction purchaser, their fellow Barwars, and the Government. In 1834, Collector E. P. Smith stated:

> The atmosphere of the courts, however much it is the fashion to decry them, has charms for the Muneer Zamindars, and some of the parties appear resolved to seek that mode of redressing their own grievances, or, what is more frequently the case, of harassing their more fortunate adversaries.[85]

L. H. Newnham, who carried out negotiations with the auction purchaser, and whose principal previous experience was in the western districts of what is today Uttar Pradesh, found the Barwars "the disciples of some village attorney who has taught them to turn the law against even the rights of the realm."[86] One of the *lambardars* of the *tappa*,

Rupan Singh, argued that the maxims of English law had brought the *tappa* to its state of disorganization, since many argued cases within the *tappa* on the basis of "decrees of court and English laws."[87]

During 1826–27, Barlow was instructed to carry out a field by field survey of the rights of the former zamindars and their underholders. Consequently, revenue was divided on the basis of this survey, and the 2,500 Rajput underholders, rather than the hundred ex-zamindars, were held responsible for payment. By having them pay directly to the Government, it was hoped that a major source of dispute within the *tappa* would be resolved. However, litigation, internal fighting, and refusal to pay the Government demand continued. In general, as in the Ghamar taluk, the Rajputs, after considerable internal dislocation and dispute, were able to prevent the auction purchaser from taking their *sir* land or from enhancing the rent. In addition, the Barwars appear to have been able to fend off the Government. In the process, undoubtedly some of the Rajputs were impoverished. The *sazawal* reported that in 1824 the combination of the attempt to collect arrears in revenue, the extra revenue demand, and the flooding which caused severe crop damage had rendered the zamindars and the cultivators destitute. They could not borrow from the moneylenders due to the uncertainty of their position. The former zamindars could not collect their share of the crop from their tenants.[88] On investigation of this report, Barlow confirmed the fact that some of the Rajputs were, indeed, reduced to beggary: "One of them, I regret to observe, by name, Boondasing, who was brought to my tent, has already become a beggar, naked and absolutely destitute of any means of subsistence."[89]

It is, of course, impossible, without statistics, to know how widespread the destitution was or if, in fact, Boonda Singh wasn't "put up" as an exhibit to influence Barlow. My guess is that there was some destitution of the Rajputs, given the uneven distribution of land and the differential effects of Government efforts to collect revenue. It is my impression, however, that more of the Rajputs maintained themselves, and when the final settlements were made, they were no worse off than they had been at the end of the eighteenth century. Many were even better off because of the introduction of cash crops like sugar cane, indigo, opium, and tobacco.

Thus, in the Maniar *tappa,* it would appear that members of the Barwar Rajput lineage were able to maintain their position in the local social system in spite of extensive governmental pressure. Undoubtedly, some particular families of Rajput fortunes and social position declined, but other Barwars replaced them, not outsiders. In short, viewed internally, although the personnel changed in the roles of the system, structural change appears not to have taken place at this point. This process of circulation, of course, was not new in Maniar or Eastern Uttar Pradesh. Individual fortunes and family fortunes changed from generation to generation, through the vagaries of the number of male children in a household who were to inherit the property. In addition, disease, famine, and warfare affected individuals, families, and segments of lineages in different ways, leading to changes in position. However, the structure of the system remained the same. The British merely added another set of variables to the system, which in the two cases we have examined were not sufficient to change the system by the middle of the nineteenth century.

### Case Study III: Lakhnessar Pargana and the Sengar Rajputs

Lakhnessar, a pargana in Ballia district of over 35,000 acres is the most famous case of a Rajput lineage being able to maintain its position in spite of over a hundred years of pressure from the rajas of Banaras and from the British. It was held by a lineage of Sengar Rajputs, of whom there were over 32,000 in Lakhnessar and adjacent areas in 1891.[90] After inconclusive military action against the Sengars, Balwant Singh, the Raja of Banaras in pre-British times, was content to levy a lump sum of revenue of twenty thousand rupees payable by the Sengars as a corporate body. Jonathan Duncan continued this plan after he was unsuccessful in trying to get any information on what the pargana of Lakhnessar was capable of paying. He wrote in 1789:

Luknesser constitutes a small but remarkable exception to almost all the rest of this zemindary, being entirely occupied by a Brotherhood of Raijpoots of the Sengoor tribe, who have long affected to hold themselves in a great degree independent of Government, and the military spirit they one and all possess has engaged them to resist the officers of Government in so much that it cost Raja Bulwunt Sing much trouble and bloodshed before he could reduce them to pay even the moderate Mokwrory, Jumma or fixed rental of about Rs. 20,000 per annum . . . . It is still an exception to the country at large by not paying in the same proportion of the natural produce as the other Purgunas do, and as I think they might still resist any attempt on the part of government to fix the assessment upon their country, on principles similar to those which the rest of the country is generally subject, I have refrained from making any innovation in their settlement . . . . Each petty landholder has been in the habit of turning his house into a stronghold.[91]

In 1799, Routledge, the collector in Banaras, had to collect revenue arrears of over fifteen thousand rupees from the pargana with the aid of a military detachment which leveled some of the stone houses individual Sengars used as their forts.[92] In 1801 the pargana was sold at auction to the Raja of Banaras, Oudit Narayan Singh, who was unable to collect the revenue and had the sale annulled.

For a number of years the Government collected the revenue directly from representatives of the Sengar Rajputs, and although from time to time arrears of revenue occurred, the Government in effect did not know from whom they were due as no official internal allotment of the revenue demand had been made.[93] Barlow, the collector in Ghazipur, was unable to force those he assumed to be defaulters to appear at his office.[94] He found that when he went to the pargana, the Sengars would not tell him who "owned" what land, and he found no boundaries or measurements of fields.[95] The arrears were never collected, no suits in the courts started, and no auction sale carried out because of the lack of records and documents on which to base legal or administrative action.

In 1843 when a survey of records and a field by field survey of rights was being carried out in the Banaras region, E. Wilmot, the collector of Ghazipur District at the time, wrote to his superior:

> I have the honour to bring to your notice that the zemindars of Purgana Luknessor . . . are unwilling to give in the Putwaries Papers required according to the Sudder Board's printed circular number three.
> I have endeavoured to explain to them, but in vain that their rights would not in any way be interfered with, by their giving in these papers . . . .
> They claim they always have been exempt from furnishing putwaries papers. I request your orders.[96]

In essence, Wilmot's superior told him to leave the Rajputs of Lukhnessor alone.[97] Lukhnessor continued, as one commissioner of Banaras put it:

> . . . a 'terra incognita,' which had yet to be subjected to British rule . . . free from the nuisances of Revenue and civil court administration . . . .
> There are no shares, no boundaries, no putwarrees papers, no sales, no executions, nothing to designate the pergunnar as a British possession . . . .
> It is one proof out of many how little governing natives requires . . . . Of course, if the Civil courts once got into the pergunnar, it would be utterly ruined in a twelve month, but happily the chaos is so complete that there is really nothing for the courts to go upon, and this republic of relations is allowed to settle its affairs in its own way.[98]

In 1909, the Sengars continued to hold almost 85 per cent of the land of the pargana, divided into 537 mahals.[99]

It is impossible to know on the basis of available records how typical were the Sengars, Kausiks, and the Barwars in their ability to prevent the Government and auction purchasers from collecting revenue or rent. It is clear, however, from the cases of Lakhnessar, Maniar, and Ghamar and from data from Ungli and Chandawak in Jaunpur and Saidpur Bhitri in Ghazipur that determined physical opposition and recourse to the courts by a lineage or a major part of a lineage could prevent the loss of control of the land.

Central to the ability of some Rajputs to oppose auction purchasers and the Government was the Rajputs' domination of subordinate castes within their territories. In 1801, Raja Oudit Narayan Singh, who had purchased Lakhnessar at auction complained:

> . . . the Singrahs have put a stop to and prevented the inhabitants and cultivators ploughing their lands; the few spots in which they [the cultivators] have sown they [the Sengars] have overan [*sic*] and eaten up with their cattle . . . . When any cultivators attempt to plough their lands, they are beaten and their bullocks taken away and their ploughs broken.[100]

## Case Study IV: Narwar Taluk and the Rajputs

The actions of a group of Rajput zamindars of Narwar taluk in Jaunpur which came to light in 1816 indicate the extremes to which Rajputs could go in control of their dependents and subordinates. The zamindars, about two hundred men, women, and children cultivated one-third of the land themselves; this was the most valuable land in the taluk, being situated near wells, tanks, and ponds, to facilitate irrigation. The zamindars invariably used the irrigation facilities first, thereby often cutting off their dependents' use of water until it was too late. The dependents plowed, sowed, and cultivated the zamindar's land as *begar* (forced labor). As a result of what appears to have been rather harsh treatment of their subordinates, even for the times, land was going out of cultivation. The zamindars planted the uncultivated land in orchards from which they derived income by selling fruit.[101] The zamindars for a while succeeded in getting their revenue reduced on the grounds that it had been overassessed in the original settlement. Barlow felt that, in reality, it was underassessed, as the zamindars paid only eight annas an acre on their land, rather than the six to eight rupees an acre others paid. No Government revenue was levied on the orchards. A land speculator who wanted to lease the taluk under a long-term farming arrangement offered to pay the government a *jama* (revenue) of 5,500 rupees, rather than the 3,300 rupees the Rajputs were paying. He argued he could do this by charging a reasonable rent of six to eight rupees on *sir* land, cutting down some of the orchards, and bringing under cultivation some three hundred acres, which had been allowed to become waste because of the departure of cultivators. Murlazzah, the speculator, stated:

> If the lands of the Zamindars be taken away from them, and if we get possession of the gardens, and the Ryots who have fled return to populate the place, the revenue of the government can be very well discharged and we can set a profit of one or two hundred rupees.[102]

Central to Murlazzah's plan was strong support from the Government who were, in fact, to eject the zamindars. It would appear the Government was unwilling or unable legally to do this.[103] As the Narwar taluk consisted of only ten villages with a total of two hundred Rajputs or ten to fifteen families, as compared to forty to sixty villages and thousands of Rajputs involved in Maniar, Lakhnessar, and Ghamar, an auction purchaser or farmer could perhaps harass the zamindars sufficiently to get direct control over the cultivators. In a situation like Narwar, where the cultivators were absconding and were clearly at odds with the zamindars, I would speculate that a new holder who recruited his own cultivators and treated them well could, in fact, dispossess the former zamindars.

Zamindars appear to have frequently collected from their subordinates a whole range of customary payments. There were fees which the subordinate had to pay in addition to the rent. Payment had to be made to the zamindar before the *rabia* (dry season) crop could be cut. Fees were levied at the time of the marriage of the son of a zamindar. A fee was paid when the zamindar gave the cultivator a receipt showing he had discharged his rent obligation; and, in one instance at least, a fee was charged when the zamindar's elephant died to help defray the costs of a new one.[104] Not only were cultivators supposed to pay fees to zamindars, but artisans and merchants who inhabited bazaars were also subject to special taxes.

It would appear that harrassment, force, and violence were not the only means of control zamindars and former zamindars had over their dependents and subordinates; there were other ties as well. In order to understand the ties that existed, a more careful classification of the types of landlords and tenants is necessary.

### The Landlords

During the 1795–1850, a zamindar was regarded as the person or persons named in the collectors' records as being responsible for the payment of the Government revenue demand. The Government recognized in theory that there were others in a village or taluk who had *within* the village or taluk similar rights and duties as those recorded officially as zamindars. These were designated *pattidars* or *hissadars* ("brethren" of the zamindars, or underproprietors).

The principles of the Regulations drawn up by Jonathan Duncan and enacted in 1795 were clear in accepting the idea that large corporate bodies to which the English legal term "coparceners" was applied could be landholders. In theory, under the Regulations, in these corporate landholding bodies, questions relating to common property were to be decided by the common will of the sharers. Clause 1 of Section 17 in Regulation II of 1795 makes it clear that the names to be entered in the *kabuliyat* (agreement to pay the revenue) were to be determined by common consent of all who had a share. Later two kinds of corporate landholding systems came to be recognized and labeled by the British courts in Banaras, *pattidari* and *bhaiyachara*.[105]

The *pattidari* estate was one in which descendants of a common ancestor had divided the lands of their ancestral patrimony following genealogical principles; usually some lands such as orchards, tanks, and some waste land was held in common. The *pattidars* in a particular estate continued to recognize ties to the corporate body, but it is my impression that by the middle of the nineteenth century in many *pattidari* areas the *pattis* (the primary or original divisions which followed major lines of descent within the corporate bodies) tended to be thought of as quite separate. In the settlement of 1789–90, as discussed above, Duncan recorded certain members of the corporate groups as "zamindars," and they were entered in the revenue roll as being responsible for the collection of revenue from their cosharers in *pattidari* estates and for its payment to the Government. This led to considerable confusion, as it tended to elevate a person who was at best *primus inter pares* above his cosharers. Twenty or twenty-five years after the Regulations of 1795, the word "zamindar" tended to be dropped as a description for the person responsible for revenue collection from his cosharers and its payment to the Government and the term *lambardar* came into use. The term is derived from the English word "number" and can be translated as one who has a number in the *jamabandi* or revenue roll. The *lambardar* was intended to be the representative in a village, *patti*, or taluk of the rest of the cosharers within the unit from which the revenue was to be paid. By 1830, the term came to be used in the sense that zamindar was used in *pattidari* estates. The office of *lambardar* appears to have become hereditary and transferable and not tied to a particular person. There are accounts of a *lambardar* being a minor, a widow, and an auction purchaser.[106]

The Regulations unwittingly encouraged disputes between the zamindars and *lambardars* and other members of the corporate holding group over the distribution of income on profit from the community-held lands of the estate and the distribution of revenue due from each shareholder. It is my impression that in smaller estates or in a village, or in part of a village in Banaras and Jaunpur, the recorded revenue payers generally were able to establish their rights as sole zamindars, and those who were *pattidars* and hence, cosharers, became legally like fixed-rate tenants. In the larger corporately held estates, such as Lakhnessar and Maniar, the cosharers tended to prosper because instead of one or two zamindars or *lambardars* there were thirty or forty, and any one or two could not concentrate enough power to subdue completely the cosharers in the estate.

Some idea of the potential numbers of individuals involved in these larger estates can be seen from a case in 1819 in the Zamania pargana, Ghazipur District. The land was divided into seven *thoks* or major subdivisions. The *thoks* were divided into 23 *pattis*. In the *jamabandi,* 83 individuals were recorded as zamindars; but on investigation, it was found that there were 791 others who claimed *pattidari* status and a share of the land and its produce based on the principle of common descent. Of the 83 zamindars, 44 were recorded as *lambardars*.[107]

*Bhaiyachara* estates were somewhat differently regarded legally than *pattidari* estates. In *bhaiyachara* estates, unlike *pattidari* estates, the land was jointly and commonly held undivided; only the produce was divided according to shares based on principles of genealogical descent. As in *pattidari* estates, some cosharers were elevated to the roles of zamindar or *lambardar* under the British at the expense of their brethren. The internal conflicts between members of the corporate holding group and the zamindars or *lambardars* were of the same type as in the *pattidari* estates. Even though there is much discussion of *bhaiyachara* landholding in the literature, it is my impression that by 1850 the actual number of such estates was rare in the Banaras region.

A ruling of the Board of Revenue of 1807 would appear to have hastened the decline of the number of *bhaiyachara* estates. This ruling prohibited the sale of part of a legally undivided estate which had fallen into arrears. The Board of Revenue stated clearly:

> All states for which one engagement has been entered into, are to be . . . considered in toto for the revenue assessed upon the estate at large. Where an estate is held by two or more individuals, the payments which are made are to be carried to the account of individual proprietors.[108]

Under this principle the board observed that in an undivided *bhaiya-chara* estate the interest of one of the proprietors could not be sold for recovery of arrears due from the estate at large.[109] By this ruling, the Board of Revenue encouraged the partition into separate estates of both *pattidari and bhaiyachara* estates.

The significance of dispute among the cosharers of estates is seen in Table XI. As can be seen from this table, disputes within the estates, between members of the holding body, or between former zamindars and auction purchasers were thought to be the significant cause for the failure of the Government to realize the revenue in fourteen cases out of the twenty-nine recorded. Misappropriation of assets could also involve internal fighting and might be the expression of underlying conflicts.

TABLE XI

REASONS FOR REVENUE ARREARS BY TYPE OF HOLDER IN TWENTY-NINE
ESTATES IN BANARAS IN 1843

| Reasons | Zamindar | Mortgager | Auction Purchaser | Total |
|---|---|---|---|---|
| Misappropriation of assets . . . . . . | 3 | 3 | 3 | 9 |
| Poor management . . . . . . . . . . . . | 2 | 1 | . . | 3 |
| Overassessment . . . . . . . . . . . . . . | 3 | . . | . . | 3 |
| Disputes among zamindars or *pattidars* . . . . . . . . . . . . . . . . . . . . . | 8 | . . | . . | 8 |
| Disputes between mortgager, or auction purchaser, and zamindars or *pattidars* . . . . . . . . . . . | . . | 2 | 4 | 6 |
| Total . . . . . . . . . . . . . . . . . | 16 | 6 | 7 | 29 |

Source: A.C.R.O., Banaras Commissioner's Office, Banaras Revenue Files, Vol. 25, File 175, Davidson to Morrison, n.d.

In addition to *pattidari* and *bhaiyachara* estates, there were zamindari estates in which one person or family had established, through a long-standing grant, purchase, or tradition, the right to be recognized as sole proprietor of an estate. He or his agents collected the revenue from individuals who were in legal fact his tenants. However, through the working of the principle of equal inheritance of sons of their father's property, an estate which had a sole proprietor would become in several generations time like a *pattidari* or *bhaiyachara* estate. In thinking about the kinds of landlords and the varying proprietary interests, it is best to think of them in cyclical terms and as part of a continuing process rather than as a fixed type, forever immutable. As with the joint family, there is a development cycle in the types of land proprietorship in the period 1795–1850. One could start with one estate consisting of twenty villages with one man as sole zamindar. If this man had four sons and they held the land jointly as one property, the income went into one pocketbook and the expenses, both personal and of the estate, went out of one pocketbook; but by the next generation the land could become a *bhaiyachara* estate. Let us say the first son had four sons; the second son, three sons; the third son, two sons; and the youngest one, one son. In the second generation, from the sole ancestor, there would be now ten actual or potential shares. As Indian inheritance is usually per stirpes not per capita, the shares would be uneven, the four sons of the first son each having one-sixteenth of the estate, the three sons of the second son each having one-eighth, and the one son of the younger son having one-fourth of the estate.

If they decided to pool the produce and divide it by the above principle, the estate would be *bhaiyachara*. If they actually divided the land rather than the produce, it would be *pattidari*. Let us say that in the fourth generation the great-grandsons of the sole zamindar wanted a partition clearly made of the land or produce of the estate. In fact, if not in law, the owners of each of the shares became sole zamindars on their share. They were individually held responsible for payment of their share of the land revenue. They could individually sell or mortgage their land, and the cycle of zamindari to *pattidari* or *bhaiyachara* back to zamindari would be set up again.

## The Tenants

In much of the literature on the agrarian systems of India, a primary classification is made between zamindars (landlords) and ryots (peasants, cultivators). This dichotomy is relatively useless in understanding rural social structure in nineteenth-century Eastern Uttar Pradesh. Viewed from the perspective of the Raja of Banaras, the Raja of Dumraon, or other large landholders, members of a lineage of land-holding Rajputs, such as the Barwars or Sengars, could be thought of as ryots since they lived on their home farms which they cultivated with the labor of their sons or tenants. Taking the perspective of a landless worker, the Barwar or Sengar was a zamindar and not a ryot. The "tenants" I will initially define in general terms as those whose major source of income came from cultivating land on which they paid cash or a share of the crop to another individual who in turn paid revenue to the Government. A tenant was someone who was not entered in the *jamabandi* as being responsible for payment of the Government revenue and who by custom and law was not considered to be a member of a corporate proprietory body as a *pattidar* or other subproprietor.

The general term in the records of the early nineteenth century which was applied to this class of "tenants" in the rural population was *asami*, a "cultivator, a tenant, a non-proprietary cultivator; also a dependent."[110] After the revision of records, field surveys, and drawing up of village papers which were part of the settlement operation of 1839–42, *asamis* appear to have been those tenants who were entered in the village record of rights (*khewat*) as occupying and cultivating a particular piece of land or lands. *Asamis* were drawn from all castes. For example, in Mirzapur in 1852 a Brahman, an Ahir (cowherd) and a Koeri (gardener) were listed as *asamis* of a village, cultivating five, four, and seven bighas respectively.[111] In a *patti* of a taluk in Ghazipur in 1849 the castes of 84 *asamis* were recorded as shown in Table XII.

In the Regulations of 1795, two kinds of tenants were recognized, *paikasht* and *chhappar-band*.[112] According to H. H. Wilson, *paikasht* tenants were:

. . . a migratory or non-resident cultivator, one who cultivates lands in a village to which he does not belong by birth or hereditary claim, and holds his lands either for a stipulated term, or at pleasure of some member or members of the proprietory body.[113]

A *paikasht* tenant was contrasted with a *chhappar-band* tenant whom Wilson defined as "a resident cultivator."[114] After the settlement of 1838–42, the terms, *shikami* and *khud-kasht* tenants, are also used in the records to describe tenantry. A *shikami* tenant appears both legally and by village custom in Eastern Uttar Pradesh to have been a tenant-at-will

## TABLE XII

"Asami" Caste Composition in a Ghazipur Taluk*

High caste:
Brahman  ........... 10
Bhumihar ........... 15
Rajput  ............ 3
28

Middle caste:
Ahir  .............. 17
Koeri  ............. 13
Baniya  ............ 9
39

Low caste:
Bind  .............. 2
Teli ............... 2
Kohar  ............. 1
Mallah  ............ 1
6

Unclean:
Bhar  .............. 6
Chamar  ............ 3
Dhobi .............. 1
Kalwar ............. 1
11

on land recorded as the *sir* land of the zamindar. A *shikami* tenant plowed, sowed, and cultivated *sir* land, often with the plow, cattle, and seed of his zamindar. The *shikami* tenant often was a household or agricultural servant as well.[115]

A particular field of *sir* land of the zamindar might be cultivated by laborers employed to cultivate and paid a wage, or by laborers performing *begar* (forced labor), or it might be let to a *shikami* tenant who paid in produce or cash for the right to cultivate the *sir* land. It was likely, as it is in the present, that the same person worked as a wage employee on some *sir* land and cultivated other *sir* as a tenant of the landlord. As far as British revenue officials were concerned, the legal definition of a *shikami* tenant centered on the question of what was recorded in village account books. If a tenant was recorded as customarily paying rent on a specific piece of land to a particular zamindar, he was not a *shikami* but a *khud-kasht* tenant. However, if a tenant annually

* Source: A.C.R.O., Banaras Commissioner's Office, Ghazipur Revenue Files, Vol. 65, No. 687, Deputy Collector to Trench, 9 April 1849.

made independent arrangements to rent land, at varying rates, then he was a *shikami* tenant.

*Khud-kasht* tenants were occupancy tenants whose names were entered in the *patwari*'s records and in the *jamabandi* of the village. The fields they cultivated were known and marked on the village map, and they paid a fixed rent. They could not be ejected unless a court order had been obtained after proof of failure to pay the rent had been established. Theoretically, *khud-kasht* tenants' rights could have originated in a number of ways. They may have been cultivators or zamindars who lived and worked in the village before the present zamindars established their control. Many Rajputs, Bhumihars, and Brahmans were *khud-kasht* tenants, but many were of lineages different from the zamindars. *Khud-kasht* tenants were also drawn from traditional cultivating and herding castes, such as Koeri, Kurmi, and Ahir, who at some time in the past were brought as occupancy tenants to cultivate waste land. Some *khud-kasht* tenants owed their occupancy rights to performing specific duties as carpenters, blacksmiths, potters, or water carriers and received permanent tenancy rights to land as part of their compensation for performing their craft duties. Some village servants, particularly Brahmans, but often artisans, at one time held small pieces of land in villages as *muaafi* (revenue- and rent-free lands). Under British rule, *muaafi* lands were steadily converted into lands which were held by *khud-kasht* tenants.

Until the 1840's in what is now Uttar Pradesh, there was little concern with establishing precise classifications of tenantry and defining mutual rights and obligations, other than the very crude distinction between *khud-kasht* and *shikami* tenants. It was not until the land settlements of 1878–85 that a careful attempt was made to define and record the rights of various kinds of tenants in Eastern Uttar Pradesh.

## Opposition to the New Landlords

As suggested above, an auction purchaser who wanted to take over his newly acquired lands and collect rent or produce from those who actually cultivated the land faced several potential kinds of opposition— first and foremost, direct physical violence from dispossessed zamindars. In 1816, the collector in Banaras reported there were 15,800 Rajputs in Jaunpur who had lost their lands and who were under arms against the Government and auction purchasers.[116]

In 1828, the Magistrate of Jaunpur reported that between 1822 and

1825 there were seventy convictions "for murders, etc. produced from the system of selling lands to realize arrears of revenue."[117] In 1841, the Kausik Rajputs of Barra Gaon in the Chit-Firzopur taluk killed two agents of the auction purchaser who were trying to collect rent from the cultivators.[118]

The Rajkumar Rajputs of the Ungli taluk in Jaunpur carried on a running battle with the Government and the auction purchaser Sheolal Dube and his descendants for over twenty years. They fought the police and the agents of the auction purchaser, absconded with crops into Oudh, and consistently refused to pay revenue to the Government or rent to the auction purchaser. The Rajkumars went armed at all times and kept large numbers of armed retainers. They illegally collected transit duties from travelers and merchants. The Rajkumars kept drug ships and refused to pay license fees on shops. They stopped every boat on the Gumpti River and taxed goods and passengers. In addition, they appear to have spent considerable time fighting among themselves.[119]

Sheolal Dube, who was a powerful *tahsildar* (revenue-police official) in charge of the Ungli taluk from 1795 to 1808, managed, largely through illegal means, to bring most of the Rajkumar holding to auction, which he then secretly bought in the names of his son-in-law, son, and agents. When the *tahsildari* system was changed, after many abuses came to light, particularly during the investigation of the activities of the British collector James Barton,[120] the *tahsildars* were relieved of their police power. Dube could then no longer control the Rajkumar ex-zamindars. In a number of the specific cases detailed by Robert Barlow, acting collector in 1818–19, Dube or his agents failed to pay their revenue, and the Government tried to auction the auction purchaser's rights, but rarely did a bidder stand forth to take the estates. The estates were directly managed by the Government and a *sazawal* collected the revenue. They had less success than Dube in collecting the revenue. In those cases when an auction purchaser was found, the latter usually absconded in a year or two with what they could collect from the Rajkumars, but never paid the Government.[121]

After twelve years or more of inability to collect on the part of the Government or auction purchaser, the Government endeavored, in most cases successfully, to get members of Rajkumar lineages to buy back their zamindar rights.

In estates where an auction purchaser or a jagirdar opposed the former zamindars forcibly, the major question of conflict was over the rent or revenue to be paid on the former zamindar's *sir* land and the control these men exercised over their former dependents, the *shikami* and the *khud-kasht* tenants.

In Chit-Firzopur in Ghazipur District, even after sale for arrears of revenue, the Kausik Rajput zamindars continued to collect income from *sair* (zamindar's tax on the products of tanks, orchards, and waste land) and the *asamis* paid much of the rent due from the former zamindars' *sir* land.[122] In Saidpur Bhitri, the jagirdari of Ausan Singh's descendants, the former zamindars continued to fight to maintain their control of their *sir* lands for two generations. Lushington, who was deputed to settle disputes in Saidpur Bhitri reported in 1832:

> The disputes concerning rent are innumerable. The Sayer is in possession of the strongest whichever that may chance to be at the moment, and if I am to believe the evidence given up on oath, the Ryots are subject to demands of illegal aboabs [additional taxes above the legal rate] both from the agents of the Jageerdars and the descendants of the old maliks.[123]

The developments in Saidpur Bhitri exemplify a widespread process. Even in the face of sustained and strong opposition from the former zamindars, the jagirdar or auction purchaser, by the 1830's, was able to collect 175,000 rupees more than the taxes. This then became his profit. At the same time, many of the former zamindars maintained their economic position. Lushington explained this paradox as follows:

> It is quite certain that this has been effected as much by raising rents as by extending cultivation. Wherever the tenant had the power of resisting this increase, it was resisted and the dispute remains to this day. Wherever the party was poor either in purse or in spirit, it took effect. Hence it would be found very generally throughout the Pergunah that the Rajpoots have been at odds with the Jageerdar's family from the first, whilst the koiries, the koormars, the aheers and others have gone on quietly paying whatever the Putwarree demanded.[124]

In many parts of Saidpur Bhitri the Rajputs cultivated large quantities of land and were called zamindars by everyone.[125] The jagirdar apparently encouraged *asamis* to move about the land; this broke the hold of the former zamindar on his former dependents and enabled the jagirdar at a later date to enhance the rent demanded from the tenant.[126]

James Barwise, an indigo planter in Jaunpur, who appears to have speculated in farming zamindaris on which the Government could not realize the revenues, complained in 1844:

[The former zamindars] are always anxious to designate as their seer land much that is not so, and to fix nominally a low rate upon all that they so designate . . . . The zamindar kept two sets of papers, one which he collected by, the other for depositing in the collector's office.[127]

Barwise claimed that not even a tenth of the *chhappar-band* tenants of the Koeris, Kurmis, and other cultivating castes had their names recorded, even though their names were in the settlement officer's *khasara* (field book). In the records they filed with the Government, the zamindars had their own names rather than those of the tenants entered as being the cultivators.

Barwise thought two or three thousand bighas were thus entered as *sir* land on which the zamindars paid a nominal rent of eight annas, rather than the four or five rupees which the zamindars collected from the *asamis*. When Barwise tried to "correct" the *jamabandi,* the former zamindars threatened the low caste *asamis* that their houses would be destroyed by fire if they paid their rents to Barwise.[128] According to Barwise, the former zamindars cultivated the land they took from *asamis* by *begar* (forced labor).

Barwise was murdered, and the leader of the former zamindars was tried for the crime but acquitted.[129] The taluk of Raja Bazaar, which Barwise tried to farm, was involved in litigation from 1822 to 1863. After Barwise's death, his dependents continued to claim their rights as zamindars.[130] It is clear that Barwise thought that as a European he would stand a better chance of subduing the zamindars, than would an Indian, because he had easier access to the courts and the administration.

Badlapur, a taluk on the border of Oudh is one of the few examples that I have come across of an extensive taluk being effectively taken over by an outsider, Sheolal Dube and his descendants. Just before the Permanent Settlement, Badlapur had as its zamindar Saltanant Singh, a Rajkumar Rajput whose ancestors had created a petty kingdom in the area by subjugating former Rajput zamindars who were Bisen, Bachgoti, Bais, and Monas.[131] In 1839, the Commissioner of Banaras reported to the Sadar Board of Revenue of the Northwestern Provinces:

The cultivators here [in Badlapur] are a powerful body; their rights in the soil are so close and firm that all attempts to destroy or shake it off have failed. They have been oppressed doubtless but they could not be ousted; excessive rents have been taken or tried to be taken from them but they were ever able to offer legal resistance which has baffled the new zamindar, who was yet powerful enough to dispossess many of the old zamindars. This refers of course only to cultivators who have a prescriptive right in their holding subject to the payment of a rent at a fixed rate, and their rights have been confirmed. Sheolal Dobey and his successors have introduced a numberous class of inferior Ryots who cultivate the more lucrative crops such as tobacco, poppy and sugar cane. These are mere tenants at will and pay a very high rate of rent.[132]

**Summary**

Identifying the "dispossessed" is not a clear or a simple task. Some Rajputs, such as the Raja of Haldi, lost their zamindaris and were in a reduced economic state; but such dramatic falls in economic and social status appear not to have been the norm. Most of the Rajputs whose zamindari rights were sold continued to live as they lived before in their villages and taluks, dominating lower-caste cultivators and offering sustained and at times effective opposition to auction purchasers. Several key facts explain this situation. Legally, what was at issue were rights, not physical entities. This meant that after an auction of landed rights, the "seller's" legal status was changed from zamindar to ex-zamindar; however, he was not physically driven from his property. He could, and and usually did, continue to live in his home area with his agnatic kin in his lineage. The purchaser usually was an urban resident and tried to manage his purchased estate from a distance through agents.

In order to maximize the auction purchaser's profit, the agent had to accomplish three things. He had to break the hold, usually maintained by a mixture of custom and force, which the former zamindars had over other occupants of the estate. He had to get the *asamis* to pay raised rent. In addition, in many cases, he had to reduce the amount of *sir* land held by the former zamindars and also raise the rate of revenue paid by the former zamindars on their *sir*. In many instances, the former zamindars held the potentially most productive fields, since their *sir* land was near irrigation facilities and capable of growing cash crops such as sugar cane and poppy.

The key to the accomplishment of the auction purchaser's goal was his ability to break the power of the former zamindar, which was closely related to the number and internal organization of the corporately organized Rajput lineages. If the Rajput lineage was a small one and had already been disrupted by the rajas of Banaras in the eighteenth century, as was the case in much of the present Banaras District, the auction purchaser could succeed. If there was considerable and persistent internal conflict among members of the lineage, and the agent or auction purchaser was adept at playing on this internal conflict, he might weaken sections of the lineage sufficiently to accomplish some of his ends, as was the case in Saidpur Bhitri. However, as in the case of Lakhnessar, Ghamar, and Maniar where the members of the Rajput lineages were numerous and could compose for a time their internal differences, they could frustrate the goal of the auction purchaser.

With the sale of their property, the legal position of the traditional zamindars changed; but in many cases their economic, social, and political position within their villages and taluks was little affected, particularly from the perspective of those inside the village or taluk. It didn't seem important to low-caste cultivators or landless workers if the Rajput who for generations had dominated them was legally a zamindar, an ex-zamindar, or a tenant. The adage told to me by a Chamar (untouchable leather or agricultural worker) held in the nineteenth century as it does in the twentieth: "Living in a village with Rajputs is like living under a thorn bush."

A final set of questions remains to be answered before the history of the relations between the Government, the auction purchasers, the ex-zamindars, and the tenants is clear. The key question is: Why did men who made money in government service, the new professions, trade, and from land continue to invest in land, even in the face of the difficulties which were likely to occur? The usual explanation for the purchase of landed estates on the part of the "new men" and others is cultural. In traditional Indian society, wealth and status attained outside of agriculture were transmitted into landed status, since other kinds of activities, such as trade and service, were not of as high social status as being a zamindar. This certainly was a factor leading men to purchase estates between 1795 and 1885. However, it was not the only one. With all the attendant difficulties of control, land appears to have been a good investment.

From the fragmentary evidence available, the price paid for land appears to have risen sharply after 1795. Based on the transactions recorded for 1837, the average price paid was fifteen times the annual revenue demand.[133] In Ghazipur, the price of land sold in private sales rose from 29 rupees and 8 annas per acre as the average for 1843–52 to 52 rupees and 12 annas per acre as the average for 1873–82. The price of land sold at auction in the same years rose from 12 rupees and 14 annas per acre to 30 rupees and 5 annas per acre.[134]

From 1795 to 1850, the price of rice more than doubled and the price of barley increased 50 per cent. Only wheat prices remained fairly stable.[135] At the same time, the production of a number of valuable cash crops increased. The most important of these was sugar cane, which had become an extremely profitable crop by the end of the eighteenth century.[136] The growing of cane expanded markedly from 1800 to 1840; for example, between 1814 and 1832 the quantity of raw sugar shipped from Ghazipur District rose from 251,000 to 335,000 maunds.[137] Robert Barlow, Collector of Ghazipur District in 1818, wrote that the average net profit on a bigha of sugar cane was 17 rupees and 12 annas on a total investment of 27 rupees and 4 annas. This compared with profits per bigha of 4 rupees and 4 annas on *urhar* (a lentil), 4 rupees on indigo, 2 rupees and 9 annas on barley, 2 rupees and 6 annas on rice, and 1 rupee and 11 annas on wheat.[138]

The rise in agricultural prices and the expanded production of crops like sugar cane resulted in the utilization of some of the considerable waste land in the region, either virgin land or land once cultivated which had reverted to grass, weeds, and scrub jungle.[139] Since the revenue demanded from estates was permanently fixed in 1795, the profits which accrued from shifting to new crops, from the rise in agricultural prices, and from the bringing of waste land under cultivation went to the cultivator, the zamindar, or ex-zamindar, but not to the Government.[140]

The rise in land prices, particularly between 1795 and 1850, would seem to be associated with this expansion of the agricultural economy. While only speculative at this point because of the paucity of data, the answer to the question of why men continued to buy land would appear to be that it was a good investment. With the assumption of an expanded agricultural economy in mind, we can now go back to our starting question: What happened to the "dispossessed"? The overall answer may well be that nothing happened, as it would appear theoretically possible that there was enough enhanced value in agriculture for the former zamindars to profit along with the auction purchasers. In effect, the two contending parties could come to an agreement to split the increased income, leaving enough to the former zamindar to maintain his position within the local area and giving enough to the urban-based auction purchaser or buyer of land to support himself at an urban standard of living.

In discussion of social mobility and social change, we often tend to think, consciously or unconsciously, in terms of closed systems. This model may be adequate for the study of isolated primitive societies, but not for India in the early nineteenth century, or for the Banaras region as a case in point. Hence, unlike a hydraulic pump, the change in one part of the system, that is, the rise of one group or class, did not necessarily mean the concomitant fall of another.

NOTES

1 Quoted in Sulekh Chandra Gupta, *Agrarian Relations and Early British Rule in India,* (Bombay, 1963), p. 117.
2 *Report of the United Provinces Zamindari Abolition Committee* (Allahabad, 1948), I, 81.
3 Quoted in Percival Spear, *Twilight of the Mughals* (Cambridge, 1951), p. 117.
4 W. W. Hunter, *The Annals of Rural Bengal* (New York, 1868), pp. 19–73.
5 The research on which this paper is based was carried out at the Commonwealth Relations Office India Office Library (C.R.O.) and the Allahabad Central Record Office (A.C.R.O.), January, 1958, to July, 1959, supported by a fellowship granted by the Humanities Division of the Rockefeller Foundation. Time for analysis and write-up was provided by a fellowship granted by the Guggenheim Foundation. I would like to express my appreciation to Shri Shri Nath Singh who collaborated with me in the research at the Allahabad Central Record Office, and whose knowledge of the rural life of Eastern Uttar Pradesh was invaluable. I have published the following articles relevant to this topic: "The Initial British Impact on India: A Case Study of the Benares Region," *Journal of Asian Studies,* XIX, 418–31; "From Indian Status to British Contract," *Journal of Economic History,* December, 1961, pp. 613–27; "Political Systems in Eighteenth Century India: The Banaras Region," *Journal of American Oriental Society,* LXXXII, 312–20.
6 See W. H. Moreland, *The Agrarian System of Moslem India* (Allahabad, 1929), p. 81.
7 H. S. Jarrett (trans.), Abul-Fazl-I'allami's *Ain-i-Akbari,* (2nd ed.: Calcutta, 1949), II. The second edition was corrected and further annotated by Sir Jadu-Nath Sarkar.
8 *Ibid.,* pp. 173–75.
9 John Beames (ed.), Henry M. Elliot's, *Memoirs on the History, Folk-lore and Distribution of the Races of the Northwestern Provinces of India* (London, 1869), II, 204.
10 Wilton Oldham, *Historical and Statistical Memoir of the Ghazeepoor District* (Allahabad, 1876), Part I, pp. 48–52.
11 W. Crooke, *The Tribes and Castes of the Northwestern Provinces and Oudh* (Calcutta, 1896), II, 64–70.
12 Elliot, *op. cit.,* p. 117.
13 Oldham, *op. cit.,* Part I, pp. 97–118, and Part II; H. R. Nevill, *Banaras: A Gazetteer* ("District Gazetteers of the United Provinces of Agra and Oudh," Vol. XXVI [Lucknow, 1922]), pp. 137–45, 195–204; V. A. Narain, *Jonathan Duncan and Varanasi* (Calcutta, 1959).
14 A.C.R.O., Banaras Commissioner's Office, Miscellaneous Revenue Files, Vol.

17, *Basta* 100, D. B. Morrison, "A Few Remarks on Mr. Jonathan Duncan's Settlement of the Banaras Province, 29 March 1842." There is no consistency in the way the records in the Allahabad Central Record Office are kept. The records used in this paper have not been organized, listed, or indexed by an archivist. They were bundled up about 1920 from district offices and deposited in Allahabad. For the convenience of future researchers, I have tried to give as much meaningful information as possible about the location of each record.

15 Oldham, *op. cit.*, Part I, pp. 100–2.

16 For examples of grants recognized by the Raja of Banaras, see: A.C.R.O., Records of the Ghazipur Collectorate, *Basta* 28, Lushington to Commissioner, 24 January 1832, and Commissioner to Lushington, 8 February 1832; *ibid.*, Banaras Commissioner's Office, Correspondence and Proceedings of the Resident at Banaras, Register of Settlement Made for the Years 1197–1206FS, Book 134, *Basta* 47, p. 15; *ibid.*, Proceedings of the Resident at Banaras, Vol. 28, *Basta* 27, Duncan to Governor General, 1 February 1790; *ibid.*, Vol. 8, *Basta* 21, letter from Neave, 2 June 1788; *ibid.*, Banaras Revenue Records, *Basta* 110, File 38 (2).

17 A.C.R.O., Banaras Commissioner's Office, Register of Settlement of Pergannah Atgawan 1197–1206, Book 134, *Basta* 47, pp. 115, 125, 235.

18 *Ibid.*, Residents' Proceedings, *Basta* 23, Register No. 17, 6 March 1789.

19 C.R.O., Bengal Revenue Consultations, Range 51, Vol. 25, consultation of 3 October 1788 on letter of Duncan to Governor, 12 September 1788.

20 A. Shakespear (ed.), *Selections from the Duncan Records* (Banaras, 1873), I, 44–45.

21 *Ibid.*, p. 47.

22 A.C.R.O., Banaras Commissioner's Office, Residents' Proceedings, *Basta* 23, Register No. 13, 27 January 1789; *ibid.*, Correspondence and Proceedings of the Resident at Banaras, Register of Settlement Made for the Years 1197–1205FS, Book 134, *Basta* 47.

23 V. A. Narain, *op. cit.*, p. 39.

24 The details of Duncan's settlement are well covered in Narain, *op. cit.*, pp. 52–145. The basic selections from British documents on the period are in Shakespear, *op. cit.*, I.

25 A.C.R.O., Banaras Commissioner's Office, Correspondence and Proceedings of the Resident at Banaras, Register of Settlement Made for the Years 1197–1205FS, Book 134, *Basta* 47, Mongra pargana.

26 *Ibid.*, Katihar pargana.

27 Narain, *op. cit.*, p. 236.

28 *Ibid.*, p. 84.

29 Minute of James Stuart, *Papers Regarding the Judicial System in the Bengal Presidency, 1814–1818* (London, n.d.), p. 48; C.R.O., Bengal Revenue Consultations, Appendix 7, No. 26A, 24 February 1809, "General Statement of Lands Sold in the Bengal Behar and Beneras in 1213FS."

30 A.C.R.O., Ghazipur District Records, Copies of Miscellaneous Correspondence, 1797–1807, *Basta* 46, sales of 7 October 1799.

31 C.R.O., Judicial Letters to Bengal, 1804–1812, p. 221, letter of 21 February 1810.

32 C.R.O., Home Miscellaneous Series, Vol. 775, W. Cracroft, "Report on the Judiciary in Gazepore," 22 August 1814.

33 Wilton Oldham, *Tenant-Right and Auction Sales in Ghazeepoor and the Province of Benares* (Dublin, 1873), p. 6.
34 William Irvine, *Report on the Revision of Records and Settlement Operations in the Ghazipur District 1880–1885.* (Allahabad, 1888), p. 157.
35 Cohn, "The Initial British Impact on India," pp. 418–32.
36 C.R.O., Home Miscellaneous Series, Vol. 775, p. 134, Jaunpore Judicial Report, 15 August 1815. *Dharna* was the practice of starving oneself in order to force someone to stop doing something. *Kaor* was the practice of threatening harm to a Brahman, usually a widow, to bring supernatural punishment on an opponent.
37 These tables are based on revenue records of the region in the India Office Library, Commonwealth Relations Office, London, and the Allahabad Central Record Office. The data is incomplete for several reasons. The materials in Allahabad are voluminous. In the records of the Commissioner of the Banaras division for the year 1895, there are over five hundred volumes regarding the area, mostly pertaining to the period after 1830. Most of these records are unindexed. The district records of Banaras, Jaunpur, Ghazipur, Ballia, and Mirzapur for the period 1795–1857 have also been centralized in the Allahabad Central Record Office. There are approximately 470 volumes of District Revenue Records.

With the collaboration of Shri Shri Nath Singh, these volumes were surveyed and all transactions of land transfers by public auction found were recorded. The largest number of cases of specific sales were found for the Banaras District, in which information on 162 separate sales was found. Of these, 131 relate to the period 1830–50. Seventy-one transactions are in Jaunpur, all but one of which is between 1830 and 1850, 21 are in Ballia Ghazipur, all from 1830–50, and 29 are in Mirzapur, all for the period 1843–44. From about 1830, collectors had to file a certificate with the Banaras Commissioner's Office, stating for each sale the name of the village, villages, or mahals sold, the government *jama* on the estate, the pargana in which it was located, the amount the estate was in arrears, the name of the seller, the name, caste, occupation, and residence of the buyer, and the price paid by the buyer. Unfortunately, not all certificates give all this information, particularly in relation to caste, occupation, and residence of the buyer.

Information on land sales in Banaras is found in: Proceedings of the Board of Commissioners for Bihar and Banaras, No. 21A, 4 February 1817; Banaras Commissioner's Office, Miscellaneous Revenue Records, Vol. 3, File 9; *ibid.*, Banaras Revenue Files, Vol. 10, File 68; Vol. 16, Files 106, 108; Vol. 18, Files 113, 116; Vol. 19, File 140; Vol. 23, Files 151, 158, 160; Vol. 24, Files 170, 172; Vol. 25, File 182; Vol. 28, File 204; Vol. 30, Files 216, 217; Vol. 34, Files 247, 250, 251; Vol. 35, File 254; Vol. 36, File 256; Vol. 40, File 270; Vol. 43, File 294; Vol. 47, File 301; Vol. 51, Files 321, 324, 325; Vol. 52, File 327; Vol. 53, File 337; Vol. 57, File 351; Vol. 59, File 362; Vol. 62, File 320; Vol. 69, File 400; Vol. 76, File 440.

For Ghazipur-Ballia, pertinent records include: Banaras Commissioner's Office, Ghazipur Revenue Files, Vol. 34, File 548; Vol. 35, File 561; Vol. 36, Files 567, 568, 571; Vol. 38, File 583; Vol. 39, File 586; Vol. 42, File 599; Vol. 43, File 606; Vol. 55, File 649; Vol. 56, File 650; Vol. 58, Files 660, 664; Vol. 61, Files 672, 673; Vol. 65, File 883; Vol. 71, File 723; Vol. 75, File 732.

Land sales in Jaunpur are described in: Proceedings of the Board of Commissioners for Bihar and Banaras, Vol. 10, No. 34, 4 November 1816; Banaras Commissioner's Office, Miscellaneous Revenue Files, Vol. 11, File 99; *ibid.,* Jaunpur Revenue Files, Vol. 44, pp. 3, 70; Vol. 45, pp. 63, 65, 135; Vol. 46, pp. 24, 76, 78, 84, 88, 89, 125, 177, 186, 213, 215, 234; Vol. 47, p. 248.

Information on land sales in Mirzapur is found in: Mirzapur Revenue Files, Vol. 9, Files 562-77, 610-23.

For a general indication of the nature and scope of documentary materials available in the Allahabad Central Record Office, see Douglas Dewar, *A Handbook to the English Pre-Mutiny Records of the United Provinces of Agra and Oudh* (Allahabad, *ca.* 1922), pp. 258–387; G. N. Salltore (ed.), "Banaras Affairs, 1788–1810," in *Selections from English Records* (Allahabad, n.d.), I; *Press List of Pre-Mutiny Records: Banaras Correspondence, 1776–1789* (Allahabad, 1955).

38  Dewar, *op. cit.,* p. 2.
39  For a discussion of the types of under civil servants in the eighteenth and early nineteenth century, see Cohn, "The Initial British Impact on India," pp. 420–21.
40  Nevill, *op. cit.,* pp. 53–54.
41  A Member of the Family, *An Account of the Govindram Mitter* (Calcutta, 1864), p. 7.
42  *Ibid.,* p. 8.
43  *Ibid.,* p. 12.
44  *Ibid.,* pp. 11–25; and Nevill, *op. cit.,* p. 54.
45  Irfan Habib, "Banking in Mughal India," *Contributions to Indian Economic History,* I, 2.
46  *Ibid.,* 19.
47  B. B. Misra, *The Indian Middle Classes* (London, 1961), p. 32.
48  See George A. Grierson, *Bihar Peasant Life* (2nd ed.: Patna 1926), p. 413, for *mahajan.* See Henry Yule and A. C. Burnell, *Hobson-Jobson* (London, 1903), for the use in English of the terms *sarraf* and *mahajan*; most of examples used to illustrate the term *sarraf* are pre-nineteenth century. The three examples given for the use of *mahajan* are nineteenth century.
49  D. R. Gadgil, "Origins of the Modern Indian Business Class: An Interim Report" (mimeographed report of the Institute of Pacific Relations, New York, 1959), pp. 4–15.
50  N. C. Sinha, *Studies in Indo-British Economy One Hundred Years Ago* (Calcutta, 1946), pp. 32–33.
51  For example, the Jagat Seths; *ibid.,* p. 18.
52  L. C. Jain, *Indigenous Banking in India* (London, 1929), pp. 18–19, and Shakespear, *op. cit.,* pp. 28–34.
53  H. Sinha, *Early European Banking in India* (London, 1927), p. 24.
54  A.C.R.O., Mirzapur Collectorate Pre-Mutiny Records, Vol. 231, letters from commissioners sent to deputy collectors regarding Kantit estates; *ibid.,* E. A. Reade, "Minutes on Purgenneh Kantit," 12 June 1850, Par. 8.
55  *Ibid.,* Par. 9.
56  *Ibid.,* Par. 13.
57  *Ibid.,* Par. 2.
58  *Ibid.,* Reade to Roberts, 5 October 1850.
59  A.C.R.O., Banaras Commissioner's Office, Mirzapur Revenue Files, Vol. 4,

File 641, Serial 1, "Mr. Moore's Memo January 19, 1857." Moore gives twelve examples of this kind of indebtedness.

60 See Mr. Thomason's dispatches in "Joint Stock Banks in the North West Provinces," *Selections from the Records of the Government of the North West Provinces* (Calcutta, 1858), II, 14.

61 *Ibid.*, 24.

62 Spear, *op. cit.*, pp. 82–83.

63 The narrative of the rise of the family of Mansa Ram and his descendants is based on Oldham, *Memoir*, Part I, pp. 97–119; A. L. Srivastava, *The First Two Nawabs of Oudh* (2nd ed.: Agra, 1954), p. 42, *passim*; A. L. Srivastava, *Shuja-ud-Daula* (2nd ed.: Delhi, 1961), I, 24–31; A.C.R.O., Duncan Records, Vol. 46, *Basta* 8, "The Raja of Banaras Family"; *ibid.*, Records Relating to the Family Domains of the Maharaja of Benares, Vol. 190(4) Basta 976; C.R.O., Home Miscellaneous Series, Vol. 201(1), p. 79, W. W. Bird's report on the Pergunah Bhadahi, 25 May 1827; *ibid.*, Vol. 202, p. 139; *ibid.*, Vol. 203, p. 34; Imperial Record Office, *Persian Correspondence* (Calcutta, 1930), V, 306. I have discussed the rise of the family and its internal political and economic policies in "Political Systems in Eighteenth Century India," pp. 312–20.

64 Oldham, *Memoir*, Part I, p. 105.

65 Rajani Ranjan Sen, *The Holy City (Benares)* (Chittagong, 1912), pp. 13–14.

66 W. C. Bennett, Orders of Government No. 898A 1-710 of 1889, Resolution of the Revenue Department, 15 June 1889, in P. C. Wheeler, *Report on the Revision of Records of the Settlement Operation in the District of Jaunpur, 1877–1886* (Allahabad, 1886), p. 6.

67 A.C.R.O., Banaras Commissioner's Office, Ghazipur Revenue Files, Vol. 73, File 727, P. C. French to E. A. Reade, 31 October 1850.

68 *Ibid.*, Miscellaneous Judicial Records, Vol. 4, File 86, Thornhill to H. C. Tucker, 22 August 1854.

69 H. H. Wilson, *A Glossary of Judicial and Revenue Terms* (London, 1855), p. 485. For discussion of *sir* land in the Banaras Region, see: A.C.R.O., Banaras Commissioner's Office, Miscellaneous Revenue Files, Vol. 5, No. 201, Gubbins to Tucker, 8 July 1854; *ibid.*, Wyatt to Gubbins, 8 July 1854; *ibid.*, Tucker to Board, 14 July 1854.

70 A.C.R.O., Ghazipur Revenue Records, Vol. 82, *Basta* 173, File 764, "Partition Statement of Taluquh Ghamur," 8 July 1844; H. R. Nevill, *Ghazipur: A Gazetteer* ("District Gazetteers of the United Provinces of Agra and Oudh," Vol. XXIX [Lucknow, 1922]), pp. 192–93.

71 Nevill, *Ghazipur*, p. 193; and A.C.R.O., Banaras Commissioner's Office, Ghazipur Revenue Files, No. 764, Salmon to Thackeray, 25 November 1808; *ibid.*, Ferguson to Bentick, 3 October 1828; *ibid.*, Wilmot to Smith, 7 September 1841.

72 A.C.R.O., Banaras Commissioner's Office, Ghazipur Revenue Files, Vol. 48, File 620, H. C. Tucker to Commissioner, 27 November 1832; Oldham, *Memoir*, Part II, p. 151.

73 A.C.R.O., Banaras Commissioner's Office, Ghazipur Revenue Files, Vol. 102, File 1488, Part I, Barlow to Commissioner, 14 March 1821.

74 Oldham, *Memoir*, Part II, p. 21.

75 A.C.R.O., Banaras Commissioner's Office, Ghazipur Revenue Files, Vol. 48, File 620, H. C. Tucker, 27 November 1832.

76 *Ibid.*, W. L. Melville to H. MacKenzie, 10 January 1826.
77 A.C.R.O., Banaras Commissioner's Office, Ghazipur Revenue Files, Vol. 102, File 1488, Part I, "Translation of Proceedings of Collector of Ghazipur of the 30th Aug. 1822."
78 *Ibid.*
79 *Ibid.*, Ghazipur Revenue Files, Vol. 28, No. 80, "Letters Issued by Mr. Lushington, Officer Superintending Settlement at Sydpore Bhittree," letter of 26 April 1832.
80 *Ibid.*, Banaras Commissioner's Office, Ghazipur Revenue Files, Vol. 102, File 1488, MacKenzie to Board of Revenue in Central Province, 22 April 1822.
81 *Ibid.*, Barlow to Board, 9 July 1825.
82 *Ibid.*, Barlow to Board, 23 July 1825.
83 *Ibid.*, Barlow to Board, 16 May 1826.
84 *Ibid.*, L. H. Newnham to Barlow, 12 February 1822.
85 *Ibid.*, Ghazipur Revenue Files, Vol. 48, File 620, E. P. Smith to Commissioner, 10 October 1834, Par. 4.
86 *Ibid.*, Par. 9.
87 *Ibid.*, Par. 4.
88 *Ibid.*, Vol. 103, File 1488, Part II, "Translation of a Petition of Suzewal of Tuppa Mannier," 23 July 1824.
89 *Ibid.*, Barlow to Tilghman, 9 June 1925.
90 H. R. Nevill, *Ballia: A Gazetteer* ("District Gazetteers of the United Provinces of Agra and Oudh" Vol. XXX [Allahabad, 1907]), pp. 225–31; W. Crooke, *The Tribes and Castes of the Northwestern Provinces and Oudh* (Calcutta, 1896), IV, 313–14; Oldham, *op. cit.*, Part I, p. 59.
91 C.R.O., Bengal Revenue Consultations, Range 51, Vol. 32, consultation of 18 February 1789 on a letter of Duncan to Cornwallis, 1 February 1789.
92 *Ibid.*, Range 73, Vol. 52, consultation of 3 September 1799 on letter of Routledge to Cowper, 20 August 1799.
93 A.C.R.O., Banaras Commissioner's Office, Ghazipur Revenue Files, Vol. 88, File 1051, Barlow to Dunsmore, 23 June 1819.
94 *Ibid.*
95 *Ibid.*, letters of 2 July 1819, 20 August 1819, and 14 September 1819.
96 *Ibid.*, Wilmot to Morrieson, 20 February 1843.
97 *Ibid.*, Morrieson to Sudder Board of Revenue, North-Western Provinces, 27 February 1843.
98 *Ibid.*, H. C. Tucker to Sudder Board of Revenue, North-Western Provinces, 18 April 1856.
99 Nevill, *Ballia: A Gazetteer,* p. 228.
100 A.C.R.O., Banaras Commissioner's Office, Miscellaneous Revenue Records, Vol. 16, *Basta* 100, p. 123, letter from Raja Oudit Narayan Singh, n.d.
101 *Ibid.*, Ghazipur Collectorate, Vol. 1, *Basta* 2, Barlow to Deane, 25 November 1816.
102 *Ibid.*, Proceedings of G. H. Barlow on Deputation, 14 November 1816, "Questions Put to Gholam Moorluzzah."
103 *Ibid.*, Proceedings of November 24, 1816 and Comment on Paper Number Three; *ibid.*, Proceedings Behar and Banares Commissioner, 31 December 1816, letter from Collector of Benares, 19 December 1816.
104 *Ibid.*, Banaras Commissioner's Office, Miscellaneous Revenue Files, Vol. 17,

*Basta* 101, Deane to Dowdeswell, 10 December 1803. Also see George A. Grierson, *Bihar Peasant Life* (2nd ed.: Patna, 1926), pp. 319–20 for terms used for various kinds of additional cases in Bihar.

105  In this discussion I am following A.C.R.O., Banaras Commissioner's Office, Ghazipur Revenue Files, Vol. 101, File 1487, F. M. Bird, "Note on the Putteedaree Tenures of Benares," 25 November 1832, Pars. 1–4.

106  *Ibid.*, Vol. 65, No. 687, Wilmot to Morrieson, 7 September 1842.

107  *Ibid.*, Ghazipur Collector's Office, Miscellaneous Revenue Files, Files 1–11, "Petition by Zemindar of Ph. Zaminia."

108  C.R.O., Bengal Board of Revenue, Consultations, Range 76, Vol. 3, Board's Resolution No. 8, 17 March 1807.

109  *Ibid.*

110  Wilson, *op. cit.*, p. 35.

111  A.C.R.O., Mirzapur Collectorate, Vol. 236, No. 15, "Letters Issued by the Deputy Collector Regarding Kantit Estates," Roberts to Reade, 13 April 1852.

112  See Bengal Regulations VIII, Sec. 60, 1793; II, Sec. 10, 1795; VIII, Sec. 18, 1819; XI, Sec. 32, 1822.

113  Wilson, *op. cit.*, p. 389.

114  *Ibid.*, p. 110.

115  A.C.R.O., Banaras Commissioner's Office, Miscellaneous Revenue Records, Vol. 5, File 20, Serial 1, Tucker to Sudder Board of Revenue N.W.P., 14 July 1854, Par. 12.

116  Oldham, *Tenant Right and Auction Sales*, p. 3.

117  *Ibid.*, p. 3.

118  A.C.R.O., Banaras Commissioner's Office, Ghazipur Revenue Files, Vol. 46, File 616, Wilmot to Smith, 3 August 1841.

119  *Ibid.*, Proceedings of the Commissioners of Bihar and Banaras, Vol. 9, Proceedings of 21 October 1816, Letter No. 162 from Robert Barlow, 18 September 1816; *ibid.*, Banaras Revenue Records, Vol. 2, *Basta* 110, Board of Commissioners of Bihar and Banaras to Dowdeswell, 15 May 1818; *ibid.*, Officiating Collector Jaunpur, to Board of Revenue, 15 January 1819.

120  Bernard S. Cohn, "The British in Banaras: A Nineteenth-Century Colonial Society," *Comparative Studies in Society and History,* IV, 190–92.

121  A.C.R.O., Banaras Revenue Records, Vol. 2, *Basta* 110, Office of the Collector, Jaunpur, to Board of Revenue, 15 January 1819.

122  *Ibid.*, Banaras Commissioner's Office, Ghazipur Revenue Files, Vol. 46, File 616, Thomason to Elliot, 29 April 1841.

123  *Ibid.*, Ghazipur Revenue Records, Vol. 28, No. 80, "Letters Issued by Mr. Lushington, Office Superintending Settlement at Sydpore Bhitri," letter of 26 April 1832.

124  *Ibid.*

125  *Ibid.*, 22 September 1832.

126  A.C.R.O., Banaras Commissioner's Office, Ghazipur Revenue Files, Vol. 5, Part III, File 621, Lushington to Curve, 15 May 1834.

127  *Ibid.*, Proceedings of the Sudder Board of Revenue, North Western Provinces, Vol. 263, No. 12, October 4, 1844, Barwise to Board, letter of 21 July 1844.

128  *Ibid.*

129  P. C. Wheeler, *op. cit.*, p. 48; Holmes and Company, *The Bengal Obituary* (Calcutta, 1848), p. 387.

130 "Raja Mahesh Narain Singh *vs.* Kshnanand Misr," in Edmund P. Moore, *Reports of Cases Heard and Determined by the Judicial Committee and the Lords of His Majesty's Privy Council on Appeal from the Supreme and Sudder Dewanny Courts in the East Indies* (London, 1863), Vol. VII.

131 Aditya Narain Singh, "Biography of Saltant Singh," a manuscript in Hindi written in 1952–53.

132 A.C.R.O., Proceedings of the Sudder Board of Revenue, North-Western Provinces, Vol. 224, 9 May 1843, letter received from Commissioner of Benares between 1834 and 1840.

133 The figures for sale price are based on the 283 transactions discussed on pp. 71–78; the compilation of price statistics on land sales and subsequent discussion of agricultural prices was done by Mr. Peter McGregor.

134 *Ghazipur Settlement Report*, Appendix, pp. 156–60.

135 The figures on agricultural prices are based on a wide variety of reports and undoubtedly are only approximations. For price statistics see: A.C.R.O., Banaras Commissioner's Office, Miscellaneous Records, Vol. I, *Basta* 98; p. 10; *ibid.,* Mirzapur Collectorate, Pre-Mutiny Records, Letters Issued, Vol. 72, p. 15; *ibid.,* Ghazipur Collectorate Copies of Correspondence Relating to Ghazipur District 1817–1818, p. 291; *ibid.,* Ghazipur Collectorate, Copies of Miscellaneous Correspondence 1820–27, letter of Barlow Tilghman, October 1823; *ibid.,* Banaras Commissioner's Office, Miscellaneous Revenue Files, Vol. 13, *Basta* 105, File 79, Appendix 10; and Nevill, *Banaras: A Gazetteer,* p. 49.

136 Shakespear, *op. cit.,* I, 36; A.C.R.O., Banaras Commissioner's Office, Correspondence and Proceedings of the Resident at Banares, Register of Settlement Made for the Years 1197–1206FS, Book 134, *Basta* 47, p. 113 for examples.

137 A.C.R.O., Ghazipur Collectorate, Copies of Miscellaneous Correspondence 1844–1858, E. P. Smith to H. Sweterhan, 29 October 1834.

138 *Ibid.,* Copies of Correspondence Relating to Ghazipur District 1817–1818, Robert Barlow, "Tables of Gross Produce of a Beegah of Land in Ghazipur" and "Tables of the Expenses on the Cultivation of a Beegah of Land in Ghazipur," 26 July 1818.

139 Narain, *op. cit.,* pp. 3–51; Shakespear, *op. cit.,* I, *passim.*

140 A.C.R.O., Ghazipur Collectorate, Copies of Miscellaneous Correspondence, 1820–1827, Barlow to Tilghman, 1 October 1823, Par. 12.

# Chapter V

# From Raja to Landlord: The Oudh Talukdars, 1850-1870

*Thomas R. Metcalf*

---

Most studies of social change in rural India under British rule have focused upon the institution of caste and upon the character and extent of social mobility. In the process such useful concepts as "Sanskritization" and "Westernization" have been formulated, and a considerable body of literature has grown up, much of it devoted to exploring the relationship between these two concepts.[1] This preoccupation with questions of caste and mobility can, however, easily obscure other types of change which took place in the structure of rural society as a result of British rule. One of the most important of these, at least in Bengal and North India, relates to the position in society of the great landholders, known as talukdars or zamindars.[2] The most striking feature in the fate of this landlord community under the British, was neither the decline, except in a few places, of the traditionally dominant groups, nor the rise of new men, but rather the persistence in positions of power of the old landed classes by a process of adaptation to the altered political and economic conditions.

Among the various landed classes of North India perhaps the most numerous and powerful were the talukdars of Oudh. A force to be reckoned with by nawabs, British district officers, and harassed peasant cultivators alike, they towered above rural society in Oudh for decades. This paper is a study of the way in which this group maintained its old status in the new environment of British rule by a thoroughgoing transformation of their relations with each other, with the Government, and with those beneath them on the land. The talukdars were still the dominant figures in the countryside in the later days of British rule, as they had been at annexation in 1856; but the bases of their power and the sanctions by which it was sustained were of a new and different character.

Before annexation, the Oudh talukdars cannot properly be regarded as landlords. They built estates, amassed followers, and contended with the nawab's officials for the control of the land revenue. But their power came not so much from the ownership of land as from the control of the resources, in men and material as well as land, of a given locality. Their estates have been called "little kingdoms," and the talukdars, as little "kings" or rajas, were not owners of land but rulers of men— leaders in time of war and arbiters in time of peace of all those subject to their sway.[3] The physical symbol of this quasi-independent political status can be found in the sturdy mud fort, fortified with cannon and surrounded on every side with dense growths of jungle, which lay at the heart of every talukdari estate. In the safety of this fort the talukdar could defy his marauding neighbors, and often the nawab's officials as well; from it, accompanied by his bands of armed retainers, he could venture forth to prosecute his own quarrels. In 1856, the British counted 623 forts in Oudh, of which 351 were in a state of good repair.[4]

Nor were the talukdars of 1850 like the English gentry of the time, a stable and cohesive group of men, bound together by mutual interests and institutions and bulwarked by centuries of prescriptive right. The term "talukdar" was applied rather indiscriminately to all those who had succeeded in the scramble for power on the local level, and this included a very diverse and fluctuating group of men. Most numerous were the heads of the old Rajput lineages, long-settled and widely scattered in each district. These Rajput families often remained talukdars generation after generation, for their position was sustained by the deferential support of their numerous kinsmen; but even in these old families factional disputes or the dissipation of the family patrimony among several heirs could easily reduce once powerful families to penury. In addition, by the mid-nineteenth century the talukdari ranks contained many self-made men, of various castes, who had taken advantage of the increasing weakness of the nawabs of Oudh to seize control of sizeable local areas and recruit large bodies of armed retainers. The

Mehdona estate of Faizabad, for instance, comprising property assessed at two lakhs of rupees, was put together during the first half of the nineteenth century by two brothers, Bukhtawar and Darshan Singh, the eldest of whom began service as a trooper in the Oudh Cavalry. Darshan's son, Man Singh, continued up to annexation to expand the estate, largely through abuse of his official position as nazim, by quietly incorporating into his private holdings villages for whose revenue he was responsible to the nawab.

The first challenge to the traditional position of the talukdar came with the British annexation of the province in 1856. Determined to monopolize the military force of the state and to retain in their own hands the powers of law and order, the British set out to deprive the talukdars of their quasi-independent political position. They dispatched troops to reduce the talukdars' forts, and they ordered the talukdars to disband their bodies of armed retainers. Neither move was immediately successful, but the importance placed upon them, when, as the Judicial Commissioner readily admitted, these forts were unlikely to prove formidable to the forces of the British Government, indicates the extent of the British determination to eradicate the memory of those "lawless times" when the talukdars exercised military power.[5]

At the same time, the British set out to lower the social and economic position of the talukdars. In the eyes of the British these men were not only potential competitors for dominance in the countryside, but a parasitic and oppressive class which stood squarely in the path of all agrarian improvement. Hence, during 1856, a great many of the talukdari estates were settled with the village communities on the pattern of the adjacent North-Western Provinces. Man Singh, for instance, emerged from the summary settlement with only six villages to his name, and many of the old Rajput families fared but little better.[6]

Barely fifteen months after the annexation of Oudh the Sepoy Mutiny broke out, and by the middle of June, 1857, apart from the Residency in Lucknow, British authority in Oudh had ceased to exist. The talukdars thus found themselves presented with an unparalleled opportunity for reasserting their old position. One year of British rule, while sufficient to arouse their hostility to the new government, was not long enough to break their political power. Many talukdars still lived within the walls of their forts and had only to dig up their concealed cannon in order to make good their independence. Hence, no sooner had the rebellion broken out than the talukdars resumed the villages they had lost at annexation, and by September the bulk of the talukdars were in open revolt.

The hostility of these men was only to be expected, and their motives for joining the rebellion were relatively clear-cut. What is more remarkable, and more revealing, is the behavior of the so-called village proprietors, the talukdars' former "tenants" or "subjects." When the Mutiny broke out, the British assumed that these men would remain loyal, for they had been befriended in the settlement of 1856. In fact, however, over wide areas of the Oudh countryside these villagers rallied to their local talukdar's standard and willingly submitted to his leadership. In June, 1857, Captain Barrow, District Officer in Pratabgarh, who had sought shelter with Raja Hanwant Singh, stood by dumbfounded as the village proprietors of the previous year trooped into the raja's courtyard to pledge their allegiance. This disillusioning experience marked the end of village settlement in Oudh. The British came away from the Mutiny convinced that the talukdars were the natural leaders of the people, and that their superiority and influence were a necessary element in Indian rural society. To fight against the power of such men, they concluded, was both dangerous and fruitless. And so in 1859, when the Mutiny was finally crushed, the talukdars, despite their rebellion, were put back into possession by a "most unreserved and liberal settlement" of all those villages they had held on the eve of annexation.[7]

That some of their old tenants supported the rebel talukdars is an unquestioned fact. However, it is by no means obvious, as the British assumed, that this support of the talukdar during the Mutiny implied any desire to see him restored with fresh powers on a permanent and legal basis. Indeed, as we shall see, fierce opposition to the Talukdari Settlement flared up among the villagers in several districts during 1859–60. Most often the villagers seem to have thrown in their lot with the talukdar because he was the unquestioned leader of the locality, or the chief of their clan, a man of power and position whose authority they would not think of defying. No doubt some villagers gave reluctant support to the talukdar in order to secure protection for their lives and property during the time of disorder. Also, many were drawn into the rebellion on altogether different grounds—a sense of fellowship, perhaps, with the mutinous sepoys, many of whom came from Oudh, a loyalty to the deposed Oudh dynasty, or simply a desire to prosecute old feuds with their neighbors—and fell in with the rebel talukdars only as a matter of mutual convenience. Particularly in the old Rajput taluks, where strong deferential ties of loyalty, if not of kinship, bound the village leaders to their talukdari overlords, much support was forthcoming to the talukdar simply because he was the traditionally acknowledged leader of the locality. As "raja," and often head of the local Rajput lineage as well, he commanded by his very position the allegiance of those beneath him.

The suppression of the Mutiny and the subsequent restoration of the talukdars radically altered both the nature of talukdari power and their relationships with their tenants. When the talukdars regained control of their estates during the 1859 settlement, they stepped into a transformed political environment. They had been decisively defeated in battle and their homeland was now a conquered country. They could no longer put forward any pretensions to independent "rajaship." At the same time the British proceeded to complete their conquest of Oudh by introducing into the province all the apparatus of the modern state. The talukdars' forts were leveled, and their armed retainers permanently disbanded. In their place the British provided their own army and police force; they set up a complete civil administration in each district, and they opened courts to arbitrate and punish according to the laws of British India. As a result the talukdars were stripped of the bulk of those quasi-political functions they used to exercise as petty rajas. There remained only the new role of landlord.

Accustomed as they were from home to the idea of a landed aristocracy as an integral part of society, the British had no difficulty in conceiving of the talukdars in this role. Indeed, after the disillusioning experience of the Mutiny, they were anxious to see them flourish as landlords and directed much of their policy in Oudh toward this goal. But the talukdars could not be made over into a group of landlords without in the process effectively redefining the term "talukdar" and giving it a new social content. This can be seen most clearly in the way in which the British took upon themselves the task of deciding who was a talukdar.

Initially, in 1860, the Chief Commissioner of Oudh, Charles Wingfield, told his subordinates, engaged in compiling a list of the talukdars in their districts, that the term should be understood as meaning "an opulent landholder," and hastened to add, "I should not consider any man who paid less than Rs. 5,000 as an opulent landholder."[8] Even this admittedly arbitrary rule was, however, by no means rigorously adhered to. Several talukdari claimants paying over five thousand rupees in land revenue were disqualified, largely on the ground that their holdings were partitioned among several cosharers or were liable to such partition in the future.[9] In similar fashion several landholders were awarded talukdari status despite revenue assessments below the five thousand rupee minimum. In such cases, the decision was usually justified on the ground that the applicant was a man of high social standing, often the chief of a clan, and the owner of an estate which had descended undivided in his family for several generations. As Wingfield noted in approving the application of Karamat Hosein of Kataria, whose assessment was only 2,763 rupees, "it seems clear that Nubbee Bux [Karamat's uncle] was always regarded and treated as a talooqdar. The estate is a small one but it is sufficiently extensive to have gained for the owner the estimation and treatment of a talooqdar both from the neighbors and the Government officials [of the old administration]."[10] The process of definition was completed by Act I of 1869. By the provisions of that act a list was prepared of all persons entitled to the status of talukdar. When completed, it contained 276 names.[11] Thereafter, a talukdar was a person whose name was on this list, or an heir of such a person. The society of the talukdars had become close and exclusive; no amount of opulence could henceforth gain a newcomer admission.[12]

In this fashion, within little more than ten years, the British changed the character of talukdari status almost beyond recognition. What had been a vague and fluctuating title, applied in a haphazard fashion to those who had succeeded in the scramble for power in the countryside, had now acquired a precise legal meaning. It denoted those of the defeated rebels of Oudh whom the British for reasons of imperial policy had pardoned and admitted as an act of administrative favor to the privileges of a special position on the land. To be sure, most of the new British talukdars were the same men who had held the title in the last years of the nawabs, and the criteria used for deciding claims to talukdari status were based to a large extent on previous nawabi usage. Those whose preeminent position in the old order was unquestioned or who could produce evidence that they had formerly been addressed as talukdars had little difficulty in gaining recognition under the new regime. But the British did give the lands and title of talukdar to favorites of their own choosing, including one Bengali babu from Calcutta;[13] and what is more important, in order to fulfill their policy objectives, they did not hesitate to apply their own rules to the decision of talukdari claims. The five thousand rupee limit, for example, reflected their determination that the new talukdars should be above all a wealthy landed class, while their insistence that a talukdar must be the sole owner of an undivided estate, preferably one descending by the rule of primogeniture, reflected their belief that a landlord community could only flourish by adhering to the laws of inheritance of the British aristocracy.

Although the British imposed this new legal position upon them by force of arms, the talukdars themselves readily accepted it. At the outset, during 1858, before the new policy had become clearly enunciated, the talukdars remained suspicious, for they knew only too well that they were rebels with no claim to mercy at the hands of an avenging government. However, once they realized their military position was hopeless, and saw that they would be well treated under the new government, they quickly abandoned their attempt to recover by rebellion their old political power. They set out instead to exploit their position as a privileged class of landlords within the British raj. And the amount of power at their disposal in this new role was by no means inconsiderable. Especially after the award in October, 1859, of *sanads,* or patents, endowing them with full proprietary rights in their estates, the talukdars possessed extensive powers over the tenure and cultivation of land, the collection of rent, and the exaction of fees and services, which they could use to enforce their will over those who lived upon their property. Indeed, in some ways, the position of landlord was more powerful than that of petty raja, for the talukdar now had what he had never possessed before, the support of the Government, with its invincible legal and administrative apparatus.

The village zamindars, as we have seen, had willingly followed their talukdari overlords into battle in 1857, for the latter had not then, despite the 1856 land settlement, suffered any marked diminution in power and prestige. Two years later, however, after he had seen his talukdar defeated and discredited as a political leader, the villager was willing to fight for his independence. Hence, the British decision to restore the talukdars to power met with fierce and stubborn resistance from the subordinate holders. The resistance took the form of a refusal to pay the talukdar his rent, or the payment at best of only the Government revenue demand plus 10 per cent talukdari *malikana,* or allowance.[14] During 1859, this agitation became so widespread and embittered that the Government on several occasions had to warn recalcitrant tenants that continued recusancy would be met by force. Indeed the decision to issue *sanads* to the talukdars reflects in large measure the realization that in no other way could the Government so effectively show the discontented villagers that the new settlement was permanent and final.[15]

When the village zamindars discovered that they had no hope of overturning the Talukdari Settlement, they simply shifted their ground, rather than abandon the struggle, and fought to preserve for themselves the largest possible amount of independence as privileged tenants or underproprietors. This immediately touched off a protracted conflict, which was only resolved in the 1870's with the establishment of a new set of relationships between the talukdars and their subordinate tenants.

When confronted with this agrarian strife, the British tried to hold the balance even between the two contenders, and more particularly to preserve the old village holders from further damage to their position, such as a reduction to the status of tenants-at-will. Therefore, while awarding *sanads* to the talukdars, they bound them to secure all holders under them in the possession of all the subordinate rights they had hitherto enjoyed. To make sure that this provision was carried out, the Governor-General, Lord Canning, ordered that the rights of these inferior holders as they existed before annexation should be defined and recorded, and the rental demand of the talukdar against such persons should be limited to a fixed sum for the duration of each thirty-year settlement.[16] This process was known as subsettlement, and those who could lay claim to its privileges were called underproprietors. Eventually in 1864, after considerable controversy and protracted negotiations with the talukdars, it was agreed that underproprietary rights were to be protected if they had been enjoyed at any time during the twelve years prior to annexation. This decision was given legal form, and the rules relating to underproprietary right defined, in the Oudh Sub-Settlement Act (XXVI of 1866).[17]

This attempt at legal protection by no means put a stop to the antagonism between talukdar and village zamindar. Partly this was because such influential men as Charles Wingfield (Chief Commissioner of Oudh, 1859–66) continued to give tacit encouragement to the talukdars. He tried, for instance, throughout the discussions on the subsettlement question to confine the award of underproprietary rights within the narrowest possible bounds. More important, however, was the fact that the talukdars were determined to break the power of these privileged tenants. This can be seen most clearly by looking closely at one or two important estates.

The Mehdona estate of Maharaja Man Singh in Faizabad District, a large and scattered property of recent origin, contained a great many former village proprietors reduced to the status of tenants. Relations between the talukdar and these former village holders had never been smooth, but the Mehdona family had never completely obliterated the rights of the former zamindars. The estate was too vast and had grown too rapidly to enable sufficient pressure to be brought to bear at any one point, while the talukdars themselves were continually distracted by the demands of their official duties as nazims. As a result the ex-zamindars enjoyed favorable rates averaging 25 per cent below those paid by ordinary cultivators.[18] No sooner had the summary settlement of 1859 been completed, however, than the maharaja set out to squeeze more money out of these privileged tenants. Often this was done by refusing to issue a *patta* or written lease to the tenant until he acquiesced in an enhancement of his rent. The tenants on their part responded by withholding rent and thus forced the talukdar to default on his revenue payments. In November, 1859, Man Singh was in arrears to the extent of 52,120 rupees on the revenue demand of the preceding four months.[19]

This conflict flared up in a particularly acute form during 1867–68, just after the passage of the Sub-Settlement Act. The storm center was Amsin pargana, located along the southern bank of the river Ghagra. The pargana was in the possession of a powerful and pugnacious clan of Barwar Rajputs, who had once owned 159 villages, but who during the years just before annexation had lost all of them, mostly to the growing Mehdona estate. In 1867, while their claims to subsettlement were being adjudicated, the Government introduced into the pargana a revised and enhanced revenue demand, amounting to 73,633 rupees, as part of the regular settlement of the province. In such circumstances the talukdar would normally be entitled to increase his own rental demand on ordinary cultivators to twice that amount, that is, to the full net assets of the estate. To protect those claiming underproprietary rights it was proposed that wherever subsettlement cases were still pending the talukdar should limit his rental demand to the revenue demand plus 5 or 10 per cent. Instead, the maharaja issued notices of enhancement to all his tenants, underproprietary claimants and avowed cultivators alike, demanding that they pay rent henceforth at double the revenue demand plus 8 per cent.[20] The Barwar tenantry stubbornly resisted this attempt to reduce them arbitrarily to the status of ordinary cultivators. A special settlement officer, who was sent into the pargana to induce the recalcitrant Barwars to pay at least part of their rent, reported desparingly that they were "obstructive from spite" and would pay nothing at all.[21] This recusancy, exasperating though it might have been to an harassed settlement officer, was in fact not so much an act of spiteful defiance of the Government as a measure of the deep-rooted enmity between the Barwars and the maharaja, and it reflected above all their growing desperation in the face of the maharaja's persistent attack on their privileged position.

In the end, the Barwars lost most of their suits for subsettlement. But in the process they exacted a heavy toll from the maharaja. Throughout the proceedings they invoked every legal stratagem to delay a final decision on their subsettlement cases, often absenting themselves for months and then appearing in court just in time to avoid an ex-parte decree. And in so doing they also forced a delay in the decision of the suits for arrears of rent or for failure to pay at the enhanced rates brought against them by the maharaja, for the courts were clogged with subsettlement cases. During this period—and the subsettlement cases were not finally decided until February, 1869—the maharaja was called upon to pay Government revenue at the enhanced demand, while he was not permitted to oust the leaseholders, or to collect directly from the cultivators, and the underproprietors on their part withheld payment of even the old rent. Furthermore, even when the claims for subsettlement were disallowed, the maharaja had little hope of collecting the large arrears of rent to which he could lay claim, for many of the defaulters had absconded with their valuables and he could find almost no property to proceed against.[22] As a result, the maharaja found himself driven ever more deeply into debt. In February, 1866, he had borrowed 31,000 rupees at 15 per cent annual interest, and during the subsequent three years he was obliged to petition a variety of banks and moneylenders for ever increasing sums in order to meet the continuing heavy Government demand upon him. By August, 1870, his total debt, together with accumulated interest, amounted to some three lakhs of rupees.[23]

The stubborn resistance of the Amsin underproprietors was duplicated widely on other talukdari estates. The subordinate holders on the Raja of Pirpur's estate, for instance, were so determined in their opposition to the talukdar that not only did they withhold their rent for years, they even forced the talukdar at times to employ police guards in support of his authority.[24] The underproprietors elsewhere were often more successful than the Amsin Barwars in winning legal recognition of their privileged status. In Faizabad District as a whole, 860 villages were decreed in subsettlement to a total of ten thousand underproprietary shareholders. This meant that nearly one-fourth of the total area of the district, and upwards of one-third of the talukdari villages were held in subsettlement by the former proprietors.[25] The British settlement officers at the time spoke with pride both of the total area under subsettlement in Faizabad, which was among the largest in Oudh, and of the generosity of the talukdars in liberally conceding subordinate rights. P. Carnegy, in particular, who was in charge of much of the Faizabad settlement proceedings, prided himself on the spirit of conciliation he was able to evoke among the talukdars and singled out Man Singh for special praise for his assistance in bringing about a compromise settlement of many underproprietary claims.[26] Yet neither the figures of subsettlement nor the enthusiasm of the settlement officials can hide the fact that the successes of the tenantry in this contest were more apparent than real.

One clear indication of the inherent strength of the talukdar's position can be found in the working of the highly-touted "compromise" subsettlement agreements. Invariably they turned out to be far more advantageous to the talukdar than to the tenants they were supposed to protect. Before these agreements were concluded, the village proprietors on such estates as those of Maharaja Man Singh were occupying and managing their holdings subordinate to the talukdar, but on terms which left them a considerable margin of profit. They consented to these *razi nama* or compromise subsettlements on the understanding that their position would remain essentially unchanged. In fact, however, the proportion or percentage of the Government revenue which the underproprietor was to pay was alone fixed; that is, he committed himself to pay the Government revenue plus a percentage of from 10 to 50 per cent. Consequently, whenever the Government demand was raised, the entire burden fell upon him. And as the talukdar had no interest in keeping assessments low, for he profited from every enhancement, the revenue demand was often set at such a high level that the underproprietor, who had also to bear the risks of collecting from the cultivators beneath him, was left with no margin of profit. Indeed, as

early as 1873 the Commissioner of Faizabad was insisting that unless
the subsettlements, including the compromises, in his division were
carefully revised, the underproprietary communities could not be
maintained.[27]

The position of the talukdar was further strengthened by the Government's willingness to come to his assistance whenever he got into
difficulty. Although many talukdars suffered acute financial embarrass-
ment when their attempts to raise rents resulted only in the diminution
of their actual receipts, the Government was always ready to come to
their rescue. In 1870, for instance, the Government took the heavily
encumbered Mehdona estate under its own management, and four
years later lent it three and one-quarter lakhs of rupees at moderate
interest to enable the maharaja to clear off his old debts. Moreover, in
its role as manager the Government was as willing as the talukdar to
resort to severe measures in order to collect the rents from underproprietors. On several occasions arrests were even made of "the most
notoriously recusant of the subproprietors."[28] And where tenants held
reduced rates only by favor of the talukdar, without any legal claim
based on a former proprietary title, the Government exerted itself vigor-
ously to bring rents up to the level of those paid by ordinary cultivators.

Although this pattern of conflict between talukdar and underproprietor
was widespread in Oudh during the 1860's, it was by no means universal.
On some estates the talukdar's authority was never questioned by a
quiescent tenantry, while on others the underproprietors were so much
the masters of the property that the talukdar was little more than a
helpless figurehead. The most striking instances of unchallenged talukdari power can be found in Gonda and Bahraich districts. These two
districts were unusual in that much of their area was either forested or
had only recently been reclaimed from the Terai by the talukdars themselves. The vast Ikauna estate of Bahraich, for instance, which was
conferred on the Sikh Raja of Kapurthala after the Mutiny, had
originally been granted to a *risaldar,* or lieutenant, of the Delhi sultan
Firoz Shah with a mandate to reduce it to order and reclaim it from the
jungle. The bulk of the cultivators on the estate were either pacified
forest tribes or had been placed in their holdings by the descendants of
the original royal grantee and possessed no rights in the land other
than those they had obtained through the talukdar's favor and protection. Even where the subordinate holders on the estate had managed to
preserve some small rights in the soil, moreover, they were deterred

from putting claims forward by the threatening attitude adopted by the agents of the Sikh raja, who made it clear to possible claimants that their only hope of obtaining any concessions was to look to the talukdar and not to the courts. As a result, no underproprietary rights of any sort were decreed on the Ikauna estate during the revised settlement.[29]

The geographical location of the Bahraich and Gonda districts, cut off by the river Ghagra from the seat of government at Lucknow, also facilitated the talukdars' claims to unfettered independence, for it considerably hampered the nazims of the Oudh government in their attempts at interference. The Balrampur Raj family, for instance, with large estates in both districts, had over the years gradually absorbed the rights of the other members of the brotherhood. By annexation, the raja, living in almost regal splendor, had become so powerful that none of the subordinate holders dared defy him, though they still resented his pretensions to almost absolute ownership of the soil. As W. Capper, the Commissioner of Faizabad, remarked in 1873:

> The clan feeling is strong and is opposed to anyone bringing a suit in court against the Maharaja. It is known that though a kind landlord on the whole, he would unhesitatingly do all in his power to crush anyone who asserted a right against him, and it is thought that his personal interest with all the hakims of the district and with the authorities at Head Quarters is great. So that the man claiming a subordinate interest in the land will long hesitate before he brings a suit to be judicially tried, and perhaps dismissed, when he feels he would be at the mercy of a powerful landlord now converted into a foe.

Awards of subsettlement within the estate were in consequence confined to a very few villages.[30]

On the Birhar and Kapradih estates of Faizabad, by contrast, the underproprietary community was so strong and united that the talukdar was never able, even with British assistance, to enforce his authority effectively. Although acknowledging him as their head, for the talukdar was the chief of the brotherhood, the underproprietors kept the powers of village management completely in their own hands. The Birhar and Kapradih estates were largely subsettled as a result, the talukdars were continually in debt or in arrears on the Government revenue demand, and the estates were often brought under Government management. Kapradih, for instance, was attached for arrears of revenue in 1866; yet the Government fared no better than the talukdar in subduing the recalcitrant underproprietors on the estate. In 1876, after ten years of

Government management, they owed arrears of rent amounting to over fifty thousand rupees, and the British officials sent to collect revenue from them often returned empty-handed.[31] With regard to one portion of the estate located in Sultanpur District, the Deputy Commissioner reported in 1879 that "these underproprietors were generally defaulters under the Oudh Government and they have not given up the habit yet." Much of this rescusancy, he acknowledged, had legitimate economic causes:

> There are no less than 75 pattis [shares] and more than 80 houses of the underproprietors and all of them seething with children. Of the whole cultivated area the underproprietors hold less than one fourth and that is their only means of livelihood, for the rest of the rental . . . goes towards liquidating the Government demand and cesses and the malikana of the talukdar and the village expenses.[32]

He concluded despairingly that with the underproprietors and those under them united in this way against the Government, it was impossible to enforce payment of rent in the usual way by the attachment of crops: "Police would have to be quartered in the villages and certainly there would be open resistance and probably direct violence." Only the threat of sale, he argued, would produce any results.

While the talukdar and underproprietor were fighting each other for mastery of the countryside, the ordinary tenant cultivators were quietly submitting to the will of their talukdari overlords. Such cultivators, who comprised the bulk of the rural population in Oudh, as settled members of the village community (*khud-kasht asamis*), had often held their land, if not at avowedly favorable rates, then in accordance with local village customs which insured them continued occupancy from generation to generation at rents fixed by usage and consensus. After the Mutiny the talukdars set out to bring the rents of all such cultivators up to the maximum the land would bear. This slow erosion of occupancy rights did not go unnoticed or uncontested. There was, in fact, heated controversy and a concerted effort to preserve for the settled cultivators some small measure of their traditional privileges. But the participants in this tenant-right struggle were all British. The contest was not between the cultivator and his landlord, but between two sets of British officials, one led by the Chief Commissioner, Charles Wingfield, the other by the Viceroy, Sir John Lawrence. It was in effect a paper war, which did not affect existing social relationships, and whose outcome, the Oudh Rent Act of 1868, simply placed a stamp of official approval on the new agrarian order.[33] The tenants themselves made no effort to challenge the growing power of the talukdar. Even on the Mehdona estate, where the underproprietors had fought bitterly, the ordinary cultivators accepted without question enhanced rents at double the Government demand or more.[34]

This passivity among the tenantry can be accounted for in part by the fact that they were too impoverished, disorganized, and politically inert to mount a concerted resistance. Organized protest was simply outside the frame of their experience. Beyond this, however, is the fact that during its early years the new settlement did not pose a significant threat to the economic position of the cultivating tenant. Population density was low, waste land was readily available, so that a person who considered himself ill-treated could always find better terms elsewhere. During the inquiries carried out by the British in 1863 and 1864 the cultivators, though they spoke proudly of their long connection with the soil, readily acknowledged the power of the talukdar and unhesitatingly conceded that he could do as he pleased. With the passage of time and the increase of population, the plight of the peasantry began to worsen; yet, even then, there was no overt sign of resistance among them until they were brought into the nationalist movement in 1920 during the Eka agitation.

By the 1870's, therefore, throughout most of Oudh the talukdars had made good their claims to mastery of the countryside. The village zamindars had been subdued, and the ordinary cultivators reduced to tenants-at-will. The talukdars now stood forth no longer as rulers of men, or petty rajas, but as landlords bound to those beneath them by the ties of rent and revenue. To be sure, they did not completely abdicate their old position of social and political preeminence. Indeed they could not do so, for the ingrained habit of deference to their social superiors was too deep-rooted among the peasantry, and their own traditions of local leadership and responsibility were too persistent to permit wholesale change. Moreover, the British were anxious to see the talukdars, as "natural leaders" of the people, play some role in local administration; and so from 1861 onward they awarded to many of them the powers of honorary magistrates over their estates. The talukdar-magistrate was empowered on the civil and criminal side to try offenders brought before him in petty cases by the police, and on the revenue side to hear suits for arrears of rent, exaction, and ejectment involving his tenants. Although the talukdars often performed the duties of this post in a lethargic and haphazard fashion, they meted out at all times a good deal of rough and informal justice to those living under them and enforced their decisions where necessary by the stout arms and clubs of their bands of personal retainers.

By 1870, the role of the talukdars in North India had substantially changed. Their earliest role, that of locality leader or petty raja, found its last effective expression in the joint enterprise of 1857, when talukdar and villager marched together against the British. After their restoration in 1859, the talukdars saw their forts destroyed and alien courts established within their domains. Little was left for them but the position of landlord, and they seized upon it with vigor. As the protracted struggle with the underproprietors shows, the talukdars after 1860 had little interest in retaining the deferential respect of those living on their estates. Under the changed conditions of British rule, when such loyalty would benefit them hardly at all, they preferred to seek the more tangible returns of increased cash rentals, and to exploit their powers as landlords.

In their progress from raja to landlord, the Oudh talukdars show how a high-status group, by radically altering the bases of its power, could maintain a dominant position in Indian rural society. It appears that adaptability and a willingness to accommodate to new ways are features not only of upwardly mobile caste groups, or ambitious individuals, but can be found in traditionally dominant groups as well and can indeed help perpetuate that dominance.

## NOTES

1  Two seminal studies of this process are Bernard S. Cohn, "The Changing Status of a Depressed Caste," in McKim Marriott (ed.), *Village India* (Chicago, 1955), pp. 53–77, and M. N. Srinivas, "A Note on Sanskritization and Westernization," *Far Eastern Quarterly,* XV, No. 4 (1956), 42–62. Much of this work has now been conveniently summarized in M. N. Srinivas, *Social Change in Modern India* (Berkeley, 1966).

2  The Persian term *zamindar* (*zamin,* "land"; *dar,* "holder"), although applicable to any landowner, is by usage applied in Bengal to large landlords and in North India only to small landholders (e.g., village coparcenary communities). The Arabic term *ta'alluqa* signifies dependency or attachment to a superior. In Bengal the term *talukdar* is used in its literal sense to denote the subordinate holders or dependents of the great zamindars. In the upper Ganges valley it has been used since the early nineteenth century to refer to those large landholders subordinate only to the officers of Government.

3  B. S. Cohn, "Political Systems in Eighteenth Century India: The Banaras

Region," *Journal of the American Oriental Society*, LXXXII, 315–17. Cohn, however, restricts the usage of the term "taluka" to the "territory controlled by a lineage of agnatically related kin of the same biradari," whereas the Oudh usage is somewhat broader.

4 National Archives, New Delhi, Foreign Consultations, 31 October 1856, Nos. 136–52, Secretary to the Chief Commissioner of Oudh to Secretary to the Government of India, 3 September 1856.

5 *Ibid.*, M. C. Ommanney, Judicial Commissioner, Oudh, to Sec. C. C. Oudh, 18 August 1856.

6 Overall, the talukdars lost 9,900 of the 23,500 villages they had held on annexation. They were treated most harshly in the districts of Faizabad and Sultanpur, and most liberally in the districts of the Bahraich Division. See the "Report on Settlement Operations in Oudh," 24 June 1859, Appendix E, Political Collections to Dispatches, Vol. 17, Part II, Collection 37, India Office Library, London.

7 See Thomas R. Metcalf, *The Aftermath of Revolt: India 1857–1870* (Princeton, 1964), pp. 134–73.

8 Uttar Pradesh State Archives, Board of Revenue Records, Oudh General, File 1964, Sec. C. C. Oudh to Commissioner Lucknow, 24 April 1860.

9 See, for instance, the case of Jaggernath Baksh and Basant Singh, who held estates assessed at 32,000 rupees in Pratabgarh District, but were not awarded talukdari status because they were only two out of a large brotherhood who jointly owned the Nain estate; and the share held by these two was itself further subdivided among other cosharers. See B. R. Records, Oudh General, File 4, Part II, Commr. Rae Bareli to Financial Commr., 20 January 1870.

10 B. R. Records, Oudh Faizabad, File 634, Sec. C. C. Oudh to Settlement Commr., 13 October 1863. See the case of Raja Mehpal Singh of Umri, Pratabgarh District, whose claim was upheld despite a *juma* of 3,600 rupees on the grounds that he was chief of the Bilkaria Rajputs and that the rule of primogeniture had prevailed in his family for many generations (B. R. Records, Oudh General, File 4, Part II).

11 For the text of the act see Chhail Bihari Lal, *The Taluqdari Law of Oudh* (2nd ed.; Allahabad, 1921), pp. 397–422. The original list of talukdars is included as Appendix G, pp. 565–74. Three additional talukdars were added to the list during the 1870's.

12 It should be noted that there was no prohibition on the sale or transfer of talukdari holdings, with the result that many talukdars were reduced over the years to only a portion of their 1859 properties, several enlarged their estates, and a few taluks were extinguished altogether.

13 The Bengali was Dakhinaranjun Mukherjee, who was awarded part of the confiscated estate of Shankerpur and was later instrumental in founding the talukdars' association. Several European planters and the Sikh Raja of Kapurthala also received confiscated estates.

14 See, for instance, a letter of 1 December 1858 from an officer in Hardoi District reporting that the 1856 settlement had "so thoroughly broken up the talooks that the mokuddums [village zamindars] who then got settlement now get up their backs at the talookdars" (B. R. Records, Oudh General, File 396). See also B. R. Records, Oudh Faizabad, File 115, Offg. Depty. Commr. Faizabad to Commr. Faizabad, 6 December 1858.

15 For references to original sources see Metcalf, *op. cit.,* pp. 149–50.

16 Sec. Govt. India to Sec. C. C. Oudh, 19 October 1859, *Parliamentary Papers* (London, 1861), XLVI, 429.

17 For discussion of the controversies surrounding this act, and for the text of the act itself, see Chhail Bihari Lal, *op. cit.,* pp. 517–43, and Chap. III of the Introduction, taken from J. G. W. Sykes, *Compendium of the Law of Oudh Specially Relating to the Talukdars* (Calcutta, 1886). Sykes defines subsettlement as an arrangement whereby when there are two distinct interests in land the holder of the superior interest is admitted to engage and is responsible for the land revenue thereof during the currency of the existing settlement and is entitled to receive from the holder of the inferior right a fixed sum representing such revenue and a further fixed sum in respect of his profits and the cost and risk of collection; the inferior holder has a permanent heritable and transferable right in such land conditional on his regular payment of such sum.

18 A. F. Millett, *Fyzabad Settlement Report* (Allahabad, 1882), pp. 449–50. See also W. H. Sleeman, *A Journey Through the Kingdom of Oude in 1849–50* (London, 1858), I, 149–50.

19 B. R. Records, Oudh Faizabad, File 6, Depty. Commr. Faizabad to Commr. Faizabad, 18 November 1859.

20 *Ibid.* For discussion of the Amsin settlement, see the memorandum by P. Carnegy, Settlement Officer, Faizabad, 5 November 1867.

21 *Ibid.,* J. Woodburn, Assistant Settlement Officer, to W. E. Forbes, 28 October 1867.

22 *Ibid.,* Capt. J. Erskine, Offg. Settlement Officer, Faizabad, to Commr. Faizabad, 25 February 1870.

23 *Ibid.* For a list of Man Singh's debts, with the name of the creditor and the date on which it was incurred, see Depty. Commr. Faizabad to Commr. Faizabad, 26 August 1870, and further letter of 15 September 1870.

24 B. R. Records, Oudh Faizabad, File 11, Part I, G. Elphinstone, Settlement Officer, Faizabad, to Commr. Faizabad, 20 April 1870.

25 A. F. Millett, *op. cit.,* Appendix No. 4, p. 17A. Slightly different figures are given in the *Gazetteer of the Province of Oudh* (Lucknow, 1877), I, 435. Fractional portions of a further 847 talukdari villages were also held in subsettlement.

26 B. R. Records, Oudh Faizabad, File 11, Part I, P. Carnegy, Annual Faizabad Settlement Report, 7 May 1864. See also his Faizabad Divisional Settlement Report for 1868–69, in Records of Commissioner's Office, Faizabad, Bundle No. 77, File 12.

27 B. R. Records, Oudh Faizabad, File 11, Part II, Commr. Faizabad to Personal Assistant to C. C., 23 December 1873. For discussion of the deteriorating condition of the underproprietors under the revised settlement, see *Gazetteer of Oudh,* I, 436; and B. R. Records, Oudh Faizabad, File 11, Part III, Sec. Govt. India to Sec. Govt. North-Western Provinces and Oudh, 11 August 1882, commenting on the Faizabad Settlement Report.

28 B. R. Records, Oudh General, File 853, Commr. Faizabad to Sec. C. C. Oudh, 30 September 1872. The arrests noted here took place on the estates of Mehdona, Kapradih, and Sehipur.

29 For the history of the Ikauna estate see *Gazetteer of Oudh,* I, 116–17 and 190–95. The Nanpara estate was also granted to a *risaldar* and subsequently colonized in much the same fashion. *Ibid.,* 123–25.

30 B. R. Records, Oudh Faizabad, File 11, Part II, Commr. Faizabad to Personal Assistant to Commr., 23 December 1873. For discussion of the Balrampur estate, see *Gazetteer of Oudh,* I, 179 and 216–19.

31 B. R. Records, Oudh Faizabad, File 23, Part I, Depty. Commr. Faizabad to Commr. Faizabad, 12 May 1876. On subsettlement and recourse to Government management in Birhar taluk, see A. F. Millett, *op. cit.,* pp. 437–42.

32 B. R. Records, Oudh Faizabad, File 23, Part I, Depty. Commr. Sultanpur to Commr. Rae Bareli, 6 August 1879.

33 For discussion of this controversy, see Metcalf, *op. cit.,* pp. 187–96, and Jagdish Raj, *The Mutiny and British Land Policy in North India, 1856–68* (Bombay, 1965).

34 B. R. Records, Oudh Faizabad, File 6, memo by P. Carnegy, Settlement Officer, Faizabad, 5 November 1867.

Chapter VI

# Social Effects of British Land Policy in Oudh

*Thomas R. Metcalf*

One of the most significant aspects of British rule in India was the opportunity it afforded for the growth of new social ties and new types of social groupings among the Indian people, in addition to the traditional bonds of caste and kinship. Everyone is familiar with the rise of the urban intellectual and professional "middle classes," such as the Bengal *bhadralog*, but the same processes were at work, though perhaps in less striking fashion, in rural society as well. The most important agency of change was land policy.

When they first gained power in India, the British did not understand the character of the traditional agrarian system, with its complex web of customary rights, in which the state and each of the various individuals connected with the land, from talukdar or zamindar down to the cultivating ryot, possessed different rights and claims, but none held title as owner. They viewed Indian rural society, naturally enough, through their own preconceptions and applied British agrarian terminology to the Indian scene. They spent much time in earnest debate over the question as to whether the land revenue was a tax paid by a landowner to the Government for protection or rent paid by a cultivator to the Government acting as his superior landlord. And at the time of settlement, the British revenue officials regularly engaged in arduous search for the "rightful" proprietors of the soil. The logical outcome of this determination to find private property rights was the wholesale creation of such rights throughout the country. No sooner were the settlement proceedings completed in any district than a detailed record of rights was drawn up and those who had engaged to pay the revenue demand were proclaimed the holders of a heritable alienable property.

Even where, as in the North-Western Provinces, the village community was the settlement holder, and individual interests were submerged in that of the group, such rights were still defined and the cosharers were permitted at any time to enter into direct relations with the Government. As a result of this process, the British brought about a radical simplification of the old tenure system. The jungle of ancient customary rights was replaced by an ordered system of precise legal definitions, and the old irregularities of tenure were smoothed out into a series of arbitrary categories. Where the pattern of landholding had once been complex, diffuse, and customary, it was now simple, clear-cut, and artificial. What is most important for our purpose, however, is the fact that by smoothing out variations in tenure and separating the various groups on the land into distinct categories, the British gave to sizable numbers of people for the first time some common legal and economic ties, some potential common interest in the defense or improvement of their newly won status.

British revenue policy did not, indeed it could not, by itself produce a sense of social cohesiveness or internal group solidarity among any particular set of tenure holders. It only made possible such a development by marking off various groups of people from each other in new ways and providing them with some common interests. The extent to which members of these new social groups thought of themselves as such and acted together as cohesive social units is another question, and one which must be squarely faced in examining the character of social change in rural India, for it is only too easy to fall into the trap of mistaking labels for social reality. The study of Indian land tenure, as has been recently pointed out, has been particularly subject to the failure to distinguish between groups composed of individuals organized for some social end and having enduring social relations and groups composed of individuals having like characteristics—legal, political, economic, or cultural—which make an observer classify them as having a social cohesiveness.[1] The mere fact that a contemporary British official, or an historian, thought he saw or expected to see some group of Indians acting in a novel "modern" way, usually defined ethnocentrically in European interest group or class terms, does not by any means imply that the Indians so described necessarily thought of themselves in these terms or behaved in this fashion. Indeed, the presumption is all the other way. We must, in other words, proceed with caution and keep clearly in view the difference between functioning social groups and administrative constructs.

Some indication of the nature of the problem, and of the pitfalls which abound on every side, can be gained by examining briefly the case of the occupancy tenants of the North-Western Provinces. Although there had long existed resident cultivators (called *khud-kasht asamis*) possessing some tangible rights in the soil, usually involving fixity of tenure and favorable rents, the position of these men had always been regulated only by the local customs of each village. Anxious to give some legal precision to these vague customary rights, the British under Act X of 1859 awarded to every ryot who had cultivated or held land for a period of twelve years a right of occupancy in that land at "fair and equitable" rates, liable to enhancement only if they were below the prevailing rental of the area, or if the value of the land and its produce had increased other than by the effort of the ryot. The twelve years' rule, however, was highly arbitrary. Mere lapse of time had never previously been the criterion by which occupancy rights were determined, nor were its privileges at all uniform. By this act, therefore, the British created a new and highly artificial social grouping in rural India—those who had held land for twelve years or more—and sharply demarcated it from those who had held land for less time regardless of the actual nature of their tenure.

One might assume that because this tenurial category existed it had some social reality. Certainly this relatively well-to-do and privileged group of cultivators had ample cause to come together in some sort of protective tenants' association, for the landlords, emboldened by prosperity and rising land values, mounted a continual assault on their privileged position during the later decades of the nineteenth century. However, no such development took place. There was no Indian counterpart to the Irish Land League, no flood of protests and petitions into the chambers of the Legislative Council, and little evidence of agrarian class warfare directed against the landlords. There were, of course, occasional sporadic outbreaks of violence, but no concerted mass movements which might indicate the existence of an articulate peasantry conscious of its class interests. Even the revolt of 1857, with its widespread appeal in the countryside, never partook of the character of class warfare. Indeed, one of the most striking features of this outbreak was the loyalty to their aristocratic leaders found among the peasantry.[2] The traditional ties were far stronger than the sentiments of class antagonism one might expect to find, and upon which the British had hoped to capitalize at the time of the outbreak.

This lack of class sentiment among the peasant cultivators reflects in part the fact that they had neither the means nor the motivation to conceive of themselves as a separate group. Preoccupied with the struggle for existence, they had been for centuries accustomed to accept uncomplainingly a subordinate position in society. Nor were there any leaders sufficiently educated and interested in the fate of the peasantry to bring home to them some consciousness of their plight until the young Nehru's "wanderings among the kisans" sparked the Kisan Sabha movement in 1920.[3] Most important, however, is the fact that peasant loyalties and ambitions had other outlets more appropriate to the context of village India than class struggle. Their energies were channeled through subcaste loyalties into localized factional disputes and into contests for precedence within the ritual hierarchy, a phenomenon most marked among those ill-defined middle reaches which contained the bulk of the peasant cultivators.

Among the rich and powerful landlord community, by contrast, the likelihood was far greater that the new tenurial distinctions would find expression in new social ties and that avowedly "landlord" sentiments and feelings would take root. The most striking instance of such a development is that of the talukdars of Oudh. At annexation a diverse collection of Rajput chieftains, Muslim immigrants, and court favorites of various castes, united by nothing except the desire to exploit the resources of their estates to the full and to hand over to the nawab as little as possible, the talukdars within ten years of the imposition of British rule possessed a distinctive tenure and seemingly "modern" associational ties, symbolized in the British Indian Association of Oudh, a model voluntary society to which all the talukdars subscribed.

Much of the talukdars' success is the result of the exceptionally favored treatment and encouragement they received at the hands of the British Government. When they restored these men to power after the Mutiny, the British did not simply confer upon them a full and unfettered proprietary title to their estates and then leave them to fend for themselves. They set out to make them not only landlords, but a cohesive landed aristocracy. After 1858, the British directed their policy in Oudh to insuring that the talukdars possessed sufficient wealth, legal status, social position, and hereditary continuity to be in reality, as they were often and proudly described, the "Barons of Oudh." To be sure, the objectives of this policy were largely political—to create in Oudh a stable conservative bulwark for the British raj—but behind it lay a vision of the talukdars, whom Canning in 1858 had called "the ancient, indigenous and cherished" leaders of their country, as the Indian counterpart of the English landed gentry, with the style of life and social cohesiveness of that group.[4]

Some of the elements in this policy, such as the five thousand rupee minimum land revenue payment for the award of talukdari status, have already been described in my earlier essay.[5] This entire process of definition and restriction of talukdar status, which culminated in the explicit listing of all talukdars under Act I of 1869, was specifically designed not only to enhance the self-esteem of the individual talukdari landlords but to facilitate the growth of a sense of belonging to a distinctive group. Their *sanads*, or patents, solemnly awarded by the Viceroy at a durbar in Lucknow in 1859, and their vested legal status as the members of a closed community, marked off a unique yet uniform talukdari tenure, and thus accentuated both the bonds binding them together and those separating them from the other groups on the land.

But the British did more than merely create a special talukdari tenure in Oudh. They lavished upon the talukdars an affectionate regard which took the form even of measures to save them from the consequences of their own folly. The first step in this direction was the talukdari succession law of 1869. After giving the talukdars unfettered rights of ownership through the *sanads*, the British discovered that this decision could easily lead to the collapse of the talukdari system, for these men, like most Hindu landholders, customarily divided their property among all their heirs and now might even be tempted to bequeath their estates to favorites outside the family. Under this act, although the talukdars retained the right to dispose of their estates as they saw fit during their lifetime, they bound themselves to observe the law of primogeniture in inheritance.

The British came again to the rescue of the talukdars with the Encumbered Estates Act of 1870. Under this act an insolvent talukdar could vest the management of his estates in the Government for a period of up to twenty years. While under management, the estate would be secure from attachment or sale; and all income, beyond the Government's revenue demand and a fixed maintenance allowance for the talukdar, would be used to liquidate the encumbering debts and liabilities. Upon their discharge, the estate would be restored to the talukdar. No one in the Government had any great fondness for the principle of this act, as it cut directly across their belief in the beneficial effects of a free market economy, and involved as well a confession that the talukdari system was too weak to stand upon its own feet; yet the measure was passed, for the British had staked too much on the talukdari system to stand idly by and watch these great estates pass into the hands of urban moneylenders. The British, then, not only gave the Oudh talukdars a uniquely privileged tenurial status, but also artificially sustained the whole community through special "nursing" legislation. By securing the principle of primogeniture and by preventing the forced sale of estates, they insured that the talukdars would remain a stable hereditary group outside the disintegrative forces of the market.

We must now ask to what extent these measures were effective. How far did the talukdars respond to the British vision of themselves as a cohesive and responsible landed aristocracy? Were they in fact as well as in name the "Barons of Oudh"? The nature of the organization they formed to give concrete shape to their new status, the British Indian Association of Oudh, gives us a good insight into the substance of the ties between them and is therefore worthy of some detailed analysis.

The association was founded in Lucknow in March, 1861, and modeled in form on an English voluntary society. It had an elected President and Vice-President, a Secretary, and an Executive Committee; business was brought before the meeting by motions properly made and seconded; and proposals were voted upon by a show of hands, the majority view being adopted. A general meeting of the society was held annually, and committee meetings took place regularly as business required throughout the year. From the start, attempts were made to include all talukdars as members. This goal was achieved in February, 1864, when endowment deeds were obtained from all talukdars in which they pledged themselves to pay an annual subscription to the association at the rate of eight annas per hundred rupees of their land revenue tax. With the final closing of the talukdari ranks under Act I of 1869, membership in the society was limited to bona-fide talukdars, although talukdari villages sold to outsiders still continued liable for dues payable to the association.

The talukdars viewed their association primarily as a petitioning body, designed to represent their interests before the authorities in matters of law and administration. The basic motivating force behind its founding was unquestionably fear of losing their newly won privileges. The talukdars detected in the Government's every move a potential threat to the Talukdari Settlement, and they devoted the bulk of their energies to securing what they regarded as their due rights in the field of land tenure. Invariably, the periods of greatest activity on the part of the society coincided with those occasions, such as John Lawrence's tenant right investigations during 1864–66, when talukdari rights over the land were under attack.[6] The strongest and most lasting ties between the talukdars, it would appear, were negative or defensive in character, and included only the small area of common interest defined by their privileged tenurial status.

The talukdars, however, also took pride in proclaiming their dedication to "the cause of reform and enlightenment."[7] They saw in the patronage of social reform and education a useful way of enhancing their new image of themselves as a progressive modernizing gentry and of showing the British at the same time that their trust had not been misplaced. Almost the first act of the association, for instance, was to enlist the influence of the talukdars in the campaign against female infanticide and to adopt stringent sanctions against estate officials or others found conniving at its continuance.[8] The association was responsible also for the founding in 1864 of Canning College, Lucknow. On that occasion, the talukdars jointly agreed by legal covenant to pay eight annas per hundred rupees on their land revenue demand to the college as a perpetual endowment. This donation, which was later broadened to include the Colvin Taluqdars' School, was the talukdars' major corporate philanthropic activity and gave to the college committee by the 1880's an annual income of 42,000 rupees. In 1909 the rate of subscription was raised to twelve annas per hundred rupees.[9]

The founding of Canning College reveals the talukdars at their most perceptive and far-sighted. By this act, they showed some recognition of the fact that success under the new order required mastery of English language and learning rather than of the traditional martial skills. As one talukdar put it, "I behold in my mind's eye the glorious day when, in *our* old age, we shall see our children coming from the halls of the College, with their mental faculties fully developed and their manners polished."[10] Had this vision been realized, the college could well have become not only the premiere educational institution of the province, as soon occurred, but also the seedbed for the growth of those shared experiences and values which could transform the talukdars into a cohesive and effective rural elite. Unfortunately, however, the bulk of the talukdars took little interest in the college they had founded. Soon after its establishment, the Government had to step in and collect the arrears of talukdari subscriptions due to the college, a practice soon regularized by the conversion of the college subscription into an additional educational cess. Nor were the sons of talukdars at all prominent on the rolls of the college. In 1868, only 24 talukdars and 27 petty zamindars had sons in attendance, as compared with 291 government servants, 128 private servants, 55 professional men, and 42 traders.[11] The following year the Director of Public Instruction reported despairingly:

> . . . it is very much to be regretted that more of the class which ought to be the most enlightened and most anxious to understand the wishes and objects of Government, do not attend school . . . . The Wards Institution in connection with Canning College is so excellently managed, and such care has been taken by those who have charge of it to meet the wishes of parents and guardians, that only some extreme reluctance to part with their boys or a sad indifference to education can account for the talukdars as a body not gladly taking advantage of it.[12]

Social reform, in similar fashion, never inspired the talukdars to much concerted action. Their interest in the subject was fitful and half-hearted at best, and more often than not the result of strong Government pressure. In 1863, for instance, appalled by the enormous expenditure lavished on the marriage of one talukdar's niece, when thirty-five thousand people were fed for six days, the Chief Commissioner urged the association to devise and enforce some measures for the reduction of marriage expenses. Such lavish weddings, he pointed out, were responsible for much talukdari indebtedness and were also at the root of infanticide.[13] The talukdars duly took the matter under consideration and in February, 1864, adopted a series of resolutions on the subject. The rules were by no means excessively stringent, for they permitted a talukdar to spend up to half his annual income on a wedding; but, more importantly, they were directed toward one caste only, the Rajputs, and their implementation was effectively left to the joint action of the members of that caste.[14] However, the Rajput talukdars were reluctant to act unless the Rajput families of the North-Western Provinces with whom they often intermarried would also agree. In pursuit of this objective, the Government of the North-Western Provinces sent copies of the Oudh resolutions to all "Heads of Chuttree Families" in that province, and the Commissioner of Gorakhpur even convened a meeting of the leading Rajputs of the division in order to point out to them the evils of lavish expenditure and the advantages of reduction.[15] The most significant aspect of this whole affair is not so much the pressures exerted by the British as the fact that marriage was preeminently a subject for caste regulation. Rajput talukdars married not other talukdars, but other Rajputs. Indeed, the Oudh resolutions specifically stated that Kshatriyas should not give their daughters to people below their rank. Although the talukdar association took the initiative in sponsoring the marriage resolutions, effective action could only be taken by a group whose members normally intermarried and who could make sanctions stick; and this group neither included all the talukdars, nor was confined within the borders of the province of Oudh.

The British Indian Association was, then, something more than a simple voluntary society, uniting a group of like-minded people behind some limited cause of social reform or in defense of some particular interest; and yet at the same time it was clearly something less than the institutional expression of the shared ties and values of a genuine aristocracy. This intermediary position can perhaps best be seen by comparing this association with the numerous other voluntary societies which sprang up in all the major cities of North India in the years after the Mutiny. Like the talukdars' association, these societies almost always espoused such "modern" causes as Western education, suppression of infanticide, and the reduction of marriage expenses. However, these groups were invariably ephemeral and often the hothouse creations of local British officials. They usually attracted only the few urban Western-educated individuals, often government employees, among them a preponderance of displaced Bengalis, who had followed the British. And they left little legacy other than a prodigious amount of talk. The talukdars' association was, by contrast, far from ephemeral. Although it was often in a feeble condition, its organizational framework continued in existence, with officers, records, and most importantly, funds, the latter guaranteed by the pledges the talukdars had signed in 1864. The association could therefore easily be revitalized whenever the occasion demanded, and it is still alive today, despite zamindari abolition, although in a much attenuated form.

The role of the British in sustaining the association was important, but not all-important. They took no part in its founding, but from the start they gave the society their consistent support, for they saw in it an excellent way of encouraging in the talukdars a sense of responsibility and collective action. As Charles Wingfield, the Chief Commissioner, commented in his Administration Report for 1862–63, "by frequently meeting together, and by the habit of free discussion, the landed gentry of Oudh will learn to divest themselves of their old prejudices and jealousies, and to cooperate in schemes of social and material improvement."[16] The British also aided the association in more material ways as well. In November, 1861, barely six months after the founding of the society, Canning gave to the talukdars the spacious Kaiserbagh Palace in Lucknow, confiscated from the former king, Wajid Ali Shah. This gift, which provided the society with a meeting place and offices, and the individual talukdars with town residences, added a much needed physical base to the new sentiments of talukdari "cooperation." Later, in 1878 when the association encountered difficulty in collecting the annual subscription from many of its members, the Government agreed, albeit reluctantly, to collect these dues as a surcharge on the land revenue demand.[17] Furthermore, from 1861 right up to the 1930's, the Government usually consulted the association before proceeding with major legislation in Oudh and usually incorporated their suggestions into the enactments. Such official patronage cannot but have greatly enhanced the prestige and status of the organization and insured its continued viability.

The talukdar association, like most voluntary societies, depended heavily for its successful functioning upon the quality of its leadership. While the talukdars were certain to produce from time to time a good many outstanding figures because of their wealth and traditions of local dominance, there was no guarantee that such men would take an interest in the affairs of the association. Fortunately, in its initial years, the association had two exceptionally capable leaders: its first Secretary, Babu Dakhinaranjun Mukherjee, and the Vice-President, Maharaja Sir Man Singh.

Mukherjee, a Kulin Brahmin from Bengal who had studied at Alexander Duff's English school, was awarded a confiscated estate in Oudh after the Mutiny by Lord Canning. A member of the British Indian Association in Calcutta—at the time the most advanced political organization in India—Mukherjee was largely responsible for the foundation of the talukdari society, which he modeled upon and named after the earlier organization. As Secretary, he conducted the correspondence and managed the newspapers (one in Hindustani and one in English) published by the talukdars.[18] In all of this, Mukherjee was typical of many transplanted Bengalis who carried Western liberal ideas and modern techniques of organization to the major cities of Upper India and laid the foundations for modern political activity throughout the region. But as an outsider he had difficulty gaining the confidence of the older talukdars, and though versed in technique he could contribute but little prestige to the new organization. Mukherjee's work was, however, ably complemented by that of Maharaja Man Singh as Vice-President.

Talukdar of Mehdona in Faizabad, Man Singh was the driving force behind the talukdars' association throughout the 1860's. He was active in all of the association's activities and financed many, including the publication of its English newspaper, the *Oudh Gazette,* out of his own pocket. As the Commissioner of Faizabad noted in 1874, "He was the leading talukdar of Oudh, and after the Mutiny was looked to as the channel of communication between the Government officials at Lucknow and the talukdars, and was the lever by which that somewhat inert and obstructive body was moved in the direction that was then sought . . . . He worked with body and soul in the political field of the day and has left his mark heavily on the legislative and administrative policy of this province."[19] He was largely responsible, in particular, for drawing up the final list of talukdars which was incorporated into Act I of 1869. Indeed, much of the reason for the increasing disorganization of his estate, and its hopeless indebtedness, can be found in the extraordinary amount of time and money he devoted to public affairs.

Mukherjee's resignation from the secretaryship in 1866, and Man Singh's death four years later, were severe blows to the association. These blows were the more heavily felt because the members of the society had already in January, 1865, abdicated their responsibilities for the subsequent six years to an extraordinary Special Committee, authorized to act fully on their behalf in the defense of talukdari rights and privileges and to carry out "all the purposes for which the society was established."[20] Although this committee was set up at the most heavily attended general meeting in several years, with the objective of making possible a more effective and concerted response to the challenge posed by John Lawrence's tenant right investigations, its establishment nevertheless signaled the end for some time to come of widespread talukdari participation in the affairs of the association. During the subsequent decade, the bulk of the talukdars were preoccupied with the survey and settlement operations then in progress and with the assertion of their authority over their estates, and hence were quite content to leave their association in the hands of those who had time and inclination for political activity. As a result, Mukherjee's resignation in April, 1866, precipitated a grave crisis, from which the society was only rescued by the generosity of the Maharaja of Kapurthala, who took charge of its treasury, and by the continued willingness of Man Singh and the Maharaja of Balrampur, the President, to shoulder the burdens of its administration.

Kapurthala, a Sikh prince who had been awarded large confiscated estates in Oudh after the Mutiny, had never previously taken any interest in talukdari affairs; but now when his aid was solicited by the other maharajas he joined with them to form a select steering committee within the Special Committee. The three maharajas apportioned the duties of the association among themselves according to a *dastur-al-amal,* a body of regulations framed at Kapurthala in April, 1866. Under it, the President retained his largely ceremonial position, the Lucknow secretary of the Kapurthala maharaja assumed responsibility for the collection and safekeeping of the society's funds (for the maharaja himself rarely left his Punjab state), and Man Singh, as before, undertook the bulk of the administrative work, including all negotiations with the Government. The Special Committee met from time to time to ratify the decisions of the three maharajas, but exercised little independent initiative.[21]

Until Man Singh's death in 1870, these arrangements served the society adequately. Indeed, they were highly successful in enabling the committee to carry out its appointed task—the defense of talukdari interests at a time when the legislative framework of the Oudh settlement was taking final shape. Through the persuasive advocacy of Man Singh, who received a K.C.S.I. in 1867, and the columns of the influential *Oudh Gazette* (soon rechristened the *Lucknow Times*), the talukdars made their voice heard effectively in the chambers of Government. The association also took upon itself at the same time the pleading of talukdari law cases and maintained agents in Calcutta and London largely for this purpose. The 1866 regulations even committed the association to bear the expenses of those cases which were of general concern to the talukdari community. Three reasons were given for this decision: "The first is that the society will be fully informed of the affairs of the talukdars. Secondly, the lawyers and counselors who work for the society will not take cases from the opposite party. Thirdly, many people may not otherwise file their cases due to laziness, inadequate finances, or short-sightedness."[22]

Despite this flurry of activity, the association languished increasingly with the passage of time. This process, which had begun in 1865, became marked after 1870, when the society lost its most dedicated leader, and the resolution of the most disputed settlement questions deprived the association of what had been, in the eyes of most talukdars, its major *raison d'être*. The feeble state of the society in the 1870's can be seen in the rapid falling off in the profits and readership of its newspapers,[23] in the difficulty encountered in collecting subscriptions, and in the irregular publication of its proceedings. The comments of the Secretary on the latter subject, when the proceedings for 1865 to 1870 were belatedly published in 1873, are revealing:

> The reports of the "Anjuman" from its establishment were published regularly up to January 4, 1865. Afterwards the reports were not published due to the resignation of Babu Dakhinaranjun Mukherjee, former Secretary . . . . This report of the proceedings of the "Anjuman" for 1865–70 is compiled from the papers present in the office of the "Anjuman." There was a delay in securing these papers due to the death of Maharaja Man Singh. Five bundles were obtained in August 1872 through the Superintendent of the Faizabad Court. The remaining were either destroyed or eaten up by insects. Moreover, in 1872 the basement of the Qaiser Bagh was flooded due to heavy rains . . . and very few papers could be saved. These proceedings are transcribed from those papers.[24]

In assessing the overall significance of the Oudh British Indian Association, then, it is evident that during the nineteenth century it was never the central focus of interest of the majority of the talukdars. Their interest fluctuated in direct proportion to the exent to which they considered their landed rights and interests threatened by the Government. It was highest in the early days of the association, when such meetings were an exciting novelty and the fate of the Talukdari Settlement was still uncertain. Over 200 talukdars out of some 270 attended the general meeting of November, 1862, and one member was moved to remark enthusiastically that, "The benefits already gained by us from the Association are of a nature well worth any expense, however great. Besides the utility we derive from it as talookdars and as British subjects, is there any among us who will gainsay the service it has done to our *izzat* and good name?"[25]

Even then, however, the association was hardly a model voluntary society, for beneath the carefully constructed democratic façade and permeating the entire organization lay many hierarchical assumptions, which the talukdars, preoccupied with considerations of status and prestige, carefully cherished. The holder of the largest taluk with an adult male head, for instance, was invariably made President and usually held the post for life. The majority, in similar fashion, regarded elections as indecent and rarely rebelled in open meeting against the decisions taken by the Executive Committee. Ultimately, as we have seen, they abdicated their powers altogether to a Special Committee, which in turn was controlled by its three most powerful maharajas.

Nor was the Executive Committee a very efficient body for transacting business. On one occasion its dilatory ways even prompted its President, the Balrampur maharaja, to point out "a few shortcomings." When a committee meeting was scheduled for a particular date, he said, "a few members come four days ahead of time and a few others come four days after the holding of the meeting." If all the members did ever get together, he continued, then "instead of discussing important matters, they waste their time in gossip and in telling stories of the past." He concluded by urging everyone to be punctual and to pay attention to business.[26] In such an easygoing environment it is no wonder that the energetic and ambitious few always dominated the proceedings of the association.

The most significant social ties of the talukdars remained throughout the nineteenth century those of caste, kin, and sect. Though the talukdars were active through their association in both education and social reform, the new shared values which emerged were limited in extent. Western education, even at the college the talukdars themselves subsidized, remained largely the preserve of the urban professional and trading classes, while social reform, wherever it was truly effective, was the work of caste groups who commanded the sanctions necessary to enforce behavior on their members.[27] The optimistic British assumption that by meeting together the talukdars would transform their social relations and values into those of a cohesive aristocratic elite had little more reality than their similar expectation that these men could as individuals be turned by the magic of private property into improving landlords. Traditional and parochial loyalties could not be so quickly and easily unseated. Indeed, even within their association, the talukdars were as often divided into caste and communal factions as united into a closely knit group.[28]

But if the ties binding the talukdars together were weak and sometimes peripheral, and interest in the association which gave them concrete shape was highly circumscribed, the talukdars still did regard themselves as a distinct and superior group within Oudh society, and the association remained active throughout the later decades of the century in the defense of their rights. This was no little achievement for a group of men who a few short years before had hesitated to venture into Lucknow for fear of their lives and whom Canning after the durbar of 1859 had privately described as "a coarse looking lot."[29] The extent of the transformation which the talukdars had undergone can perhaps most readily be appreciated by looking briefly at the status of the talukdars in the adjacent North-Western Provinces. There, although the province had come under British rule fifty years earlier, it was only at the turn of the twentieth century, with the foundation in 1896 of the Zamindars' Association, in Muzaffarnagar, and of the Agra Province Zamindars' Association in 1914, that organizations came into existence at all comparable to the British Indian Association of Oudh. And both these organizations were, at least until the 1920's, considerably smaller, more parochial, and less prestigious than their Oudh counterpart.[30]

A large part of the reason for this slower pace of development can be found in the character of British land policy in the province. While the Oudh talukdars were entrenching themselves in power and making good their claims to independence under the weak government of the later nawabs, the talukdars of the North-Western Provinces were face to face with the might of the British Government. By 1817, with the reduction of Dya Ram's fortress in Aligarh District, they were forced to acknowledge their subordinate position under the new raj. But the British did not stop with the assertion of political superiority. Under the influence of Utilitarian ideology, the settlement officers during the 1820's and 1830's brushed aside the claims of the talukdars to control of their holdings and settled the bulk of the land with the coparcenary village communities. Many talukdars were reduced to pensioners, losing all contact with the land, while those who remained were few in numbers and much reduced in power.

This policy of official hostility was maintained throughout the remainder of the century. The talukdars received no patents, no succession acts enumerating their rights and privileges, and no encumbered estates acts to save them from their follies. Although they were at times treated liberally as individuals, no attempt was ever made to foster the growth of a cohesive aristocratic class in the North-Western Provinces. Hence, it is not surprising that no such class emerged. Scattered about the countryside in a large and amorphous province which stretched from Delhi to Benares, the talukdars had no occasion to meet together or to become aware of their common interests. And of equal importance, lacking the precise definition of landlord status which the Oudh talukdars possessed, they had little to pull them together. There was no focus, such as their land patents, around which they could coalesce, no legal framework within which they could conveniently operate as a group. They were just a disparate collection of individuals who happened to live in the same province, and whom we would call landlords, but who were unlikely to think of themselves as such.

Even in the twentieth century, when political development in the province had reached a more advanced state and the two Agra landlord associations were set up, the landlords had to rely upon arbitrary qualifications for membership. The Agra Province Zamindars' Association, for instance, was open to all zamindars who paid over five thousand rupees in land revenue to the Government. This qualification, though it certainly skimmed off the cream of the landlord crop, did not in any way delineate a natural social group. The Muzaffarnagar Association, by contrast, was open to almost anyone who cared to join. Landholders, tenants, and other persons interested in the aims and objects of the association were all eligible for membership. It thus appealed only to the vaguest and most indistinct form of landlord feeling.

From the 1858 reconquest of Oudh onward, the British labored to make the talukdars improving landlords and a socially responsible aristocracy. The ideal which sustained this vision was that of the English landed gentry. The talukdars were to be the "Barons of Oudh." This ideal, however, was flawed from the start. Partly this was because British policy in Oudh was heavily flavored with mid-Victorian liberalism, with its insistence upon laissez-faire and absolute proprietorship, and this was hardly the most congenial atmosphere for the growth of aristocratic sentiments. More importantly, the cultural transplantation involved in this process was far too exotic and artificial to take root. No amount of legislative encouragement or official patronage could transform such an unwieldy and backward-looking group of Indians as the Oudh talukdars into even a reasonable facsimile of their presumed English counterparts. The enthusiastic British officials of the "Oudh School," Charles Wingfield, W. C. Bennett, and Harcourt Butler, indulged in little more than wishful thinking when they spoke, for instance, of the talukdars as a "landed aristocracy," affording "the only possible foundation for the devolution of political power."[31]

But the talukdars did respond to the new order, and they did take advantage of the opportunities which it opened to them. The basic determinant of their behavior was a desire to maintain in the new order as much as possible of their traditional position of rural dominance. Under British rule, certain old paths of power were shut off, and other new ones opened up. The talukdars modified their attitudes and patterns of action to take maximum advantage of the new paths and to minimize the losses they would suffer from the barring of the old. This was the sole justification and the full extent of their transformation. The changes in the position of the talukdar which this process of adaptation demanded were by no means inconsequential. They included a far-reaching reconstitution of their relationships with their tenants. From rajas, they became landlords. But the talukdars saw no benefit in further mimicry of the English gentry. Despite British urging, for instance, they did not become improving landlords, for agricultural improvement was not essential to the maintenance of their position of rural dominance. They attended agricultural exhibitions, spoke in glowing terms of the advantages of improved cultivation, and even purchased agricultural implements; but they then allowed this equipment to rust unused, in much the same manner as they patronized, but did not attend, Canning College.[32]

Similarly, the talukdars saw no real need to develop intimate social relationships among themselves. The British Indian Association was a useful and convenient organization for the expression of talukdari grievances to the Government. So long as it was active in the defense of talukdari landed interests it won widespread support, for the bulk of the talukdars had neither the time, the inclination, nor the legal sophistication to deal with the British Government. This limited degree of association was sufficient to enable them to maintain their dominant position in rural society. Hence, it is not surprising that all efforts to encourage philanthropic and social activities among the talukdars met with a lukewarm and half-hearted response. Convivial mingling on the grounds of the Kaiserbagh was no more required for success under the new order than were attendance at Canning College or the reduction of marriage expenses. Although the talukdars often clothed themselves in the trappings of English aristocratic behavior, such activity always had an artificially contrived look about it. Usually it was the work of some outstanding leader with a broader vision, such as Maharaja Man Singh, or else it reflected the talukdars' perennial concern with prestige and status. Much of what they did was done to satisfy their own vanity or the expectations of their British rulers.

But if these limited and partial changes in their attitudes and values gave the talukdars a position of uncontested dominance in the rural order of late nineteenth-century Oudh, they placed them at a grave disadvantage in meeting the more demanding challenges of the years of the independence struggle. When a popular and determined contender for power appeared on the scene in the Congress Party of the 1930's, the talukdars had become so habituated to their narrow landlord ways and so convinced of their own inevitable and perpetual dominance that they found it impossible to take concerted steps against a genuine threat of destruction. The talukdars today retain much of their old position at the head of rural society, but the storms of the independence era, culminating in zamindari abolition in 1951, have reduced that dominance to a much attenuated shadow of its former greatness. Bereft of the numerous levers of control their landlord position formerly gave them, the talukdars are now totally dependent upon the continuance of traditional habits of social deference and must eschew all appearance of independent political action outside the framework of the established political parties.

### NOTES

1 Bernard S. Cohn, "Comments on Papers on Land Tenure," *Indian Economic and Social History Review*, I, No. 2 (1963), 178.

2 See my earlier essay in this volume, "From Raja to Landlord: The Oudh Talukdars, 1850–1870," pp. 126–27.

3 See Jawaharlal Nehru, *Toward Freedom* (Boston, 1958), pp. 54–64; and Walter Hauser, "The Indian National Congress and Land Policy in the Twentieth Century," *Indian Economic and Social History Review*, I, No. 1 (1963), 57–65.

4 For a discussion of British post-Mutiny policy toward the talukdars, see Thomas R. Metcalf, *The Aftermath of Revolt: India 1857–1850* (Princeton,

1964), pp. 134–73. Canning's remark is in a letter of Government of India to Chief Commissioner of Oudh, 6 October 1858, cited on p. 148.

5 "From Raja to Landlord," p. 127.

6 See, for instance, the reports of the heavily attended special meeting of 30 December 1864, in *Proceedings of the Meetings of the British Indian Association of Oudh from 1861 to 1865* (Calcutta, 1865), pp. 176–88.

7 *Ibid.*, p. 167, speech of Babu Dakhinaranjun Mukherjee in a meeting of 2 March 1864. He defined the objectives of the association as being "to further the ends of good government, to aid in promoting sympathy between rulers and ruled, to exert ourselves to remove moral and social evils, and to further the cause of reform and enlightenment."

8 *Ibid.*, pp. 6–12, speech of Maharaja Man Singh in a meeting of 1 November 1861, and rules adopted at the same meeting.

9 For the foundation of Canning College, see Khan Bahadur Sheikh Siddiq Ahmad, *Tarikh-i-Anjuman Hind Avadh* (Lucknow, 1935), I, 121–23, 153–54. This work, written in Urdu, is a history of the British Indian Association of Oudh.

10 Speech of Maharaja Man Singh in meeting of 27 February 1864, in *Proceedings of the B.I.A. from 1861 to 1865*, p. 162.

11 W. Handford, Director of Public Instruction, *Report on the Progress of Education in Oudh for 1867–68* (Lucknow, 1868), p. 25.

12 W. Handford, Director of Public Instruction, *Report on the Progress of Education in Oudh for 1868–69*, (Lucknow, 1869), p. 8.

13 Sec. C. C. Oudh to Sec. B.I.A., 25 March 1863, *Parliamentary Papers* (London, 1865), XL, 171.

14 Resolutions adopted in meeting of 25 February 1864, *Proceedings of the B.I.A. from 1861 to 1865*, p. 141.

15 See the Circular Letter from Sec. Board of Revenue to all Heads of Chuttree Families in the North-Western Provinces, 6 September 1864, in the North-Western Provinces General Proceedings, 24 September 1864, No. 109, Lucknow Secretariat Archives. On the Gorakhpur meeting, see the letter of Commissioner Gorakhpur to Sec. Govt. North-Western Provinces, 31 October 1864, in the North-Western Provinces General Proceedings, November 19, 1864, No. 66.

16 *Administration Report of Oudh for 1862–63* (Lucknow, 1863), p. 38.

17 See Ahmad, *op. cit.*, I, 139–43. For original documents regarding collection of Canning College and B.I.A. subscriptions by the Government, see Board of Revenue Records, Oudh General, File 86, Part I, in the Uttar Pradesh State Archives, Allahabad.

18 For Mukherjee's career, see C. E. Buckland, *Dictionary of Indian Biography* (London, 1906), p. 304, and George Smith, *Life of Alexander Duff* (London, 1879), II, 354–55. For an account of Mukherjee's services to the association, see speeches of Man Singh and Balrampur in meeting of 12 November 1862, *Proceedings of the B.I.A. from 1861 to 1865*, pp. 98–100.

19 B. R. Records, Oudh Faizabad, File 6, Commr. Faizabad to Sec. C. C. Oudh, 23 March 1874.

20 *Proceedings of the B.I.A. from 1861 to 1865*, p. 189.

21 See *dastur-al-amal* of 5 April 1866, and report of committee meeting of 31 May 1866, in *Majmui Report Anjuman Hind Avadh* (Lucknow, 1873) pp. 5–9 and 11. This work, written in Urdu, gives the proceedings of the

B.I.A. from the beginning of 1865 to 1870. See also Ahmad, *op. cit.*, I, 357–64.

22 *Majmui Report Anjuman*, pp. 8–9.

23 Ahmad, *op. cit.*, I, 82–85.

24 *Majmui Report Anjuman*, pp. 1–2.

25 Speech of Raja Hanwant Singh in meeting of 13 November 1862, in *Proceedings of the B.I.A. from 1861 to 1865*, p. 102.

26 Speech in meeting of 14 August 1864, in Saiyid Aqa Hussan Rizvi, *Ahsan-ut-Twarikh* (Lucknow, 1865), IV, 509–11. This work, written in Urdu, is a biography of Maharaja Digvijai Singh of Balrampur. It is significant that this speech was not published in the society's own account of its proceedings.

27 The Kayasthas were particularly effective in organizing caste *sabhas*, or societies, for the promotion of social reform and education. Analysis of their activities would provide much useful comparative data for the study of this subject.

28 A few suggestive allusions to these factions can be found in Brajendranath De, "Reminiscences of an Indian Member of the Indian Civil Service," *Calcutta Review*, CXXIX, No. 2 (1953), 161–62. I have so far been unable to uncover any further references to this important subject.

29 Canning's comment was made in a letter to Sir Charles Wood, Secretary of State for India, 12 November 1859, cited in Metcalf, *op. cit.*, p. 160.

30 For information on the Agra and Muzaffarnagar associations, I am indebted to P. D. Reeves, "Landlord Associations in U.P. and Their Role in Landlord Politics, 1920–1937," a working paper of the Institute of Advanced Studies, Department of History, Australian National University, 4 May 1961.

31 Harcourt Butler, *Oudh Policy: The Policy of Sympathy* (Lucknow, 1906), p. 40. See also Harcourt Butler, *Oudh Policy Considered Historically and with Reference to the Present Political Situation* (Allahabad, 1896).

32 For a detailed account of the Lucknow Agricultural Exhibition of December, 864, and of the character of talukdari interest in it, see Rizvi, *op. cit.*, IV, 530–41. References to the talukdars' lack of interest in agricultural improvement are found in almost all the Oudh settlement reports of the later nineteenth century.

Chapter VII

# Permanent Settlement in Operation: Bakarganj District, East Bengal

*Tapan Raychaudhuri*

The facts about land control in East Bengal under the Permanent Settlement of 1793, though described in detail in the gazetteers and revenue literature, are not easily comprehensible.[1] The de facto as well as the de jure rights of the various categories of interest in land were enmeshed in an incredible maze of crisscross relationships so that it is impossible to determine with any precision who was who or what was whose. Descriptions in the settlement reports indicate that those who owned land very often did not know what land it was they owned, and those who cultivated land often did not know the title or estate of their landlords. The settlement camps were indeed regarded somewhat as lost property offices where landlords came to find their lands, and tenants came to find their landlords. Beside this picture of confusion one has to juxtapose another—the feudal, almost religious ties of loyalty and protection which bound the zamindar and the tenant to each other practically down to the time when the system was abolished. Any attempt to extract clear categories from this jigsaw puzzle and, even more, to identify structures will necessarily be an essay in abstraction. We have here no clear-cut pyramid of hierarchically arranged land rights; what we have is a fantastic amalgam of pyramids, pueblos, hanging gardens, and a few leaning towers thrown

163

in for good measure. Hence, the relationship of the simplified picture given below to what was actually going on is not always very close.

In our simplified picture, at the nearly flat top of the uneven, almost rectangular pyramid were the zamindars and the independent talukdars. Who were the zamindars and the talukdars of Bakarganj? Cornwallis and his men in 1793 believed that they had the answer to this million-dollar question. They further believed that it was a fairly straightforward answer. Writing as late as 1918, Collector Jack, with years of intensive administrative experience behind him, states with enviable confidence that the decennial and permanent settlements in Bakarganj were made with the original proprietors of the soil, to wit, the zamindars and taluk-dars, the latter being included in this category chiefly by the grace of Lord Cornwallis.[2] However, we learn from the Mughal chronicles that the Bengal zamindars of the pre-British days were erstwhile independent or semi-independent chieftains who had become *peshkash*-paying sub-ordinate allies or *mansabdars* of the empire with their administrative autonomy unimpaired. Beginning in the eighteenth century, Murshid Quli Khan and his successors had added another category: hereditary revenue farmers with full administrative authority over the area as-signed, subject to regular payment of stipulated amounts. By the mid-eighteenth century we have a functionally homogeneous class of Bengal zamindars derived from these two distinct origins, people in effective administrative control of roughly specified areas whence they collected revenue, liable to be removed at the nawab's will, but usually only if they failed to pay up the stipulated sums. These were the people whom the men in charge of the Decennial Settlement identified as the original proprietors in Bakarganj and, in some instances, physically forced to accept the settlement. Among these were two families descended from the famous Bhuiyas—the rajas of Chandradwip, once the rulers of the greater part of the district, and the zamindars of Raikathi, descendants of Raja Satrajit. The outstanding instance of zamindari rights derived from revenue farming in Bakarganj were those acquired early in the twentieth century by Raja Rajballabh during the notorious years of the Dyarchy.

A large number of zamindari estates in Bakarganj had as their orig-inal nuclei taluks granted by the Chandradwip rajas or some other zamindar of the pre-British era. The taluks were named after the original grantee or some relative of his and might consist of several villages, a single village, or a part of a village. The grant did not specify the measurement of the area concerned, but indicated the boundaries in the four directions. I would like to emphasize that the taluk was a piece of land, not a territorial unit, though it was not precisely measured. The talukdar's concern was to collect a share of the produce from this piece of land and hand over a part thereof to his landlord. This overlord might be the grantor's family or their successors in the zamindari or—in cases where the overlords had disappeared from the scene or the taluk was granted by the nawab himself—the nawab's government. If the latter was the case, there was little to distinguish the talukdar from a zamindar.

A fair proportion of the talukdars actually paid revenue direct to the nawab and not through any superior zamindar. Beveridge mentions a further criterion for distinction between zamindars and talukdars in the pre-British era: A zamindar was in effective occupation of a pargana— a territorial unit with a distinct name and history—or a sizeable portion thereof; anyone with less than this under his control was a talukdar. The distinction is significant only in that it probably hints at the political-administrative authority over a territorial unit as the *original* basis of the zamindar's rights. Over a period of years, many talukdars had added substantially to their original taluk so as to control sizeable portions of parganas, and even acquire the title of zamindar, adding "Chaudhuri" to their caste name. The useful distinction therefore would be between zamindars and talukdars paying revenue direct to the Government and talukdars paying revenue through some superior zamindar. Under the Cornwallis system, it was the latter who were "separated" from the zamindaris and established as independent talukdars dealing directly with the Government.

The "proprietors" under the Permanent Settlement thus consisted of three groups: the zamindars, the originally "independent" talukdars, and the talukdars made "independent" at the time of the settlement. Functionally, there was nothing to distinguish between the three. The social distinction weighted in favor of the zamindars was largely obliterated by the talukdars' successful efforts to climb into the higher category and be accepted as zamindars. Even Brahman talukdars began to prefer "Chaudhuri" to their time-honored caste names to affirm their claim to zamindarship—a symptom of changing social values. Following earlier practice, the zamindars' and talukdars' "tenants-in-chief" under the Permanent Settlement were also called talukdars, a fact which further aggravated the terminological confusion.

The Permanent Settlement is usually accepted as a landmark denoting a two-fold discontinuity in Bengal's history: the virtual ruin of the old families who had superior interests in land, and, simultaneously, the creation of a legally protected ownership of land vested in the zamindar which cut across and undermined all earlier patterns of land rights. In Bakarganj District, however, the evidence of family tradition as well as the Government records suggests continuity rather than discontinuity so far as "superior rights" in land are concerned. The big zamindaris appear to have been few in number in the district and throughout Bengal these usually suffered the most in the early days of the Permanent Settlement. More information was available about their revenue-paying capacity and, unlike the smaller estates, they could not hope to get away with a light assessment nor could their cumbersome machinery cope with the rigors of the law. In Bakarganj, however, only one big zamindari, Buzrugumedpur, covering 381 square miles, passed out of the original "proprietors'" hands very shortly after the Permanent Settlement owing to quarrels among the proprietors or to too heavy an assessment. The descendants of the Bhuiyas, though not totally ruined, suffered an eclipse of their family fortunes. This was a slow process spread over many decades stretching back to the pre-British era, but primarily was the result of certain peculiar characteristics of the settlement as it operated in the district.

Some of the smaller proprietors found their estates gradually eaten up, and these were eventually sold for arrears of revenue; but the majority appear to have retained their estates, and a fair number added considerably to their property during the nineteenth century. This expansion of the smaller estates was achieved mainly at the cost of the larger ones. On the other hand, the extension of the settlement operations added to the number rather than the size of the estates already in existence. New land, such as that reclaimed from the Sunderban jungles was for the most part settled directly with the cultivators on a temporary basis. The addition to the number of the estates through subdivision was not very significant.

The fact that the Bengal zamindars and talukdars acquired absolute "proprietary rights" over their land is often emphasized. How these rights were actually exercised in Bakarganj is worth examining. In 1918, only 1 per cent of the area owned by the proprietors—28,255 acres out of a total of 3,270 square miles—was held by them for their own occupation. Of this only 5,000 acres were cultivated; homesteads, forests, marshes, and the like accounted for the rest. Five per cent of the land was granted free of rent for religious purposes or as service tenures. Ninety-one per cent was leased to rent-paying tenants—79 per cent to "tenure-holders" and 12 per cent to "ryots." Of the lands leased out, only a fraction was leased to ryots on a temporary basis subject to enhancement of rent. The bulk of the land was leased to tenure holders at a rent fixed in perpetuity. The situation as described in the 1952 settlement report is essentially similar. Whatever the de jure position, neither the composition of nor the actual rights exercised by the "superior interests in land" in Bakarganj District apparently underwent any revolutionary change as a result of the Permanent Settlement.

The element of novelty in land relations under the Permanent Settlement in Bakarganj has to be sought elsewhere—in the proliferation of tenures and subtenures. From Jack's descriptions, there were three main classes of land tenures: *taluks*, grants from the zamindar or his lessees intended to create the interest of a landlord; *hawalas*, leases given by the talukdars and their sublessees to substantial men for the reclamation of forests; and *karshas*, rights granted on payment to prosperous cultivators to land in their previous occupation. The last class was apparently a unique feature in land tenure, but promotion in status of the cultivators by the grant to them of the right of tenure holders was very common in Bakarganj.

The above classification really oversimplifies matters. In fact, 162 revenue terms were used to describe the various forms of tenures and subtenures. Between the proprietor and the actual cultivator, there might be eight to twenty grades of intermediary tenures. In 1918, there were 170 tenures in every square mile of the area leased by proprietors to tenure holders. By 1952, four grades of under-ryot tenures had developed below the *karsha* tenant-cultivator; this was largely a post–World War I development. The majority of the tenures were of modern creation, though a fair number were from before the Permanent Settlement. It is necessary to emphasize that in its personal aspect the tenurial structure was not marked by any clear gradation. The same individuals or families might be proprietors as well as tenure holders, holding land under a dozen different tenures at various grades. A cultivator might hold his land directly from the proprietor or any one or more of the twenty intermediate grades of tenure holders. The same person often was landlord as well as tenant in relation to another. In fact, the proprietor, rigidly circumscribed by the permanent leases to his tenants, often saw the acquiring of subtenures, unfettered by similar restrictions, as his best chance of improving his prospects. It is at this point that the supposedly pyramidal structure of land rights under the Permanent Settlement dissolves into some indefinable shape.

The multiplicity of tenures and their gradations in Bakarganj is usually explained with reference to the district's "physical conformation." There were dense forests to be cut down and these were divided by large rivers and numerous streams into a multitude of petty blocks which were difficult to manage or to supervise. The division was made in a gradually diminishing scale to grade after grade of middlemen until the areas were sufficiently small for the reclamation of the forests to be arranged. The *karsha* tenures are explained in part by the cultivators' desire to achieve superior status, and the encouragement provided them to plant slow-growing trees like betel and coconut palms, which was impossible under insecure tenures.

However, the above-mentioned facts are not adequate to explain the continued multiplication of tenures after the process of reclamation had stopped or the continued growth of under-ryot tenures. Sociological explanations are probably relevant. Moving up the social ladder to the top story of zamindar-*cum*-chaudhurihood was an ambition fairly common to all with a bit of extra savings to invest. The purchase of a tenure, besides providing a small steady income, was often the equivalent of a firmly set little toe on a modest rung of the ladder. It is significant that many a cosharer in the tenures derived no income whatsoever from his "landed interest," yet retained it as a symbol of prestige. On the supply side, the prestige value of becoming a rent-receiver rather than a mere "owner" of lands cultivated by hired or crop-sharing laborers was probably an important influence. The better-off peasant was surely willing to pay some price to become a *hawaladar*. And this entire process of proliferation was rendered economically viable by the relatively low and unchanging rate of revenue demand which left a large surplus to be distributed among a numerous and parasitical class of rather poor intermediaries.

We are still left without an economic explanation of a primarily economic phenomenon. One can at best suggest that the successive layers of tenure holders preferred to lease out the land rather than organize cultivation themselves because the differential advantage to be reaped from the latter course was not worth the effort. And, of course, there is always the last resort: increasing pressure on land. However, one cannot help but be aware of the snag in this line of reasoning: The *karsha* ryot secured from his under-ryot 50 per cent more than what he himself paid in rent; obviously, the under-ryot derived from his toils a very low subsistence income. Why did the tenure-holding talukdar not try to skip all the intermediary layers of interests and settle directly with the under-ryot whenever possible and thus hog the bulk of the surplus? I do not have any answer to this riddle and would very much welcome some analytical light on this problem. The following extract from the District Gazetteer may be relevant to such analysis:

Under the tenure-holders come the raiyats who cultivate the land, although a large part, indeed very nearly one acre out of every three, is cultivated by the inferior grades of tenure-holders . . . . Of the total number of tenure-holders rather more than one-third cultivate all or almost all of the lands in their tenures which in the average measure only two acres . . . . The rent for which such tenures are liable amounts in the average to Rs. 3–8–5 per acre, which is substantially less than the rate paid by the raiyats. Pure middlemen hold 45 percent; and tenure-holders, who partly sublet and partly reserve, hold 20 percent, of the total number of tenures . . . . The total area held by raiyats is equal to 63 percent of the land area in the district and to 72 percent of the cultivated area. The average size of a holding is 2.51 acres . . . . Under-raiyats hold 81,784 acres or 6 percent of the area held by raiyats; their holdings . . . average little more than an acre in size.[3]

I shall now briefly discuss the main features of estate management under the zamindars and talukdars in Bakarganj in the 1930's and 1940's. It may be added that except for brief references in Bengali literary works no other descriptions of the internal organization of the zamindaris in Bengal have been published. However, the following paragraphs are not an attempt to fill this gap, but simply the result of personal observations.

Most zamindari and talukdari estates in Bakarganj were jointly owned by a large number of cosharers descended from the original recipient of the taluk or founder of the zamindari. A fact which may be of interest to demographers is that the average number of cosharers of an old estate was not nearly as large as one might expect. Family histories invariably mention frequent failures of male succession and adoptions; in quite a few cases of estates going back to the eighteenth century or earlier, the number of cosharers at the time of the partition did not exceed a dozen. The cosharers might arrange to collect the rent jointly or separately on the basis of an informal partition. Cases of formal partition were relatively rare. While the joint management by cosharers led to endless bickering, the sale of his share to an outsider by an individual cosharer was generally considered as a calamity for the rest.

Absenteeism has often been described as a characteristic feature of the Permanent Settlement in East Bengal. This description has, however, only a limited validity for Bakarganj. The Bakarganj zamindars might spend part of their life in Calcutta in rented houses, but few had houses of their own in the metropolis. "Absenteeism" usually took the form of living at the district headquarters, Barisal. Even then, rarely did all the cosharers live away from the villages. Of course, one has to remember that most zamindari estates were scattered over several parganas. The estate was named after the village where the original taluk was situated, usually the zamindar's ancestral home. The bulk of his property was often as far from this village as it was from Barisal. Therefore, living in Barisal did not necessarily mean "absenteeism" and living in the village home did not necessarily imply any great interest in the estate or the tenantry. Besides, the town-dwelling zamindar also invariably spent some time—usually at least the autumn months—in his village. The zamindar's chief estate office might be in his village home or in the district headquarters. And wherever the zamindar lived, there was a constant flow of tenants with their numerous *arzis* or petitions so that he could never be entirely cut off from the life on his estate.

In fact, however, absenteeism was not a matter of the zamindars' physical absence from the vicinity of their estates. The zamindar might never stir from his village home and yet take only a very casual interest in the management of his estate; and this appears to have been the state of affairs in most cases. The management of the estates was usually entrusted to hired managers, often retired petty Government officials who had knowledge of revenue matters. In earlier times, the *diwan* performed a similar function, but one gathers that until about the turn of the century the zamindars took a greater degree of personal interest in the management of their property.

There were several categories of officials in the zamindar's estate office, though their functions were not very clearly distinguished. The *diwan* or *sarkar* (chief financial officer), *naib* (deputy *diwan*), and *bakhshi* (paymaster) were the main functionaries at the chief estate office, assisted by a number of *muhuris* (clerks) and *gumashtahs* (agents). Generally, the zamindar had a small *kachahri* or office in each pargana or mahal where he had sizeable properties. The local *kachahris* were under the *tahsildars* or rent-collectors, assisted by *muhuris* and *gumashtahs*. All these petty functionaries generally held tenures under the zamindar at less than the usual rent, besides being paid very low salaries. The *tahsildars* and *gumashtahs* were often entitled to a commission on the collections. Control of the various mahals was maintained through tours of inspection undertaken by the zamindar or by functionaries from his central office. Such tours invariably speeded up collection and helped settle outstanding difficulties with the tenants. The functioning of the zamindars' *kachahris* was almost untouched by the British influence. The language used in the records was Persian until the 1860's and a highly Persianized Bengali afterwards. The hours of work were in accordance with old practices—in the morning and in the early hours of the evening after a long break for siesta. Records and accounts were kept in old-style *bahis* (ledgers), bound in cloth; files were practically unknown. The zamindar's *kachahri* was probably a survival of older extinct forms of Indian administrative practices. Informality and flexibility were the keynotes of the system, and its efficiency was determined almost entirely by the ability of the man at the top. If he were weak or inefficient, nearly everyone cheated, and the estate would be well on its way to being sold for arrears. Only a few were influenced by considerations of personal loyalty to the zamindar.

This last statement would not apply to the bands of "feudal" retainers maintained by every important zamindar down to the time of the partition. There were several distinct elements among these retainers. At the top were the *mridhas*, Muslim peasants, often well-to-do, ostensibly employed to protect the zamindar's *kachahris* and village home and to accompany the *gumashtahs* on tours of collection. They enjoyed rent-free or nearly rent-free tenures and received some form of payment in kind. They were usually armed with spears at the zamindar's expense. Besides, there were the *lathiwala*, or clubmen, often described as *kahars*, recruited from among Muslims and lower-caste Hindus. These were professional fighters—expert in the use of *lathis* (bamboo sticks) and other traditional weapons. In the disputes between zamindars over property and for dealing with recalcitrant tenants, the *kahars* were frequently used until as late as the 1930's. The frequent references to "riotings" in Bakarganj are really concerned with this type of activity. The notorious river dacoits of Bakarganj, who were never suppressed, often swelled the ranks of zamindars' retainers. It was well known that these dacoits accepted no authority other than their zamindars; this loyalty was said to derive in part from an earlier history of actual collusion.

Under the zamindari system, there were survivals of "feudal' ties from the pre-British days. Middle-class *bhadralogs* (gentry), often of humble origin, were absorbed into this pattern of relationship when they acquired zamindari estates or even extensive tenurial rights. The term for tenant under the system was *praja* which means literally "subject"; the *praja* usually addressed the zamindar as *maharaj,* "the great king," the same title as was applied to the chieftains and revenue-farming zamindars in the Bengali literature of the seventeenth and eighteenth centuries. The tenant was expected to—and invariably did—offer a present, usually a small amount in cash as *nazrana,* when he came to see the zamindar. Cornwallis had disbanded the zamindar's police force, but they effectively retained some of their judicial functions outside the system of organized British law. They also retained the de facto power of punishing their tenants through fines and corporal punishments, and little could be done to check this extralegal authority, not only because of the tenant's weak position, but also because of his basic acceptance of the situation. On its better side, this extralegal dimension to the zamindar's position meant that a certain leniency was expected of him in cases of arrears of rent resulting from genuine hardship. The zamindar who functioned as a usurer—very few did—was looked down upon. Most zamindars also organized some philanthropic activity, such as founding schools and charitable dispensaries or maintaining water tanks. There were two distinct images of zamindars, the good and the bad, and the type which sought the chief sanction for authority in the proverbial *lathi* was not very numerous.

The idea that the zamindar was his tenants' protector found institutional expression in a particular form of subtenure, the *zimbadari* system. A tenant harrassed by one zamindar sought the protection of another through a fictitious transaction. The "protecting" zamindar accepted from the tenant a sublease on the land and then leased it back to him, thus coming between the original zamindar and the tenant as custodian or *zimbadar.* His financial gain from the transaction was marginal; the rent went to the original proprietor as before, the *zimbadar* getting only the extra perquisites besides the satisfaction of being one-up on a neighbor. This medieval institution in a modern garb has flourished in the twentieth century.

Feudal pretensions were particularly marked in the zamindars' style of life. Nearly every zamindar had a palatial residence in his ancestral village. The favored style was *chak-milan,* which was in the form of a very large hollow square around which a two- to three-storied structure was constructed, complete with underground stores, armory, and the dreaded dark room (*andharia kotha*) once used as a dungeon for recalcitrant tenants. The administrative offices and the room where the festive worship of Durga and other deities was held were generally on the ground floor. The residential quarters were on the floors above, and these usually included one or more large halls for entertainment. Often enough, the ground-floor rooms served as residence for the *kachahri* staff and the host of menials invariably recruited from among the poorer tenants. As the family proliferated, fresh wings or hollow squares were added to the original building until it was a huge rambling structure. A zamindar's house with a hundred rooms was not exceptional in Bakarganj. As few of the zamindars were really rich, they could not afford to maintain these white elephants which were mostly dilapidated. The zamindars' style of life in the village may best be described as one of very shabby grandeur. Down to the turn of the century, the zamindar often donned on festive occasions bejeweled court robes reminiscent of Mughal days. Later, the dhoti-clad babu under the regal umbrella looked a rather pathetic figure.

In the district headquarters, the zamindar assumed a different style of life, less marked by feudal pretensions. He lived in very comfortable, but relatively modest, bungalows, with spacious lawns and gardens. The object of emulation here was the nineteenth-century English gentleman rather than the seventeenth-century Indian raja. In the village, the typical form of conspicuous consumption was a grandiose feast, to which all were invited, complete with fireworks, amateur theatricals, and a nautch. In town, the number of horses and horse-drawn carriages, the style in which the drawing room was furnished, the excellence of one's china and one's cook and, until 1905, intimacy with British officials were the symbols of prestige. Western clothes appear to have been very popular until the turn of the century; at least it is in such guise that the zamindars posed for oil paintings. Subsequently, the strong tide of nationalism appears to have inhibited such preferences.

Many of the Bakarganj zamindars took to Western education. Having a B.A. or M.A. at the end of one's name became an additional status symbol. There were occasional atavistic throwbacks to the days of the robber barons—the patrons and allies of the river dacoits—who scorned such effeminate refinements and always a few hard-drinking, hard-wenching "squires." But, by and large, genteel Victorian values seem to have claimed the Bakarganj zamindars for their own. One generally preferred to be known for the excellence of one's library and one's taste in music rather than for more virile traits. In fact, some of the zamindars built up very fine libraries, and several were recognized as gentlemen-scholars. In the twentieth century, vocational education became fairly popular among the Bakarganj zamindars. Quite a few qualified as lawyers, but very few actually practiced. Being educated in England became a further symbol of status, and the zamindar families produced a few barristers, doctors, and artists educated in England; but, generally, one preferred not to *earn* one's living, because it was not strictly necessary to do so. The system did not foster initiative. It is often stated that the zamindar let the agriculturist down and frustrated Cornwallis' pious hopes. How badly the zamindar let himself down is not as often emphasized.

## NOTES

1 The paper is based on data available in: J. C. Jack, *Bakarganj District Gazetteer* (Calcutta, 1918) and *Reports on the District of Bakarganj* (Oxford, 1916); H. Beveridge, *Bakarganj—Its History and Statistics* (London, 1876); *Settlement Report of Bakarganj District* (Dacca, 1952); Rohini Kumar Sen, *Bakla* (Barisal, n.d.), ostensibly a history of Bakarganj, but in fact a compendium of family histories of local zamindars; *Amar Purvapurush* (Barisal, n.d.), a history of the author's family, whose estate dated back to the pre-British era; and my article, "Some Old Documents in Barisal, East Bengal," *Indian Historical Quarterly,* 1948. The details concerning zamindari estate management and the zamindars' style of life may be treated as an eye-witness account based on things seen and heard approximately during the years 1935–47, supplemented marginally by information gathered in later years from zamindars of Bakarganj and their former functionaries.
2 Jack, *Bakarganj District Gazetteer*, p. 89.
3 *Ibid.*, p. 96.

Chapter VIII

# Integration of the Agrarian System of South India

*Burton Stein*

In this preliminary comment on the development of the agrarian system of South India, my major concern is the delineation of three "episodes" of integration of the agrarian order of South India between the ninth and the nineteenth centuries. Secondarily, I am concerned with the relationship between the modes of integration of the agrarian order and changes in some aspects of the social structure of South India.

My use of the term "agrarian system" is as a concept which permits me to treat the relationship between people, groups of people, and the land as a systemic unity, a whole. Scholarly literature on the agrarian problem in India typically lacks the comprehensive qualities which this subject requires. Some writers are aware of this need; for example, in two relatively recent works, Daniel Thorner's, *The Agrarian Prospect in India*, and Irfan Habib's, *The Agrarian System of Mughal India*, relationships between persons and the land are viewed as part of a whole. Thorner, using the term "agrarian structure," states: "The agrarian structure is, after all, not an external framework within which various classes function, but rather it is the sum total of ways in which each group operates in relation to other groups."[1] Habib, in his preface, stresses the fact that his work is "concerned not only with land revenue

175

administration . . . but also with agrarian economy and social structure."[2] Both Thorner and Habib perceive the comprehensive nature of
relationships involving land; yet both, pursuant to the specific problems
of their respective works—for Thorner the problem of the politics of
land reform, for Habib the organization of resources within the Mughal
power structure—fall short of comprehensive analyses. Older works,
such as B. H. Baden-Powell's monumental *Land Systems of British
India* and W. H. Moreland's *Agrarian System of Moslem India,* or such
regional studies as M. N. Gupta's *Land System of Bengal* and K. M.
Gupta's *The Land System of South India Between c. 800* A.D., *and
1200* A.D., never pretended to be comprehensive; though useful in many
ways, these works are limited to land tenure and revenue considerations.[3]

The concept of the agrarian system assumes a whole and developing
complex of relationships among groups of people and the basic resource,
land. Utilization of the concept demands recognition of the manifest
dependence of power, livelihood, and status upon control of land; and
any adequate analysis of dominantly agrestic societies must indicate the
way in which political, economic, and social institutions are related to
and integrated with the control of land. This relationship is illustrated
in the trade guilds in medieval South India.[4]

From the eleventh to the fourteenth century in South India, one of the
great institutions described in the stone inscriptions was that of the
itinerant guilds, called "merchants of many countries" or *nanadesi*
merchants. These merchant associations, or guilds as they are usually
labeled, ranged over the entire southern portion of the peninsula and
beyond to Southeast Asia. Among the most prominent of such associations were the Ayyavole merchants of medieval Karnataka. In their
inscriptions they boast of their great wealth derived from extensive trade
in commodities ranging from horses and elephants to precious stones
(part of which wealth was gifted to temples) and of their military prow-
ess used to protect trade caravans of asses and bullocks through the
foreboding forest land which separated the major areas of densely settled
agricultural people of South India. Their political power and status is
reflected in the fact that large villages and towns in various places
in South India were under their direct control as major market centers.

All of this we know directly from the stone inscriptions prepared
under the sponsorship of these merchants; but there is much we do not
know. Particularly, we do not know how these merchant groups carried

out their trade, that is, how the trade was organized and with whom it was carried out. Nor do we know why these great associations virtually ceased to function after the fourteenth century as evidenced by the lack of references in the inscriptions of the fifteenth and sixteenth centuries and by the lack of notice from the earliest Europeans whose vital interest was trade. I believe that I have found preliminary answers to these two questions in my work on agrarian institutions of the great period of merchant guild activity and later.

A series of inscriptions were published some years ago by the epigraphist and historian K. V. Subrahmanya Aiyer dealing with a particular kind of territorial assembly which flourished in South India from about the eleventh to the thirteenth century, the *chitrameli-periyanadu*.[5] Little notice has been taken of these inscriptions which were collected at about the same time as the great *brahmadeya* inscriptions and which admirably complement these famous inscriptions of early Brahman settlements. *Periyanadu* assemblies had two important characteristics: They had jurisdiction over a relatively extensive territory reflected in the term *periyanadu,* or "great country," and they were dominated by agriculturists as reflected in the term *meli,* the Tamil word for plow, and symbolized by the representation of a plow incised on the stones containing the inscriptions. These assemblies proudly claimed to be protectors of Brahman settlements and temples. They also claimed authority and control over merchants, including the *nanadesi* as well as local merchant groups. Here then, so far as I know, is the only description of the context in which the great, medieval, itinerant merchant associations conducted their business. Well-organized and integrated areas of settled, agricultural villages, with prosperous and respectable peasant groups, provided the major consumers of the trade carried out by the extensive medieval trade organizations. The question of what became of the great trade associations after the fourteenth century may be answered when it is understood that the nexes of their trade network were the scattered, well-developed agricultural territories of the sort in which the *periyanadu* assemblies existed. The fate of the trade associations was linked with that of the peasant-dominated assemblies, and after the fourteenth century these assemblies disappeared owing to changes in the agrarian order of South India. The particular characteristics of agrarian integration after the fourteenth century no longer permitted the existence of politically and militarily powerful trade associations. By the sixteenth century, the integration of the South Indian agrarian order, based upon warrior-dominated territories, was hostile to the kind of mobility and power of associations like the Ayyavole.

This digression is meant to indicate the way in which the proper identification of the relationships and institutions within a society with a pervasively agrarian character like medieval South India can suggest answers to questions relating to essentially non-agrarian problems. In such a society, the more systematic the concept of agrarian integration, the greater the possibility of grasping the totality of the structure and style of the entire society.

Three significant episodes of relatively stable agrarian integration may be identified for South India to the middle of the nineteenth century: the Pallava-Chola integration of the ninth to the twelfth century; the Vijayanagar integration of the fourteenth and fifteenth centuries; and the British integration to the beginning of the nineteenth century. My discussion of these episodes is meant to be tentative and suggestive; there is obvious imbalance in the treatment of each of the integrative periods examined, and comparability among the three periods is imperfect. At this stage of research, it would be improper to regard the three designated periods as anything more than empirical hypotheses. Much yet needs to be done. Thus, none of the episodes can be or need be dated precisely. At this point, my purpose is to indicate aspects of three different modes of integration of elements in the South Indian agrarian system and to note particularly the relationship between social structure and land control.

The shape of any agrarian system must ultimately be based upon two fundamental and, over any but the longest time period, unchanging elements: the state of the arts (technology) and the persistent forms of human organization. A radical change in either of these elements would cause a new order to emerge.

Broadly speaking, over the millenium with which I shall be dealing, technology and the dominant forms of human organization remain highly, even depressingly, stable. Irrigated agriculture, based primarily upon tank or reservoir storage and secondarily upon riverine sources, was the dominant and stable system of cultivation. Bullock-drawn, shallow-cutting plows were utilized in all but a few areas which required deep plowing and additional animals. The standard grain crops were rice, barley, and millets. Garden cultivation based upon rainfall in the two monsoons was usually associated with intensive field cultivation.

In addition, there were a variety of dry crops such as heartier millets and pulses which were regularly cultivated. The crops and the techniques utilized in their cultivation appear to have changed little over the entire period.

Forms of human organization also remained stable over the period except for a sustained displacement of the tribally organized, pastoral and hunting society of the forests and upland areas by caste-organized, village-based societies. The principal elements of southeastern Indian caste organization, which in modern times comprises a recognized regional variant of Indian caste, were clear in the period of the Pallava-Chola integration.[6] These elements are the tripartite division of castes into Brahman, non-Brahman, and low caste groups with a dual division in the last grouping of castes into those of the right hand (*valangai*) and those of the left hand (*idangai*).

In only one significant respect was there important change—the relationship of cleared, cultivated land to forest. The reduction of forest and the expansion of regularly cultivated land was a continuous process. This may be regarded as the ecological concomitant of the social displacement and assimilation of tribal peoples. As in any developing, tropical, agrarian system, the clearing of forest was one of the standard methods for expansion; this kind of change in environment may therefore be considered a regularized process in which the tempo of expansion is a factor of vital importance.

### Pallava-Chola Integration

During the ninth century we find the first solid evidence of an agrarian system, the dominant characteristics of which persist for the next thousand years. The nature of the agrarian order prior to this time is obscure. Legends dating from the third century contained in the early Tamil literature of the Sangam period (*ca.* third century A.D.) recount some ancient colonization of central parts of the plains of Coromandel by Vellalas, the most important South Indian agriculturists of the historical period. In one such account, 48,000 Vellala families were settled in Tondaimandalam (modern North and South Arcot and Chingleput districts) and were granted superior and permanent rights over the land for the purpose of establishing agricultural villages. This allegedly followed the defeat and expulsion of a tribal people.[7] The movement of Vellalas for purposes of colonization has been noticed elsewhere, for example, the movement, again of 48,000 families, from

Tondaimandalam to Madurai.[8] Migration legends of this sort may be based upon actual events, though this has been questioned by historians.[9] However, these legends may also be seen as ways for prosperous cultivating castes of low origin to claim an association with the respectable Sat-Sudra Vellala caste; the achievement of such status was an important accomplishment for many over most of South Indian history.

The integration of the agrarian system during the Pallava-Chola period was based upon the control of small regions by well-established, often highly organized villages dominated by Brahmans or Sat-Sudras. The major component in this agrarian integration was the relatively large number of scattered, small regions which I call "nuclear areas of corporate institutions."[10] These nuclear areas, most abstractly conceived, are ecological systems, that is, consisting of relatively intensively organized and interrelated human activities and biological and physical processes. More concretely, the nuclear areas were localities comprising a set of natural and social elements which represented the most advanced level of early South Indian life. The Pallava-Chola nuclear areas were located in those places which permitted the most regular production of surplus food because of the accessibility of water for irrigation. They existed in the drainage basins of the major rivers or in those physiographic settings in which the tank storage of rain and runoff water was possible. They were characteristically areas of relatively high population density with agricultural villages clustered closely together, surrounded by intensively cultivated fields.

Within such areas, the dominant forms of integration were achieved through two institutions: the *brahmadeya,* or Brahman-controlled circle of villages, and the *periyanadu,* or Sat-Sudra–controlled extended locality. The *brahmadeya* as an institution of early South India has been thoroughly studied by such scholars as the pioneer epigraphist V. Venkayya and the historian Nilakanta Sastri.[11] Some later scholars have exaggerated the functions and distribution of the *brahmadeya,* in part as a result of their nationalist enthusiasm; but, for the most part, the importance of these early agrarian institutions has received attention fully commensurate with their significant place in Pallava-Chola society.

The *brahmadeya,* as it is usually understood, was a type of settlement under the control of a group of Brahmans. However, it was more than this; it was a mode of agrarian integration in which several extant settlements were brought together under the management of a group of Brahmans who became the major beneficiaries of the production of the land and who made the crucial decisions about the utilization of resources within the circle of villages. Despite the tendency of scholars to conceive of all *brahmadeyas* as elaborately organized and comprehensively managed, such as the great *brahmadeya* of Uttaramerur in Chingleput District, Madras,[12] there was obviously a great deal of variation among such settlements, some of which were established on such slender resources or under such difficult conditions that they failed to maintain themselves. In all cases, the establishment of a *brahmadeya* created a comprehensive integration among a circle of established and productive villages under the central direction of a group of Brahmans.

The *periyanadu* assembly was the other core component of the nuclear area. In scope, this institution encompassed a much larger area than the *brahmadeya,* the latter institution being included in the *periyanadu,* or "great country" assembly. In function, these assemblies differed from the *brahmadeyas* in that they were not essentially management bodies over a circle of neighboring settlements, but a legislative body for what appears to be the entire nuclear area. In social composition, the *periyanadu* assembly was dominated and directed by the dominant, respectable, agricultural castes of the nuclear area, Sat-Sudras.

As indicated above, the existence and functions of the *periyanadu* assemblies have not received the same notice by scholars as the great South Indian *brahmadeyas,* though inscriptions which describe them have been known for as long. The explanations for this neglect are too complex to outline here, though I may suggest that the chief difficulty in the utilization of these inscriptions has been that South Indian historians have never attempted to systematically analyze the structure of agrarian relations and institutions. Where the *periyanadu* assemblies have been noted in the past by historians, they have generally been consigned to that limbo category of early Indian institutions called "corporate" groups and never linked structurally to other important institutions in the country or to processes of change.[13] One further explanatory point may also be that there have been fewer inscriptions dealing with the *periyanadu* assemblies than with the *brahmadeya,* which has tended to diminish the recognized significance of the former and to make their functions more difficult to understand.

The character, composition, and functions of the *periyanadu* assemblies reflected the culture and structure of the nuclear areas over which they had jurisdiction. Though dominated by respectable cultivating castes, the style of these assemblies was very nearly the same as that of the great Brahman settlements and itinerant merchant associations. This is quite clear in the language of the inscriptions which were ordered by the *periyanadu,* examples of which follow:

Lord Hari, hail Prosperity. This is the order of the *chitramela,* [consisting of] the prosperous sons of the soil and those subsisting on the cow's milk. Let this order [stand] . . . for the protection and strengthening of the sons of the land, who are born of the four castes; [may they] prosper in this world.

We, the *Chitrameli-periyanattar,* who are the sons of the earth goddess, who have studied proper Tamil language and literature and northern arts [i.e., the Sanskrit language and literature], who are the sons of the goddess of wealth, who are the lights to all quarters, who deal with sweet words in the case of the good and exorcise evil with harsh words, who prosper in this wide world bounded by the four seas, with the Lord of the Winds blowing the winds, the Lord Varuna showering the water, the Lord of the Heavens illuminating the quarters, and the people of all quarters in peace, with the lands filled with coconut, jack fruit, mango groves, plantain, areca nut, the sweet-scented flowers on the creepers, and the birds flocking in their enchanting array increasing in numbers without any waning, with justice prospering and injustice waning, with their fame spreading and . . . enemies capitulating, with their mace of just authority preceding them in all quarters without unduly disturbing, having the plow share as their god, with golden fertility . . . as their goal, conducting the affairs of their organization with tolerance and sympathy, having high and true justice as the source of their towering fame, having learnt fully the works of law, make this benefaction. As even previously the festooned gate named after the plow and earth goddess had been installed and as such the temple of the god in [the place] Chittiramelivinnagar in Tiruvidaikali in Tirukkovalur in Kurukkai-kurram in Miladu alias Jananatha-valanadu had become the responsibility of our organization, and as the endowments we had already made had changed hands (and thereby were lost) during calamities, we re-endow a *padakku* of paddy per plow and a *kuruni* of paddy per individual including from those outside the organization.[14]

Hail, Prosperity. We [are] the *Chitrameli-periyanattar,* who have the great fame for best justice, resplendent in all quarters, of the eighteen lands in the four quarters, the local merchants [and other named merchant groups] being subordinate to us. We, the above bodies, having met in full quorum . . . with unanimity made this arrangement on [a date in 1235 A.D.] . . . .[15]

The composition of the *periyanadu* varied according to the problem with which the assembly dealt. In some inscriptions, the assembly appeared to be comprised only of agriculturists; in others, the assembly included members of local and itinerant merchant associations who are specifically mentioned as subordinate to the *periyanadu*; finally, some of the *periyanadu* inscriptions were placed on the walls of temples in *brahmadeyas* in which the assembly had met to confer their support and protection upon the settlement of priests and the temple in which they officiated. That the assemblies included Brahmans at such times is obvious from the business conducted and also from the elegant composition of the inscriptions reflecting the hand of the learned priestly elite. There has been and continues to be a problem about whether these assemblies formally included members of all castes, including Brahmans, or whether the assemblies were comprised exclusively of agriculturalists of Sudra rank whose protection and jurisdiction extended over the institutions of merchants and Brahmans. Both interpretations may be supported from the *periyanadu* inscriptions.

The functions of the *periyanadu* assemblies were more comprehensive than those specified in their inscriptions which, like most South Indian inscriptions, dealt essentially with detailed grants to temples. Typical of temple endowments of this period, those of the *periyanadu* assemblies provided for the permanent grant of goods or funds to temple officials. In those records where there are no merchant groups mentioned, the grants are in grain on a regular assignment per plow; in the cases where there are merchant groups associated with the assembly, the grant would be in money as an octroi duty per standard unit of measure for the particular commodity. In addition to establishing the rates at which different groups within a territory were to support a given temple, the *periyanadu* assembly summarized and solemnized the arrangements in a stone inscription under their own authority. Moreover, it is perfectly clear that these assemblies were capable of enforcing their decisions as noted in a Nellore *chitrameli-periyanadu* inscription by K. V. Subrahmanya Aiyer. He cites the concluding portion of an inscription: ". . . such of the villages that do not obey this order shall be deemed to have committed an offense against the *Periya nadu* (Provincial Assembly): and all individuals that cultivate and hold plough should not say (by way of excuse) that the land belongs to a Brahmana lady and that they are only servants."[16] Further, Subrahmanya Aiyer has pointed to the characteristic Sanskrit passage in a number of *periyanadu* assembly inscriptions in which it is implied that the right of the assemblies to adjudicate and punish was recognized by the rulers of the country.[17]

The character of the *periyanadu* assemblies as reflected in their inscriptions and the nature of its functions make the institution extremely important in the understanding of the nuclear areas of corporate institutions in South India in the twelfth and thirteenth centuries. These assemblies comprehended, and appeared at times to control, the better-known institutions of the nuclear area, the *brahmadeyas* and the merchant associations. Their culture was that of the nuclear area as manifested by their boast of knowing and valuing Tamil and Sanskrit and in their support of dharma as reflected in their protection and support of Brahmans and temples. In the management of nuclear-area resources and the maintenance of proper and valued social institutions, the respectable agricultural groups comprising, if not dominating, the *periyanadu* assemblies shared fully with Brahman, merchant, and artisan groups.

The spatial distribution of these nuclear areas of stable South Indian settlement and civilization can only be considered approximate at this time. In the early twelfth century, the configuration of nuclear areas over South India resembled a reversed E with a long, somewhat broken line of settlement paralleling the Coromandel Coast from which three major extensions projected inward, a major one along the Cauvery River and somewhat shorter ones along the Pennar and Palar rivers. Of the major, contemporary territories, Cholamandalam in the Cauvery Basin was the most densely occupied by nuclear area institutions; next came Tondaimandalam, comprising the bulk of what has been known as the Carnatic. After these, the other two territories thus settled were Pandyamandalam, the southern portions of the peninsula from Madurai southward, and Kongumandalam, the western portions of the peninsula to the eastern Ghats, and including portions of the modern state of Mysore. The measure which I have used for this distribution is the incidence of *brahmadeyas* cited in the vast body of Pallava and Chola inscriptions.

Difficult as the delineation of nuclear areas around South India may be, establishing boundaries for any particular nuclear area is virtually impossible. The names of territories during the most stable period of Chola rule were subject to frequent changes according to the changes in rulers, conquests, and the establishment of a major *brahmadeya* which often prompted the change of name of the territory in which it was established. Terms for territorial units, *nadu, valanadu,* or *kottam,* would be changed one or more times in the course of a single reign. Names for component parts of such nuclear units were even more ephemeral.[18] It is not simply the nature of the evidence which prevents an accurate definition of the nuclear areas within South India during this period; it is the nature of the political system of the period and the absence within that system of any persistent administrative or power structure in which small territorial units required persistent labels.

The political system of South India during the Pallava-Chola period cannot be viewed as a centralized, bureaucratic one despite the excessive enthusiasm of many South Indian historians to discover such a state. The political system may best be described as a multicentered system of power in which it is possible to distinguish two kinds of power centers. The one, the nuclear area, with only the lightest links to the great warrior families of Kanchi or Tanjore, the capitals of the Pallava and Chola dynasties. The other type of power center consisted of isolated, tribally organized, upland and forest people. These people were capable at times of cooperating against the agricultural people of the nuclear areas; they were also capable at times of alliances with some nuclear-area people against others. Primarily, the forest people were antagonistic to the nuclear-area culture and society and to the warriors who exercised a loose rule over these areas; they were ever on the defensive against the more civilized and wealthy people of the nuclear areas.

The nuclear area as a center of power within the South Indian political system was the central element of that system until the thirteenth century. To that time, the Brahman- and Sat-Sudra–dominated nuclear areas were poised between the ambitious and expanding authority of the great Chola warriors and the always dangerous upland and forest peoples; and to that time, the nuclear areas held their own against the former while continuously pressing the latter peoples as forests were cleared and settled agriculture was established. And it is in terms of these two other elements of early South India that the nuclear area must be understood.

There appear to be four elements which characterized the nuclear areas. First, the nuclear areas were fundamentally independent and self-governing. A set of powerful institutions controlled these areas. Some of the institutions were based upon kinship, such as the *brahmadeyas* and peasant caste villages, and some based upon function such as the organization of artisans, like the Rathhkara,[19] and itinerant merchants, like the Ayyavole association. These institutions organized productive labor and allocated its products; they acted together in the *periyanadu* assembly and adjudicated conflicts among constituent subgroups within corporate groups of the area; they maintained a body of warriors for protection from forest raiders who stole cattle and women. Nuclear area warriors also participated in looting wars carried out by the great warriors of the country in such distant places as Ceylon.

It is important to note that the warriors of the nuclear areas were of two sorts: relatively high-caste warriors of peasant, artisan, and merchant groups who preserved their identification within larger armies and those of low-caste origin, organized in a dual division of right-hand (*valangai*) and left-hand (*idangai*) castes. In both cases, the warriors were subordinate to the dominant institutions of the nuclear area, a condition which changes drastically in the course of the next few centuries.

Second, nuclear areas may also be viewed as relatively autonomous economic units. Within the nuclear area, human and material resources were mobilized to satisfy not only the basic requirements of subsistence, but the quite elaborate requirements of sophisticated and complex political, religious, and social institutions. In addition, the nuclear areas of Chola times were responsible for transmitting at least a small share of their resources to the Chola treasury, though the nature of "revenue" organization is very obscure. Resources within a nuclear area were subject to the control of the several well-organized corporate institutions of the areas including the *brahmadeyas,* villages of Sat-Sudras, merchant associations of various kinds, artisan associations, and the few great temple institutions which existed in this early period. As pointed out above, the single overarching nuclear area institution which seemed to be capable of commanding the resources of all such bodies was the *periyanadu* assembly. As for the nuclear areas and the Chola warriors, the transfer of resources appears to be of minor importance except that the Chola rulers drew from the rich agricultural land around the capital of Tanjore, itself a nuclear area. For the most part, however, "royal" income came from looting expeditions against neighboring peoples who had developed something like the complex economic and social structure of the nuclear areas of Cholamandalam and Tondaimandalam. These peoples were the Pandyans and the Sinhalese in the South and a few centers of Telugu- and Kannada-speaking peoples to the North. To the same predatory category belong the expeditions to Southeast Asia. These looting wars were a source of wealth not only for the Chola rulers but for the various corporate bodies of the nuclear areas who contributed armed men to the enterprises, and the wars appear to have had no other purpose than the extraction of wealth either through looting or ransom; conquest and settlement were rarely undertaken. I believe that the view taken by many historians that these were pointless wars which weakened the Chola state is based on a misunderstanding of the resource base of the state. The Chola state never achieved a command over the resources of the territory it claimed to rule; indeed, it never tried, for there is no convincing evidence of machinery through which such demands could have been met.

Each of the nuclear areas tended to be a relatively self-sufficient economic unit, and economic relations beyond the nuclear area were restricted to a certain amount of trade carried out by the itinerant merchant associations, like the Ayyavole body, in which a few necessities such as salt and iron and a diverse collection of luxury items were exchanged. It addition, modest and irregular tribute was paid by some of the nuclear areas to the Chola rulers.

In social and cultural terms, nuclear areas were centers of Hindu civilization. Here, caste rules defined social relationships and provided the social processes upon which society was based. Brahmans and Sat-Sudras, particularly the various branches of the Vellala caste, the most important agricultural group, dominated nuclear-area society through their acknowledged high status and the effectiveness of their corporate institutions. Other, lower, social groupings were all related under the dual divisions of right-hand castes (*valangai*) and left-hand castes (*idangai*). In later centuries, the right- and left-hand castes acquired notoriety as disrupters of the peace and as a constant source of tension, primarily in the towns, but also in the countryside. During the Chola period, these groupings of castes were treated as low but integrated elements of nuclear area society. The terms *valangai* and *idangai* appear on many of the Chola inscriptions in connection with some of the greatest military episodes of the Cholas. They often appear as donors to important religious institutions. The origin of this dual division of lower castes and the function with which they are associated have never been adequately explained.

Broadly speaking, the dual division may be seen as two alliance systems dominated on the one side (the *valangai* or right-hand) by lower caste occupations associated with agriculture and on the other side (the *idangai* or left-hand) by occupational groups associated with artisan and husbandry functions. Each of these alliance systems provided a context for the integration of new peoples to the social order of the nuclear areas by conferring upon such new entrants a set of symbols, particularly for the status-affirming marriage and death ceremonies, and a set of support relationships upon which the new entrant could rely at times of crisis. The Chola inscriptions which refer to the *valangai* and *idangai* provide us with a rare insight into the process by which peoples never associated with caste organization were integrated into caste society.[20] These new entrants came from the forest and upland regions which abutted the nuclear areas and against which the settled agricultural village society and culture of the nuclear areas constantly pressed during Chola times. Integration of forest and hill people provided the nuclear area with a constant supply of excellent warriors whose archery was often mentioned in inscriptions; and because the process of assimilation of such peoples was gradual, they remained for most of the Chola period under the firm control of the dominant corporate bodies of the nuclear area.

The importance of agricultural occupations and groups within the nuclear areas, already evident in the nature of the *periyanadu* assembly, brings us to the final element characterizing the nuclear area. The nuclear areas were basically units of agrarian organization and management. Ultimately, these areas can be defined as regions of settled village agriculture. The nuclear area stopped where groups of peasants working their fields to the fullest extent that their technology permitted ran upon forest or upland barriers to intensive cultivation. Within a certain range of variation, all nuclear areas shared a set of characteristics. All were zones of relatively high population density separated from each other by zones of scattered populations in forests and uplands; all contained a set of highly autonomous, self-governing institutions, Brahman and Sat-Sudra settlements, caste and occupational assemblies, and religious bodies, which were linked to other similar institutions in other nuclear areas; all maintained some relationships with the Chola rulers to whom some tribute went and with whom joint looting expeditions were carried out; and all were centers of Hindu civilization where proper ritual and learning were preserved and extended. What marked the boundaries of the nuclear areas was the limit of the intensive agricultural production upon which all of the functions of the nuclear areas ultimately depended.

### Vijayanagar Integration

The agrarian integration which succeeded that of the Pallava-Chola period consisted of components of that period which were recombined and altered during the fourteenth and fifteenth centuries. Three dynasties of warrior-rulers, whose capital was Vijayanagar on the Tungabhadra River, dominated the political history of South India from 1336 to the early seventeenth century. However, denoting the agrarian integration of the period as "Vijayanagar" is not meant to suggest direct imperial control over agrarian resources. Rather, use of this appellation is meant to denote a change in the military and political structure of the South into what has been called the most warrior-dominated and warfare-oriented state ever established by Hindus.[21] Maintaining this warlike state required a fundamental reorganization of the agrarian order.

Beginning in the thirteenth century, the Chola rulers and the agrarian order over which they exerted a light overlordship began to experience a series of shocks. Perhaps the first shock came from the gradual capacity of peoples neighboring on Chola nuclear areas to resist the plundering expeditions from Chola country and ultimately to reverse the order of aggression and mount the same pressure themselves. This reversal was most notable with the people of the southernmost portion of the peninsula, the Pandyans, who, in alliance with Sinhalese warriors, caused the settled areas of the southern Chola country to be weakened through their raids. Of greater long-run consequence, however, were changes which occurred on the northern borders of Chola country in the late thirteenth and early fourteenth centuries with the expansion of Muslim power to the central portion of the peninsula. The direct effects of Muslim expansion were never significant for South India, but the indirect effects were of the greatest importance. First, aggressive and capable Muslim warriors pressed from the Gangetic area to the Kistna River, posing an imminent threat to those institutions of nuclear area culture which made these places centers of Hindu civilization. This was a threat which could not be denied, nor could it be met out of the defensive capacities of the scattered resources of the nuclear areas. A new defensive organization was required. Secondly, the intrusion of Muslim power into the central peninsula north of the Kistna caused the flight of numerous Hindu warriors into the southern regions where they reestablished themselves and formed the basis for the military defense of the South. These warriors, essentially Telugu speakers, formed the nucleus of a new local and regional elite in South India during the fourteenth and fifteenth centuries.

The most appropriate term to describe the local and regional power established by warriors between the fourteenth and eighteenth centuries is "tributary overlordship." The system of tributary overlordship seldom and only transiently approximated a hierarchy or pyramid of power relations, as when a Krishnadevaraya, in the sixteenth century, or Shivaji in the seventeenth century, could achieve wide recognition. Historically, Indian warriors had the greatest difficulty in creating the political cohesion necessary for lasting kingly power over the numerous local leaders of a region. Certain critical elements were lacking. Absent was a tradition of bureaucracy which could exercise continuous administrative and revenue control; absent too were traditions of personal loyalty which might cross lines of caste association and bind relations of warriors over an extensive territory; and absent, finally, was a universal, value-distributive institution, such as the medieval European church, which could contribute to political cohesion beyond the narrow confines of a locality. Hence, it is to the locality itself that attention must be focused in order to understand the political system in which agrarian relations and institutions operated.

Local warrior power as established in the fourteenth century was based on the balance of two countervailing factors. One was the primacy of force which permitted an ambitious and fortunate warrior to seize the position of local overlord. From among the several contenders in a locality, each with a coterie of followers, one would emerge victorious. In theory, such a man was supposed to be a Kshatriya (or of the warrior varna), but often he was not. He also could emerge, and often did, from the dominant tribal people of the area, if it was a newly-settled agricultural region, or from the dominant agricultural caste in an older area of agricultural settlement. In both cases he would depend upon his numerous tribal or caste kinsmen for support. Or, like the Telugu warriors forced from their homelands by the expansion of Muslim power, a warrior would collect a body of warrior kinsmen and move southward to win a new territory to control. Once in power, such an overlord had first to repress his rivals, second to defend his territory against predatory neighbors, and finally to seek ways to extend his authority. When it happened that such a leader was threatened by the expanding power of a more powerful warrior, the local warrior had to decide whether to resist by force and risk annihilation or to recognize the superior warrior and pay a portion of his tribute from the locality for as long as necessary. Force, frequently bloody and brutal, and ceaseless competition for power were vital elements in the system of tributary overlordship.

The second countervailing and modifying factor in this system was the need of local and even great overlords to deal with the corporate groupings within their territories and frequently to alter their ambitious plans to meet the demands of such aggregates. Since each of such groups had, in greater or lesser measure, the power to grant or withhold some or all of its support to the local overlord, they could bargain for special rights and privileges such as relief in the tribute demand, gifts to temples and shrines, economic advantages, and favorable portions of the booty to be won from wars against neighbors. Basic to all sanctions against the overlord, and a serious limitation upon his power, was the threat that part of the peasant and artisan population of the villages would leave the territory to take up residence in the territory of a neighboring warrior or even to move into the forests to survive by slash-and-burn agriculture.[22] These migrations occurred, and there are records of local warriors reducing the tribute demand in order to win peasants back to their villages and to induce them to stay.

The most important change which occurred in the agrarian system of South India under the new conditions from the fourteenth century on was the conversion of nuclear areas of the former period into areas of private jurisdiction (*amaram*) of the warrior-dominated regime.[23] The *amaram* was not a military service estate, for typically it was not granted by the rulers in Vijayanagar so much as validated by them. Warrior holders of territories designated as *amaram* were most often men who had seized existing settled territories, often the nuclear areas of the former period, or had opened new territories by burning over forest, after conquering the people there. The system of military rule which came to maturity under the first dynasty of Vijayanagar after the middle of the fourteenth century, which is described in the inscriptions and by a few European travelers, was what Kosambi has called "feudalism from below."[24] That is, warriors whose private jurisdiction had been forged by the warriors themselves, were recognized by and submitted to the overlordship of the great warriors of Vijayanagar. The system, even under the most powerful of the Vijayanagar warriors, Krishna-devaraya (1509–29), was little more than this.

There were several important consequences of the establishment of the new warrior regime. First, the integrity of the older nuclear area of corporate institutions was destroyed. The best documented example of the abridgment of formerly self-governing institutions was the *brahmadeya*. Brahman settlements continued to exist in South India under the new warrior regime; in fact, their number may have increased.

But, with increasing frequency during the Vijayanagar period, the *mahasabha,* the assembly of the *brahmadeya,* had in attendance an officer representing the major warrior of the territory who took an active part in the deliberations of the assembly and apparently often simply dictated decisions. Of those nuclear-area institutions which declined and all but disappeared under the new regime, two were the *periyanadu* assemblies and the itinerant merchant associations. The decline of the latter institution has already been discussed. The fate of the *periyanadu* assembly, with its former comprehensive control over the most important nuclear-area institutions, was undoubtedly the same, and for the same general reasons. The warrior overlord would have brooked no limitations from an assembly dominated by agricultural groups in the nuclear area. Not only were such corporate bodies traditionally too powerful to have shared authority with the aggressive new warrior overlords, but also such stable and responsible groups no longer could speak for the entire agricultural population. The reason for this was that under the aggressive and often ruthless control of warriors, the territories controlled by them rapidly expanded to include forest peoples whose protective foliation was rapidly burned over by the warriors. This, of course, was not a new process; the expansion of nuclear-area settled agriculture was an important aspect of the former period. But the new warriors were anxious to expand their resource base to the maximum, and anxious also to eliminate from their territories the forest refuge of menacing tribal peoples as well as of escapees from their settled territories, and thus drastically stepped up the expansion of their territories. The result was the inclusion of a greater proportion of forest peoples at a faster rate than before. Older, prestigious, agricultural castes and their assemblies could no longer speak for the rapidly changing population.

The warrior regime established in the fourteenth century was comprised of three essential elements, each of which reflected a fundamental change in the integration of the agrarian order. Political power, previously distributed among the principal corporate elements within the nuclear area, was now distributed among a group of warriors in a territory. The primary power-wielder in the territory was the *nayaka* whom early Portugese witnesses wrongly called "captain," implying a structure of subordinate military commands the source of which was supposed to be the Vijayanagar rulers.[25] The *nayaka* system, which was the first of the three fundamental changes in the new agrarian integration, altered the older system in two ways. First, it was a more direct management of agrarian resources accomplished by reducing the autonomous character of Brahman and Sat-Sudra villages and utterly destroying other institutions such as the *periyanadu* and artisan and merchant associations. Secondly, the *nayaka* system produced integration over a substantially larger region than had been encompassed by the nuclear areas. A *nayaka*'s territory would perhaps comprise several nuclear areas plus the previous interstices of forest or upland peoples. The nuclear areas within the *nayaka*'s territories retained their identities, often one of their former names, but surpluses previously managed within the nuclear area were now expropriated by a local leader subordinate to and dependent upon the *nayaka*. Part of this surplus was utilized to support the local leader and a body of soldiers and part of it was transmitted as tribute to the *nayaka*. The *nayaka*, on his part, was obliged to share a portion of his tribute with the great overlords at Vijayanagar.[26] Again, as in the earlier period, one cannot speak of a revenue system—a regular, predictable, and orderly transfer of a portion of wealth to a political authority—but there was a new channeling of resources and wealth through new redistributive centers among which local warriors and their overlords were of first importance.

The second major component of the new integration was a substantial growth in urbanization. Style emulation and the requirements of defense prompted even the most minor warrior to create a fortified headquarters. In comparing the Chola and Vijayanagar inscriptions one cannot avoid noting the change in the idea of "important place." During the earlier period, "place" was conterminous with the nuclear area and its constituent institutions; during the Vijayanagar period, "important place" was the headquarters of a warrior, be he the *nayaka* or a subordinate, and territorial names were frequently the same as the major headquarters town.

As a third major component, the new urbanization was also of economic and religious significance. The new headquarters might become important regional market sites. However, since military requirements were foremost in locating the warrior's headquarters, other places, better situated for trade, developed. Part of the new urbanization was a direct result of autarchic economic policies followed by the new warrior elite. Each warrior attempted to maximize his control over resources within the territory he commanded. One of the important steps taken by many of the warriors to this end was a deliberate policy of attracting artisans from other places in order to achieve self-sufficiency in the stable artisan products, particularly cloth. Autarchic economic policies plus the political requirement of breaking the military capacity of the older merchant associations contributed to the decline of these older merchant associations after the fourteenth century. In place of these older, prestigious, associations of itinerant and local merchant groups, the new trade context, based upon more and direct economic control, contributed to the rise of local merchants—a notable example of which were the Komati merchants of modern Andhra who rose from modest local merchant status to powerful regional merchants under the protection of Telugu warriors whom the Komatis followed to all parts of the southern portions of the peninsula.

Another important feature of this urbanization process was the unprecedented rise of new religious centers based upon temple worship and pilgrimage. This change reflected development in medieval Hindu sect religion, especially Vaishnavism, in which participation in the bhakti devotional religion was opened to many persons who previously had participated on the margins of organized ritual. Temple worship and pilgrimage were important aspects of the new sect religions, and major temple institutions became the centers of sect teaching and ritual. Popular, temple-centered, religious activity not only encouraged the growth of pilgrimage centers, which also became market centers of importance, but it was attended by a decline in the importance of Brahman settlements, the basic importance of which in the earlier period was to provide the same facilities. Support for the new temples of the Vijayanagar period and the urbanization attending temple development came from warriors of the region, most often men of low ritual origin whose participation in temple-oriented Hinduism reflected pretensions to higher rank commensurate with their political power. Other groups also supported the building of temples and support of temple ritual, and the temple inscriptions of the Vijayanagar period permit one to trace the emergence of new influential social groups, such as subordinate warriors and local merchants, as well as Sudra agriculturalists of the region serviced by the temple and its functionaries. As I have pointed out elsewhere, these temples themselves became centers of important agrarian developmental activity. Temples received land and money endowments to maintain ritual performances of religious institutions in perpetuity, and they became involved in schemes of productive agricultural development designed to produce a stable income flow.[27]

The system of warrior power was never a stable one, for there was constant competition among local warriors to expand their control at the expense of a neighboring warrior. Such aggression was subject only to the fitful control of greater warriors in the region culminating in a *nayaka* over a very substantial territory. Unstable though it might have been, this new integration under warriors did serve to achieve a wider integration of settled agricultural villages and the defensive capacity of South India was considerably strengthened for over two centuries.

With respect to social organization in the period, two factors deserve mention. The new urbanization associated with warrior control and temple development raised the status of local artisans and merchants whose contribution to the warrior's wealth was important and whose protection they enjoyed. These groups seized opportunities which permitted them to break away from older restraints of the dual (left- and right-hand) division of castes. Often, also, new artisan and merchant groups were brought in from elsewhere to contribute to the new warrior integration. Certain Brahmans from beyond the locality were also encouraged to migrate to a warrior's territory to serve as ritual func- tionaries, enriching the temple worship and thus enhancing the prestige of the temple and its supporters; other Brahmans served as administra- tive agents of the warrior who valued these foreigners because they were less likely to enter conspiracies and resistance activities of older, estab- lished groups of the area. Deshastha Brahmans from Maharashtra were introduced into many places in Tamil country for this latter reason. There was thus a weakening of local solidarity as the new, enlarged regions of warrior authority achieved a degree of cosmopolitanism with the addition of prestigeful carriers of other cultural traditions.

The breaking of older bonds is even more clearly reflected in the transformation of the right-hand and left-hand divisions which had been relatively stable and integrated social alliance systems through which new members of nuclear-area society were assimilated in the older period. During the Vijayanagar period, with the increased tempo of expansion of settled village agriculture into what were previously forested zones, the influx of forest peoples also greatly increased and undoubtedly strained the capacity of the alliance systems to accom- modate and adjust not only to new numbers but to the changing context of society brought into being by the assumption of warrior control. Urbanization, in particular, created a source of strain on the alliance systems and produced the pattern of disorders, the latent purpose of which, I believe, was to cause adjudication and the affirmation of traditional rights in a changing society.[28] The competitive, often violent, relationship between the right- and left-hand alliances of castes dates from this period of Vijayanagar integration. From that time, the balanced relationship between dominant agricultural interests (agricultural castes and artisan and merchant castes associated with them) and non-agricultural groups broke down. This reflected the enlarged arena of agrarian integration of Vijayanagar times under the greater exploitation of warriors and resulted in a breakdown of those social and cultural controls which had characterized the older nuclear areas.

### Early British Integration

By 1800, the English East India Company had come to control a large part of the southern peninsula. Company territory exploded in less than a decade from a few scattered holdings, most important being the "Jaghir" (modern Chingleput District) and the Northern Circars (the deltaic districts of modern Andhra Pradesh), to include most of the rest of the peninsula. In 1792, after the Third Mysore War, the Company acquired Salem, Dindigul, and Malabar. Seven years later, with the final defeat of Mysore under Tipu Sultan and the establishment of a diminished Mysore kingdom, the districts of Canara and Coimbatore were added to the Company's control. In the same year, 1799, Tanjore was acquired from the Maratha Raja; and in 1800, the Company was ceded the territories south of the rivers Kistna and Tungabhadra, comprising the districts of Cuddapah, Bellary, Anantapur, and part of Kurnool by the Nizam of Hyderabad. Finally, in 1801, the Nawab of Arcot, long a suffragan of the Company, was compelled to cede the Carnatic tracts comprising the districts of Nellore, North and South Arcot, Trichinopoly, Madura, and Tinnevelly. The Company thus disposed of the major Indian overlords who had held sway, and what remained of the elite local leadership of the Vijayanagar and post-Vijayanagar period was destroyed in the consolidation and first establishment of Company collectorates in the late eighteenth century. In short, by 1800, a new effective overlordship was established—that of "Company raj."

The following fifty years in the history of the agrarian system have been viewed by most scholars as a period of transition. South India, it has been said, was passing from the chaos of the eighteenth century into the orderly growth and progress of the nineteenth century.[29] Such a view seems untenable. It is true that inchoate and violent warrior rule was destroyed by the end of the eighteenth century; however, it was replaced by an early British rule which was only somewhat less disorganized and violent. Tax farming and village lease arrangements under the Company permitted wealthy, influential groups to exploit weaker groups within village and locality and to expropriate public funds from under the noses of the first English agents. These Englishmen were helplessly ignorant about the people they were supposed to be ruling, and they were, from the first, under severe career pressures to maintain the highest revenue flows from their jurisdictions. The early period of the Ryotwari Settlement, before 1822, did little to reduce these problems; indeed, it was not until the revised Ryotwari Settlement, decided upon in 1855 but not completed until much later in the century, that revenue problems were, if not resolved, at least reduced in importance.[30]

But, for those scholars who see the period from 1800 to 1850 as a period of agrarian transition, the crucial transitional criteria have to do with the distress of most of the peasantry arising from famines and the decline of prices between 1800 and 1850. Severe famines occurred in 1799–1800, 1804–07, 1811–12, 1824, and 1833–34. In the next two decades the most serious agrarian problem was a secular decline in commodity prices. This price crisis apparently arose from the widespread monetization of the agricultural economy without a concomitant and proportionate increase in the supply of money.[31]

Famines and the price problem resulted from a set of factors which may be said to signal a new agrarian integration. These factors included the revenue measures of the Company, especially overassessment and overcollection, poor communications with agricultural markets, and insufficient support to irrigation. To those viewing these factors and their effects as transitional, the turning point came after the 1850's when the revenue demand was reduced and the system began to be revised to encourage increased peasant investment in productive capacity, especially well construction; when cash crops such as indigo and sugarcane became more important; and when the Government undertook programs of large-scale irrigation works, constructed roads to improve communications and for general market purposes, and sought to find and encourage the cultivation of new cash crops.

Yet, the very nature of the conditions of distress between 1800 and 1850 point to basic changes in the agrarian order by 1800. Eric Stokes seems to advance this proposition when he argues that whether one looks at the Cornwallis system in Bengal, with admittedly "modernizing" (Anglicizing) objectives, or at the Munro system in Madras, with avowedly cautious and conserving objectives, there was a profound and early impact of British institutions and usages.[32] In assessing the British impact, however, care must be taken to distinguish between the mature British agrarian system of the late nineteenth century and the early variant of that system of 1800. The mature system of the late century was based upon (1) a virtually complete market-oriented, money-mediated allocation of agrarian resources—human and non-human—under (2) a framework of regulations administered by a provincially centralized bureaucracy staffed by a combination of Englishmen and Indians in which (3) conflicts were adjudicated by a judicature in which both procedural and substantive rules were statutory. This mature system grew out of conditions which were implied and given by the conditions of the late eighteenth century and the culture of the Englishmen who took the first administrative steps in India.

Two prime factors influenced the integration achieved by 1800. The first was the nature of the East India Company. As an influence, the Company was more significant in the integration of the eighteenth and nineteenth centuries than the extension of Muslim power had been in the integration by the warrior elite of the fourteenth century. The Company, like the earlier warrior elite, was not wholly external to the system which it came to dominate. The warrior elite consisted of men who valued and supported the Hindu, caste-integrated culture, and while different from and more violent than the Brahmans and Sat-Sudras who controlled the order prior to the fourteenth century, these warriors could easily maintain a place in their new order. So, too, the Company. Though it had begun its career in early seventeenth-century India with a vulnerable series of trade stations ("factories"), the intervening century had witnessed a profound change in its status. Unrecognized by the contemporary servants of the Company, whose ample records of the seventeenth and early eighteenth centuries we have, and virtually unrecognized by historians of this period, the Company had achieved the status of significant local leadership.[33] Along with the French Company at Pondicherry, the English Company had slowly, tentatively, and over the reluctance of directors in Europe expanded their influence from the walled fortresses on the coast to command a considerable hinterland. From here, they mobilized not only commodities for their trade but also extracted tribute, or, what they called, "rent."[34] In this hinterland, both

European companies operated as local leaders in essentially the same way as the Indian warriors of the sixteenth and seventeenth centuries; and while the records of the English Company at Fort St. George (Madras) are full of the frustrated reports of trade hazards in a countryside torn by warfare among local Indian leaders, it is clear that the Company, in order to protect its trade and the Indian artisans and merchants whose production was the foundation of this trade, became a powerful, political force. By virtue of the highly defensible, walled city of Madras, a well-trained body of Indian soldiers led by European officers, fleet support in the Bay of Bengal, and a revenue base on the land, the English Company had matured into a formidable political and military force in South Indian politics.

In the light of this development, the bold policies of Dupliex, head of the French Company at Pondicherry, become more comprehensible. It does not denigrate the accomplishment of Dupliex to say that he simply formulated and carried out a systematic policy for maximizing the opportunities of control afforded by the French position of overlordship in their territories. Given the increasingly vulnerable position of the French relative to British sea power, some new French policies became necessary by the late 1740's. This crisis of the mid-seventeenth century has been well established by historians. Less clearly seen, however, was the fact that neither the French nor English companies were so much establishing a new status for themselves as "Indian country-powers" as extending an already achieved position to wider limits. Sir Josiah Child, who dominated the Court of Directors of the English Company in the late seventeenth century, saw the possibility of this development precociously, but took on too formidable an adversary in Aurangzeb.[35] By the middle of the eighteenth century, the circumstances were ripe for a movement forward by the Europeans, not as foreign powers, but as well-integrated Indian powers.

Having argued that the European companies had achieved powerful positions as local leaders within the warrior-controlled political system of South India by 1750, I should note the differences between them and their rivals. First, there was a set of differences arising from the fact that they were Europeans and merchants. As eighteenth-century Europeans, they were carriers of a culture in the midst of striking florescence —a Europe moving rapidly toward modernity. In the spheres of science and technology, in political organization, in economic activities, Europe was changing with unprecedented speed. This transformation of Europe was to enable Europeans to extend their control over most of the rest of the world during the next century. The Europeans at Fort St. George and Pondicherry possessed a military capacity which provided impressive advantages over Indian competitors as well as wealth for controlling the productive capacities of an increasingly large group of Indians through a system of advances, standardized production, and continuity of leadership which brought to positions of leadership in Madras and elsewhere men of ability recruited in Europe for their prospective abilities in commerce and also for their abilities in civil administration.[36] All of these attributes gave them enormous advantages in their bid to extend their power.

As merchants, the servants of the European companies had not overtly challenged the established warrior powers of South India. The companies, sequestered in their coastal territories, had long been isolated from the mainstream of conflict among Indian warriors. European traders followed the early-seventeenth–century dictum of Sir Thomas Roe regarding peaceful trade[37] and, later, chastened by the humiliating defeat at the hands of Aurangzeb, the East India Company had come to terms with the existing system and seemed to pose no threat to the established, albeit unstable, order. Dutifully, the companies paid their tribute (*peshkash*) through the seventeenth and early eighteenth centuries, and they suffered additional charges upon their trade.[38] However, the Europeans were inconspicuously (and largely unconsciously) building political and military power within their coastal territories, and, when they did begin to reach beyond their narrow coastal spheres in the middle of the eighteenth century, they broke upon an agrarian order which was as exposed as that of the Brahman–Sat-Sudra order had been to the Telugu and low-caste warriors in the fourteenth century.

The second order of difference between the Europeans of the middle of the eighteenth century and other local leaders of the time was a result of the first. Being foreigners and involved in a trade system which was marginal to the agrarian order, the companies were not encumbered by the restraints which operated upon Indian local leaders who were closely tied to agrarian institutions. This is a fact of central importance.

As explained above, the system of local and regional overlordship which was established in the fourteenth century combined two basic and countervailing elements. One was the ceaseless competition of armed power among warriors over narrow localities as well as over broad regions. In this competition, there were no developed institutional or broad political means of stabilizing a particular distribution of power, for example, through bureaucratic continuity or hierarchies of loyalty.[39] Opposing this element of violent competition was the necessity of every local and regional overlord to heed the constituency of corporate interests within the area of his power. Local leaders relied upon the support of caste brethren and allied castes; they were compelled to recognize and deal with the interests of any other corporate entities as well, including prestigious priests and sect leaders, merchant and artisan groups, and village assemblies. And while it is true that the effective self-government of such corporate units was reduced by these warriors, these privileges were not wholly gone. Thus, responsiveness to kinship and traditional local interests had to be balanced against the full use of coercion of which the ambitious warrior might be capable. This balance worked against the Tamil, Telugu, and Maratha warriors in South India by the eighteenth century and placed them at a disadvantage against the new power ambitions of the Europeans. Without the restraints of kin and locality connections and possessed of a different set of values and institutions which were European ones adapted to the Indian context through a century of trade, the European companies were in a position to establish control over agrarian elements over most of the South by 1800.

In political terms, the most significant result of English control upon agrarian relations and institutions by 1800 was the suppression of the warrior elite of the previous four centuries. Even a casual examination of the first half-century of British rule, 1750–1800, reveals how extensive were the activities and costs of pacifying much of South India. Unfortunately, this extended period of violent "police actions" has not been adequately recognized because few of the actions were of such a magnitude to warrant the appellation "war." It is interesting to notice that what the English Company was doing in the Carnatic and southern districts of what became the Madras Presidency was also being done in the northern districts of the later Presidency by the Muslim overlords of Mysore, Haider Ali and his son Tipu Sultan, in about the same period.[40] The only prolonged campaign against the local southern overlords by the Company was that of 1799–1800, remembered as the "Poligar War."[41] These pacification campaigns resulted in the destruction of a class of local leaders who were either killed, forced to flee and lose themselves in the population, or converted to the status of "zamindar" in the Bengal fashion of the early nineteenth century.

Elimination of this traditional warrior elite by about 1800 resulted in a truncated political structure that had important implications for the next fifty years or more. The reestablishment of the earliest elite of Brahmans and Sat-Sudras in the manner of the Chola period was impossible. The pacification campaigns from 1750 to 1800 generated the need for revenue far beyond any previous level and beyond that obtainable from the older "home" territory of the Company around Madras and elsewhere on the coast or in the new territories acquired after 1750. Hence, there could be no question of reestablishing the order of the Chola period in which control of the agricultural surplus was vested with corporate groups such as the *mahasabhas* of the Brahman villages. Even if such institutions were capable of being restored to their former importance, which is highly doubtful after the centuries of domination under the warrior controllers of the land and its people, the Company was in no sense disposed in this direction. Needed instead were means to mobilize the surplus more fully than ever before for the expensive objectives of Company policy.

The initial means adopted by the Company were various forms of tax farming. Tax farming and other revenue assignment arrangements were also utilized by the Mysore rulers Haider Ali and Tipu Sultan at about the same time in their territories to the west of Madras and by warriors in other parts of India. The military capabilities and ambitions of Mysore led to two costly and difficult wars which were fought to determine whose overlordship was to prevail in the South. After the Third Mysore War in 1799, the Company was free to pursue the expansion of its control without serious challenge; however, the English did not develop an alternative to tax farming until the firm establishment of the ryotwari system in the 1820's when Thomas Munro, the chief architect of this system, had become governor of the Madras Presidency. Between 1792, when the system was first introduced in Salem by Alexander Read, and 1822, when Munro firmly established ryotwari as the revenue system for the Presidency, appropriation of the surplus varied and changed constantly.[42] The chaos attending these revenue procedures provided opportunities for Brahmans, Sat-Sudras, and some wealthy merchants to reassert themselves once again, but now under wholly new circumstances.

The Company needed links with the peasantry who came under Company control as a result of its military operations. Brahmans and respectable Sudras, and also some of the merchant castes, possessed a set of qualifications which filled the deficiencies and met the structural requirements of this early period of British agrarian management. These qualifications were: (1) They were peaceful and did not challenge British control as the warrior elite had. (2) They were literate and could follow written directives and maintain records required by the British. (3) They were prestigious members of society able not only to communicate with the peasant-villager (as the British could not) but respected by the peasantry as well. (4) They were wealthy enough to meet the British money requirements. At the very outset of British expansion, shortly after 1750, the Company had sought these qualifications in the warrior elite, but was finally compelled to recognize that their interests and those of the warriors were fundamentally divergent. Hence, respectable, wealthy, and peaceful segments of South Indian society were eagerly seized upon in the late years of the eighteenth century as the most readily available means for accomplishing the measure of control sought by the Company at the time.

These respectable groups of South Indians were not passive agents in the system of control established by the Company in the late eighteenth century. They quickly perceived the opportunities for advancing their social and economic interests under the canopy of Company protection and in the absence of the formerly powerful warriors under whose difficult subordination they had previously lived. The truncated political order which resulted from the pacification provided wide scope for the landed Brahman and Sudra groups as well as for merchants to establish themselves as a complex layer of adept and influential manipulators between the Company and the peasantry. What Robert Frykenberg has described in Guntur during the period could be replicated in most of the other districts of the Presidency.[43] This new class of agrarian leaders profoundly altered the structure of agrarian relations well into the nineteenth century.

Destruction of the warrior elite severed the integrative spatial bonds within the older agrarian system of South India. What were constituted in the place of the warriors' territories were expediently drawn, agro-administrative units—revenue districts. The British revenue district was based substantially upon preexisting, recognized tribute regions, but differed from such older areas in that Company authority—foreign in origin, mercantile in orientation, and rational in operation—bore directly upon the agrarian system.

The revenue district was to serve as the locus of British management

of the agrarian system until the later nineteenth century when there was
a rapid development of a centralized, provincial bureaucracy in the city
of Madras. From the late eighteenth century until the 1840's there was
no responsive and well-articulated centralized authority under the Company in most places. Thus, when the role of the collector, the Company
agent in charge of the district, is compared to that of the previous warrior, the difference with respect to control over local affairs was one of
degree only. The early British collectors were charged with executing
policies and regulations framed by the Board of Revenue in Madras, but
in most cases, the collectors were permitted to substantially modify these
policies and regulations to meet local requirements. Actually, the degree
of control from the Madras was quite light, and this permitted the
greatest adaptiveness to local peculiarities.

From 1750 to 1850, minute regulations from the Madras headquarters of the Company were lacking or, at best, intermittent. The
basic objectives of the Company's agents in the field, the collectors, were
the same in all of the districts: maximum extraction of the agrarian
surplus. The costs to the Company of the pacification campaigns and
wars of the late eighteenth century against the Mysore and Maratha
states required the most complete mobilization of the surplus ever
sought in the South. Company forces were mercenaries, not plunderers
as were the older armies; both the Indian sepoys and the British soldiers
had to be paid, provisions had to be purchased and transported over
substantial distances, and other charges, swollen by the exigencies of
campaigning, had to be met. The Company could not rely upon trade receipts in this troubled time, nor would the Court of Directors in London
lightly sanction sufficient special allocations from other sources to
defray the military expenses. Hence, the demand for revenue was high.
Moreover, the revenue was sought in money; grain and other payments
in kind were cumbersome and unsatisfactory. Each collector was under
the most profound pressure to transmit the largest possible money
revenue after the charges of his own administration were met, and his
performance (hence his career) was measured on this criterion alone.
As the Board of Revenue was to state in 1812: "Collectors newly
appointed to newly acquired territory, unfettered by judicial regulations,
at a distance from control, [were] excited by the hope of increasing the
Public Revenue and establishing their own official reputations."[44]

To 1800, the East India Company collectors made no systematic
and deliberate changes in the South Indian agrarian system. Under the

policy of paternalism to which the Munro administrators were committed, such programmatic changes were eschewed. Moreover, owing to the pressure of generating the maximum revenue from their jurisdictions and being fundamentally confused about the people they were governing, the collectors could do little else until about 1800. However, a profound change was underway as a result of the military actions of the Company from 1750 to 1800 which deposed the earlier warrior elite. The opportunities to Brahmans, Sat-Sudras, and other influential people to vastly deepen their control over agrarian resources and the demand for a high money revenue coupled with the continued focus upon and efforts to normalize trade receipts were the opening wedges of change. Added to these developments, the effects of the ryotwari revenue system with its emphasis upon "private property" and the early efforts to alter existing legal usages to cognize the English ideas of contract and property resulted in an agrarian revolution, or, at least, an agrarian reintegration.

The full character of the agrarian changes discussed above were to become perfectly clear by the end of the century. Aspects of this mature system have been described elsewhere and are not appropriately the subject of this discussion.

### Summary

This tentative and preliminary discussion of aspects of agrarian integration in South India is meant to set forth major elements of the argument that the development of the South Indian agrarian system may be seen through three episodes of integration between the ninth and the nineteenth centuries. As these episodes are hypotheses which have emerged from work which I have so far completed on the agrarian system of the South, and as these hypotheses will guide subsequent work, the argument cannot be concluded here, merely summarized. This summary will consider a comparison of (1) the nature of agrarian regions and the scale of integration achieved in such regions during the three periods and (2) the major elements which made for integration *within* the agrarian region in the three periods.

### *Regions and Scale of Integration*

By "the nature of agrarian regions" I mean the constellation of land-associated, social, cultural, and political elements whose congruent distribution defined an agrarian region. Here, region is taken to mean a portion of land surface which differs from others by reason of the presence of some element or a set of elements. The actual areal extent of such agrarian regions in the same period would be highly variable according to natural and other factors.

During the earliest of the three periods, the Pallava-Chola period of the ninth to the thirteenth centuries, the agrarian region was what I have called the "nuclear area" of early corporate institutions. This is a region defined in terms of a set of social and cultural elements which provided a distinctive character to landed communities over a substantial portion of South India at the time. The *brahmadeya,* Brahman village, gave this region its basic character as a sociocultural, or civilizational, unit. Here, various ethnic groupings were organized into self-governing corporate bodies under the leadership of learned Brahman assemblies, the *mahasabhas.* The corporate element giving definition to the region was even more evident in the little-recognized assembly called the *periyanadu,* or "great country" assembly, which included not only Brahmans but also the spokesmen of other influential corporate bodies, such as respectable Sat-Sudras, itinerant guildsmen, local artisans, and merchants. Each of these had an important voice in the *periyanadu* assembly which legislated for the nuclear area in matters of common concern. By the twelfth century at least, low status people of the nuclear areas were integrated into the characteristic dual division alliances of castes of the nuclear region. The ecological concomitant of the sociocultural components of these nuclear areas were those which provided means for productive agriculture based upon riverine or tank irrigation. In those places favored by such conditions, as in Cholamandalam and Tondaimandalam (present-day Tanjore and Tiruchirapalli and North and South Arcot), the distribution of nuclear areas was relatively dense; in other places nuclear areas might be widely separated. In either case, however, the nuclear areas were often in close proximity to upland and forest tracts sparsely populated by groups who lived by slash-and-burn agriculture and hunting and whose relatively primitive economy and social organization set them apart from people of the nuclear areas. While there was a tendency for the more powerful nuclear-area people to expand their territories into the hill and forest tracts, the rate of such expansion was slow and controlled. These corporate nuclear areas tended to be quite stable over time.

During the second episode of agrarian integration of the fourteenth and fifteenth centuries, the agrarian region is best defined by tributary arrangements among warriors. As compared with the relatively stable agrarian regions of the Pallava-Chola period, the territory of a warrior was evanescent and constantly changing in conformity with his fortune. It is only in the reign of the greatest Vijayanagar overlord, Krishnadevaraya (1509–29), that some degree of stability was temporarily achieved. While the extent of the agrarian region shifted in this period, depending upon the skill and power of the overlord in extracting tribute from numerous local leaders, such a unit might include one or more of the older nuclear areas plus forest and upland extensions by warriors determined to maximize the territory of their control and so strengthen themselves for the inevitable challenges from others like themselves.[45] The persistent tactic of warrior overlordship was to seize maximum control over the productive capacities of tracts which they could hold militarily. This resulted in violent competitiveness, a mark of the era. The warrior overlords attempted to control some institutions, such as village assemblies and local artisan and merchant groups, and to eliminate others, such as the older nuclear-area assemblies and itinerant guilds, since they were dangerous to their ambitions. Urbanization of three basic kinds—military, economic, and religious—accompanied the development of these warrior-dominated regions and gave them a quality quite different from the older regions.

The agrarian region of the early British period was the revenue district. These units were formed in the period prior to 1800 on the basis of military exigency and the particular treaty terms under which territories were added to Company control. In this period of British dominance of the agrarian system, there was no attempt to alter the fortuitous aggregration of lands comprising the first collectorates; they were maintained as the grouping of tribute territories which were acquired during the period of military actions by the Company from 1750.

The integrity of older warrior overlordships was undermined by the results of British military policies which destroyed the warrior elite of the previous several centuries. Deprived of the elite structure, the political system of South India in the late eighteenth century permitted a new local elite to emerge, consisting of respectable, peaceful, and prestigious men. These were not "new men" in the sense that they represented groups who had not before held prominent agrarian positions. The Brahmans, Sat-Sudras, and merchants occupied positions intermediate between the British collectors, befuddled by the society and ways of the Indians whom they had come to rule, and the mass of peasantry, denied

traditional rights and subject to excessive revenue demands. This elite
was descended from those who had dominated the earliest period of
agrarian integration. However, they lacked the great corporate solidarity and control of their predecessors, and they were in the uneasy
position of mediating the power of men who lacked basic knowledge of
the people they ruled.

The rulers of early British agrarian units—English collectors—were
directly charged with transmitting the maximum revenue from their
jurisdictions and were committed, by their basic value orientations and
the fundamental objectives of their rule in India, to a monetized agrarian
economy. The full operation of the British system did not occur until
late in the century, though the major elements of the British integration
were evident by 1800.

With respect to the scale of integration achieved under these agrarian
units, it is clear that there was a considerable increase in scale through
time. The British revenue district comprehended a large territory comprised of many of the older nuclear areas and a number of warrior
territories. These units were large and diverse. In general, the agrarian
units changed from those based upon corporately organized social groups
of the earliest period through the dominantly locality-centered, kin- and
caste-organized system of the middle period to the atomized and formally organized system of the British.

*Integration within Agrarian Regions.*

Considerable emphasis must be placed upon the *periyanadu* assembly
as the most significant agency for the integration of the corporate nuclear area. Though little is known of this institution, inscriptional evidence from a number of nuclear areas suggests that this body was
responsive to, if not dominated by, powerful groups of agriculturists
and that its competence was general over the region. Inscriptions of this
assembly indicate that the better-known *mahasabhas* of the Brahman
villages were subordinate. Yet, this cannot diminish the significance of
the Brahman institution in setting the Hindu and caste-ordered culture
of the nuclear area, nor its importance in managing agrarian resources
within the nuclear area. Decidedly less is known about the assemblies
in peasant villages (*ur*), but those for which there are extant records
suggest that Sat-Sudras occupied positions of respect and power, especially within *periyanadu* assemblies.[46] Finally, the corporate power of

artisans and merchants, while not central to the agrarian functions of nuclear areas, was considerable.

No effort has been made here, or elsewhere for that matter, to distinguish among nuclear areas of this period with respect to the degrees and modes of internal integration. We cannot be certain that all nuclear areas had comprehensive *periyanadu* assemblies or that all such assemblies functioned in the same way. It may be suggested that the nuclear areas in the vicinity of the Pallava and Chola overlords, at Kanchipuram, Tanjore, and a few other subordinate headquarters, were subject to the direct control of these warriors.

The most significant factor of internal integration in this early period was the obvious strength of corporate groups consisting of clusterings of allied castes which cooperated in various ways to maintain the overall integration of these core tracts of Hindu civilization and to manage agrarian resources under the general supervision of Brahmans and Sat-Sudras. This degree of local control under corporate groupings may have been a unique characteristic of South India in this early period; there is no evidence to support the contention of some scholars that it was widespread, and some evidence suggests that it was not.[47]

By the fourteenth century, internal agrarian organization and integration came closer to the mode of much of North India; that is, agrarian organization was based upon the relationship of groups of persons with the dominant warrior authority of the locality. Put another way, the agrarian organization which replaced the previous nuclear area could be defined by the flow of tribute from those on the land through a series of warrior overlords. In northern India, where this relationship achieved an element of stability owing to the widespread, kin-linked control of putative or genuine Rajputs, the onslaught of Muslim and then English overlordships caused most groups merely to slip down from one level of control to a lower one. A similar "structural slippage" may be said to have occurred in the South during the middle period of agrarian integration when the key groups within the earlier corporate area—Brahmans and Sat-Sudras—slipped from an important place among the local leadership to become essentially village leaders (*mirasidars* of the early British period) under local warriors. However, the structure of political and agrarian relations in the South never attained the kin-linked integration of the northern military control and was thus unstable in most places.

Warriors of South India from the fourteenth century to the late eighteenth century relied for management and control of agrarian resources upon relatively stable connections with dominant landed groups and through control over urban places. The urban places—fortified headquarters, market towns, and religious and pilgrimage towns—were created by the local warriors and their superordinate overlords as means for extracting the greatest tribute from landed communities. At the most local level, the established villages of cultivators in the older nuclear areas or in newly opened, reclaimed forest land were members of the dominant cultivating castes, tribal communities, or, more rarely, Brahmans. Such village and local leaders were required to aggregate tribute payments for more powerful leaders who dispatched agents to make collections. Such superior warriors (most of whom the British called *poligars*) occupied the first tier of urban locations—small fortified towns, hardly more than large villages, but with more diverse functions, including a local market and minor religious center. Over this level of warriors, who were usually men who represented an important segment of the local population, were the more powerful warriors, as for example the *nayakas* of the sixteenth century. These men were either of local origin and confirmed in their positions by the great overlords of Vijayanagar, or they were strangers who had carved a place for themselves through superior military capacity. In the early part of the period, the fourteenth to sixteenth centuries, these strangers were from the Telugu-speaking northern tracts; later, they were Maratha speakers from the West.

It would be wrong to conceive of these arrangements of power as orderly—a system of fixed tiers based on explicit or implicit principles. Such they were not. The forms through which warrior power of the middle period integrated the agrarian system were as varied as the diverse social contexts of South India in the period. A typology of localities in this period is one of the urgent requirements for further work on agrarian relations at the time.

The establishment of British power fixed few of the highly fluid internal integrative elements as they had existed in the middle period. In this sense, the impact of early British rule in South India may have differed fundamentally from the North. "Fossilization," in most respects, was averted by the elimination of the warrior elite to a degree that appears different from the North.[48] Yet, the internal integration of agrarian relationships bore certain elements of continuity as of 1800.

The vaguely defined and kaleidescopically changing warrior-dominated territories over which the British established control have been defined in terms of tribute flows from village and local leaders to superior warriors. The Company aggregated into subunits of the revenue district tribute territories found to exist upon their conquest, and, in a ruthless manner, the Company converted irregular, negotiated, tribute payments of money and grain into regular, fixed payments of money. Though this process was a lengthy one and not fully realized until late in the nineteenth century, ascendant Company political power permits us to posit that a new internal integration of agrarian resources and relations had occurred by 1800.

As early as 1800, the internal integration of the Company agrarian region, the revenue district, pointed to the final transformation of the impressive corporate institutions of the earliest period. From the fourteenth century, the triumphant warriors exerted pressure to break the corporate structure of South Indian agrarian life. Certain of the overarching, corporate institutions—the *periyanadu* assemblies and the itinerant guilds—were crushed, and other institutions were compelled to yield much of their authority in the middle period. This condition was required by the warriors, the fullness of whose power necessitated a reduction of corporate solidarity. Corporate institutions were further weakened by the British as a result of the tensions of the new internal ordering, especially the greater urban-centeredness, on the one side, and the atomization of crucial agrarian relations, on the other side.

The rise of the provincial capital at Madras and the twenty-odd district headquarters constituted a basic change in South India because the local elite of the nineteenth century became inextricably associated with these places. This elite of Brahmans and Sudras was able to enjoy pivotal power in the locality without checks from the other local groups, in contrast to the earlier two periods when the constituency of the locality severely limited the scope of the local elite. Validation of the local elite of the early nineteenth century came from a remote district town or an even more remote provincial city; protection of this status also emanated from these remote places, and recruitment to the local elite required access to elements which were of the British-dominated urban area—knowledge of English and related symbolic skills as well as contact, through family links or otherwise, with persons already in Company service. This heightened urban focus did not diminish the control over agrarian resources which the local elite enjoyed; it increased it. However, the fact that the ultimate sources of elite status were these urban places served to diminish the reciprocal character of agrarian relations which had previously existed. The nineteenth-century rural elite held great agrarian power with little agrarian responsibility.

Simultaneously, the internal structuring of village and locality agrarian relations was altered by vesting control over land in the hands of individual families. By the middle of the nineteenth century, one-third of the cultivated acreage in the Presidency was held by persons on zamindari or permanent tenure and the remainder under ryotwari *pattas*, or leases. Access to land holding status was open to all groups, excluding only the traditional castes of landless laborers. While it is true that the individualization of land control and the opening of this possibility to a larger segment of the population than ever before was of little consequence until later in the century, when rates of revenue were reduced and the growing population encouraged more persons to take up ryotwari land, the possibility of this fundamental change weakened older agrarian relations.

Summarizing the changes in the internal ordering of agrarian life during the three periods, it may be said that integration of caste groups through the operation of corporate social groups within a cooperative context was successively eroded. By the nineteenth century, even the very beginning of the century, the pattern of integration had become increasingly atomized and responsive to the formal rules of early Company authority.

## NOTES

1  Delhi, 1956, p. 2.
2  New York, 1963, p. vii.
3  B. H. Baden-Powell, *The Land Systems of British India* (3 vols.; Oxford, 1892); W. H. Moreland, *The Agrarian System of Moslem India* (Cambridge, 1929); K. M. Gupta, *The Land System of South India between c. 800 A.D. and 1200 A.D.* (Lahore, 1933); M. N. Gupta, *Land System of Bengal* (Calcutta, 1940).
4  See Burton Stein, "Coromandel Trade in Medieval India," in John Parker (ed.), *Merchants and Scholars* (Minneapolis, 1965), pp. 47–62.
5  K. V. Subrahmanya Aiyer, "The Largest Provincial Assemblies in India," *The Quarterly Journal of the Mythic Society* (Bangelore), XLV, No. 1, 29–47; *ibid.*, No. 2, 70–98; *ibid.*, No. 4, 270–86; *ibid.*, XLVI, No. 1, 8–22.
6  Modern analyses of the South India variant of caste organization are rare and unsatisfactory. Exceptions are the studies by M. Marriott and E. K. Gough: McKim Marriott, *Caste Ranking and Community Structure in Five Regions*

*of India and Pakistan* (Poona, 1960), especially pp. 31–36 for the "Coromandel type"; and E. Kathleen Gough, "Caste in a Tanjore Village," in E. R. Leach (ed.), *Aspects of Castes in South India, Ceylon, and Northwest Pakistan* (Cambridge, 1960), pp. 11–60. Other, more detailed statements on regional caste organization are: N. Subha Reddi, "Community Conflict among the Depressed Castes of Andhra," *Man in India*, XXX, No. 4 (1950), 1–12; C. S. Crole, *The Chingleput (Late Madras) District: A Manual* (Madras, 1879), p. 33 ff.; J. H. Nelson, *The Madura Country: A Manual* (Madras, 1868), p. 4 ff.; C. S. Srinivasachari, "The Origin of the Right and Left Hand Caste Division," *Journal of the Andhra Historical Research Society*, IV (1929), 77–85; C. M. Ramachandra Chettiar, "Social Legislation in Ancient South India," *Quarterly Journal of the Mythic Society*, XXI (1930–31), 341–53, and XXII (1931–32), 65–71; Government of India, *Annual Report of South Indian Epigraphy, 1921* (Madras, 1922), Par. 47 (hereafter cited as *A.R.E.* followed by the year of the report).

7   B. Ramaswami Naidu, "Remarks on the Revenue System and Landed Tenures of the Provinces under the Madras Presidency of Fort St. George," *Journal of the Royal Asiatic Society*, 1834, pp. 295–96.

8   M. Arokiaswami, *The Early History of the Velar Basin with Special Reference to the Irukkuvels of Kodumbalur* (Madras, 1954), p. 36.

9   K. A. Nilakanta Sastri, *The Colas* (Madras, 1955), p. 36.

10  This concept is related to and derived from the usage of the late B. Subbarao, *The Personality of India* (Baroda, 1956), p. 6, where he spoke of "areas of attraction of perennial nuclear regions."

11  K. A. Nilakanta Sastri, *Studies in Cola History and Administration* (Madras, 1932), pp. 96–175; V. Venkayya, "Two Inscriptions at Uttaramallur," in Government of India, *Archaeological Survey Annual Report, 1904–5* (Calcutta, 1908), pp. 131–45.

12  *Ibid.*

13  For example, R. K. Mookerji, *Local Government in Ancient India* (2nd ed., rev.; Oxford, 1920).

14  *A.R.E. 1900*, No. 117, from Tirukkoyilur, South Arcot, thirteenth century. A *padakku* equals two *kuruni* or one cubic foot (A. Appadorai, *Economic Conditions in Southern India, 1000–1500* A.D. [Madras, 1936], II, 783).

15  A grant to a Jain temple follows. *A.R.E., 1902*, No. 601 copied at Anbil, Tiruchirapalli District, dated 1235 A.D. I express my gratitude to Sri J. Sundaram, Epigraphical Assistant of the Office of Epigraphist, Government of India, for his aid in the translation of this and the preceding inscription; he is not responsible for the use I have made of these inscriptions.

16  Subrahmanya Aiyer, *op. cit.*, No. 4, 277–78.

17  *Ibid.*, 282.

18  There are a number of reasons for the vagueness in the names and boundaries of major areas of population and settled society. The evidence upon which virtually all of the historical reconstruction of this period rests is inscriptional—records of temples, *mathas* (seminaries), and religious settlements such as *brahmadeyas*. These records deal with grants to religious institutions and only tangentially, in the introductory sections, called *prasastis*, is there information of a non-religious nature. There is no intent in the *prasastis* to provide an accurate or even a consistent description of the political system; rather, it is the purpose of these introductory verses to affirm the hero-

credentials of the donor or some highly placed patron. Moreover, these records are not often retrospective and only rarely is there a series for one place, such as Uttaramerur, which permits charting changes over time.

19 An interesting inscription dealing with this artisan group is *A.R.E., 1908,* No. 479, of the twelfth century. It is commented upon in some detail in Par. 45 of *A.R.E., 1909.*

20 A group of inscriptions collected in Tiruchirapalli District in 1912 and 1913, reported in *A.R.E., 1913,* Par. 39, are especially interesting. These inscriptions plus others suggest that between the two alliance systems of low-caste persons there was a relatively higher status associated with the right-hand group of castes, as one would infer from the polluting nature of the left hand in India. The relatively higher status of the right-hand castes also affirms the superior prestige of agricultural pursuits with which most right-hand castes are identified.

21 K. A. Nilakanta Sastri, *A History of South India* (London, 1955), p. 295.

22 Migratory peasants seeking relief from the excessive demands of local over-lords are reported for North India for a somewhat later period by Habib, *op. cit.,* pp. 328–29, passim.

23 The word "fief" has been inappropriately used for *amaram* by many writers, e.g., T. V. Mahalingam, *Economic Life in the Vijayanagar Empire* (Madras, 1951), p. 88; the *amaram* never possessed the relatively consistent set of privileges and responsibilities of the European fief.

24 D. D. Kosambi, "The Basis of Ancient Indian History, II," *Journal of the American Oriental Society,* LXXIV, No. 4 (1955), 330–37.

25 Robert Sewell, *A Forgotten Empire; Vijayanagar* (Delhi, 1962), pp. 269 and 355.

26 *Ibid.,* pp. 354 and 365 ff.

27 Burton Stein, "Economic Functions of a Medieval South Indian Temple," *Journal of Asian Studies,* IX, No. 2 (1960), 163–76, and "The State, the Temple, and Agricultural Development in Medieval South India," *Economic Weekly Annual,* 1961, pp. 179–87.

28 I refer here to the latent, eufunctional character of social conflict for which India, medieval and modern, seems to provide excellent examples; cf. Lewis Coser, *The Functions of Social Conflict* (London, 1964), pp. 82 and 125.

29 See, for example, A. Sarada Raju, *Economic Conditions in the Madras Presidency: 1800–1850* (Madras, 1941) and S. Srinivasa Raghavaiyangar, *Memorandum on the Progress of the Madras Presidency During the Last Forty Years of British Administration* (Madras, 1893).

30 General accounts of the Madras revenue system may be found in: Baden-Powell, *op. cit.,* III, 1–50, or, for the earlier period, N. Mukherjee, *The Ryotwari System in Madras: 1792–1827* (Calcutta, 1962). Also see "Early Land Revenue Systems in Madras," in B. S. Baliga, *Studies in Madras Administration* (Madras, 1954), pp. 82–98.

31 See Srinivasa Raghavaiyangar, *op. cit.,* p. 58, for statistical data on early-nineteenth-century prices.

32 Eric Stokes, *The English Utilitarians and India* (Oxford, 1959), pp. 25–26.

33 English East India Company, Madras Record Office, Records of Fort St. George: Diary and Consultations, 1672–1760, 90 vols.; Records of Fort St. George: Despatches to England, 1694–1751, 18 vols.; Records of Fort St. George: Letters from Fort St. George, 1679–1765, 40 vols.; John Bruce,

The Annals of the Honorable East India Company: From their Establishment by the Charter of Queen Elizabeth, 1600, to the Union of London and English East India Company, 1707–8 . . . (London, 1810); Shafat Ahmad Khan, *The East India Trade in the XVIIth Century; In its Political and Economic Aspects* (London, 1923).

34  For a general inventory of these holdings see "British Acquisitions in the Presidency of Fort St. George, Madras," in W. K. Firminger (ed.), *The Fifth Report from the Select Committee of the House of Commons on the Affairs of the East India Company* (Calcutta, 1918), III, xii–xxii. For a detailed account of one such holding, see: "Report on the Tiruvendipuram Farm, 1775; from Charles Hyde, Collector for South Arcot, Cuddalore, South Arcot, 30 June 1775," Madras Record Office, Library No. ASO (D) 56. For similar activities of the French also see C. S. Srinivasachari, *Ananda Range Pillai; The "Pepys" of French India* (Madras, 1940).

35  Child, of course, was struck by the success of the Dutch in the East Indies and sought to emulate them. It is doubtful that he perceived the basic differences between the situation in India and the archipelago and the peculiarities of the Indian political system.

36  For descriptions of trade, see John Irvin, "Indian Textile Trade in the Seventeenth Century: Part II, The Coromandel Coast," *Journal of Indian Textile History* (Calico Museum of Ahmadabad), 1956, No. 2, pp. 24–42; Tapan Raychaudhuri, *Jan Company in Coromandel, 1605–1690* (S-Gravenhage, 1962), pp. 142–48; Sarada Raju, *op. cit.,* pp. 163 ff.

37  Roe, in India as an ambassador of the Company from 1615 to 1619, advised Company officials on his return: "Let this be received as a rule that if you will profit, seek it at sea, and in quiet trade; for without controversy, it is an error to affect garrisons and land wars in India" (P. E. Roberts, *A Historical Geography of the British Dependencies,* Vol. VII [Oxford, 1916], p. 37).

38  See Raychaudhuri, *op. cit.,* and Sukumar Bhattacharya, *The East India Company and the Economy of Bengal* (London, 1954).

39  Historians of the medieval period of Indian hsitory are remarkably persistent in their presumption that Indian states were centralized, bureaucratic entities. A recent example is G. Yazdani (ed.), *The Early History of the Deccan* (2 vols.; London, 1960). Nor are the analyses of those who deny the existence of centralized states but who speak of "Indian feudalism" much better. See, for example: R. S. Sharma, *Indian Feudalism, 300–1200* (Calcutta, 1965). The use of the term "feudalism" must be understood, for India, to lack the components of "fief, fealty, and faith" with which we associate European feudalism and perhaps, to a degree, Japanese feudalism, though here note must be taken of the work of John W. Hall, "Feudalism in Japan—A Reassessment," *Comparative Studies in Society and History,* V, No. 1 (1962), 15–51. I prefer to use the term tributary overlordship to describe what I believe existed over most of India for most of its history.

40  This and many other relevant details of the eighteenth century are recorded in Government of India, *Records of Fort St. George: The Baramahal Records,* (13 vols.; Madras, 1907–33).

41  R. Caldwell, *A Political and General History of the District of Tinnevelly in the Presidency of Madras from the Earliest Period to Its Cession to the English Government in* A.D. *1801* (Madras, 1881), Chap. VI ff; James Grant, "Political Survey of the Northern Circars," in Firminger, *op. cit.,* pp. 1–118; and S. C. Hill and Husuf Khan, *The Rebel Commandant* (London, 1914).

216 *Burton Stein*

42 Mukherjee, *The Ryotwari System.*
43 This process has recently been charted by two writers: Bernard 'S. Cohn, "The Initial British Impact on India: A Case Study of the Benares Region," *Journal of Asian Studies,* XIX (August, 1960), 418–31; Robert E. Frykenberg, "Traditional Processes of Power in South India: An Historical Analysis of Local Influence," *Indian Economic and Social History Review,* I (October, 1963), 122–42.
44 Sarada Raju, *op. cit.,* p. 43.
45 In an epic poem in Telugu attributed to the sixteenth-century Vijayanagar ruler Krishnadevaraya, the king advises his heir that considerable care and caution was necessary in dealing with forest peoples whom all would try to include in their territories (A. Rangasvami Sarasvati, "Political Maxims of the Emperor Poet Krishnadeva Raya," *Journal of Indian History,* VI, Part III (1925), 61–88.
46 Recent further evidence of this is noted in Noboru Karashima, "Allur and Isanamangalam: Two South Indian Villages of the Cola Times," in *Proceedings of the First Conference Seminar of Tamil Studies, Kuala-Lumpur, Malaysia* (Kuala Lumpur, 1968), pp. 426–36.
47 See A. S. Altekar, *A History of Village Communities in Western India* (Bombay, 1927).
48 See Cohn, *loc. cit*

# Chapter IX

# The Ryotwari System and Social Organization in the Madras Presidency

*Nilmani Mukherjee*
*Robert Eric Frykenberg*

When the East India Company extended its political authority over a large part of the subcontinent in the late eighteenth century, the collection of revenue, especially land revenue, became a major function of its government. Several methods of collection were tried in different places and at different times. Company officers, some with only military or commercial experience, could hardly be expected to be familiar with all the peculiarities of peoples whose complex relationships to one another and the land varied so markedly from locality to locality; yet, in making land revenue agreements with local inhabitants, they had to make decisions which were to have far-reaching consequences in the organization of each local society. These decisions touched the lives of hundreds of thousands of individuals whose traditional social attitudes and values were little known. The formulators of these new land "settlements" often failed to realize how radical their policies were, how disruptive and novel, and how foreign to the existing social institutions and customs. Such uninformed policies occasionally produced social tensions. When these consequences were realized, remedial measures were introduced, so long as Company interests were not compromised. The traditional social order was too strong to be ignored. Consciously or unconsciously, the Company succumbed to its influences. Officials had to recognize and come to terms with social forces that were often imponderable but immensely powerful.

An attempt will be made here to illustrate how these influences affected the Ryotwari Settlement in the Madras Presidency during the first quarter of the nineteenth century. The districts of Malabar and Kanara are omitted from this analysis to give it greater unity. Those two districts possessed social and ecological characteristics peculiar to the southwestern coast which were not shared by the rest of the Presidency.

The Ryotwari Settlement was an agreement made directly between the Government and the ryots or "cultivators" of land, to the complete exclusion of intermediaries. Under this agreement, the Government usually sought to receive its due in the form of a money value fixed upon the actual fields under cultivation. Since this money value was not supposed to be set according to a fixed percentage or share of the produce, but rather according to a fixed valuation of the soil in each field, supply of water, proximity to market, and other specific local circumstances, the amount of revenue realized annually varied according to conditions affecting the crop each year instead of according to the size of the harvest. In short, the share or percentage of the harvest realized by the Government each year varied because soil valuation per field remained fixed. Only by pleading flood, drought, or locusts, could the ryots hope to persuade the Government to relent and forego its fixed demands. Actually, this ideal form of the Ryotwari Settlement, often called the *makta* or fixed field assessment, was more the exception than the rule during the early nineteenth century. Much more common were the traditional *asara* (sharing) or *kailu* (heaping) forms of revenue assessment, with the money value being computed only after the Government's fixed percentage of grain had been set aside.

The ryotwari system differed basically from the zamindari or *mutthadari* system and from the *gramawari* or joint-village or village-lease system not so much in how revenue was assessed and taken from the ryot, whether by "fixed field" (*makta*) or by "fixed share" (*asara*), but by the number of nongovernmental intermediaries and agents interspersed between the Government and the cultivator or ryot. Under the zamindari system, "proprietary rights" or personal privileges and powers to collect revenue (if not in some respects to govern) from many villages were conferred by the Madras Government upon individuals under conditions which were to remain "perpetual" or "permanent." These *mutthas* or "estates" of villages, the largest sometimes consisting of many hundreds of villages, could be held so long as the Government's fixed amount of revenue was regularly paid. Under the *gramawari* or village system (called *mahalwari* in the North), the Government collected a fixed amount, a "joint-rent," from each village. No nongovernmental agents, such as zamindars, *mutthadars*, or *ijaradars* (rent contractors) interposed their services between the Government and village. The Government usually came to an agreement—or made a "settlement"—with each village by fixing its revenue demands for a period of three to ten years. Whether this agreement was made with the whole body of village ryots collectively or, as more often happened, with the leader or leaders (*pedda* ryots) of the village, who were sometimes known as "renters" (*ijaradars*), the servants of Government dealt directly with each village. Both the ryotwari and *gramawari* systems came under what was called *amani* or Government administration as against zamindari or nongovernmental or delegated administration. If one were to apply modern jargon, the former would have been the "public sector" and the latter the "private sector."

The Ryotwari Settlement was first tried in Baramahal in the 1790's after the Third Mysore War by Captain Alexander Read. Subsequently, his assistants, such men as Thomas Munro and John Macleod, extended the system to the Ceded Districts, Coimbatore, and the whole of the Carnatic. Due to opposition in the Madras Government, it was abandoned in favor of the *gramawari* or village system in 1808. Acrimony filled the air in the years that followed. Finally, a revised form of ryotwari was restored in 1819. Thereafter, the system gradually grew until it became the recognized mode of land revenue administration in South India.[1]

While it would not be entirely correct to assert that the ryotwari system originated with the Company, since land control of the ryotwari kind seems to have existed in ancient South India,[2] it is quite certain that, immediately prior to the introduction of Company rule, the prevailing mode of land control was the village system. In this tradition, each individual had been obliged to submerge his own identity and to sacrifice his own interests for the common weal of the village, as determined by the lords, the elite of that village. Village affairs were controlled by persons whose titles, by local custom, might be any of the following: *pedda raiyat, reddi, kapu, dora, patel, kadim, mirasidar, gramatamu*; often the adjective *pedda,* or "great," was prefixed thereto. These persons were the headmen, the elite of their villages. Invariably they were of high and clean caste, either Brahmans or, more often, "yeoman-warriors." They stood between the Government and the rest of the village which was composed mostly of laboring people of lower caste.

There is some disagreement as to the actual intent of the Ryotwari Settlement, as originally conceived, and its consequences. The conventional line of argument holds that ryotwari policy swept away village elite groups and that it eliminated their role as intermediaries between Government and other villagers. In short, as ryots began paying taxes directly to Government officers, members of this class ceased to function as renters (or joint-renters) and hence lost authority and influence. More recent lines of argument point out that there has been a serious misconception about the functional meaning and social role described by the word "ryot." Ryot (*raiyat*) or "cultivator" has been commonly identified, especially during the past century, with the "landless laborer" of low caste when perhaps it should have been identified more closely with the high-caste elite, the *rayalu* or leaders of the village. As far as we know, these "cultivators" or *rayatulu* were invariably from among the highborn, the farmer-warrior castes; and they usually acted as overseers in the fields while most work like plowing and threshing was carried on by their menial laborers.

That the "ryot class" in each village was considerable cannot be denied. It might even have numbered up to a third or more of village inhabitants. That there certainly were less privileged and poorer members of the ryot community in each village also cannot be denied. Such poorer members of the ryot community would most certainly be among the less contented and more ready to compete in the village, especially if they were of a different but equally high caste from the entrenched leadership of the village. Hence, in short, a more current view would argue that village leadership was not eliminated as an intermediary group. After all, village leaders could be just as effective as hereditary village and circle officers (*samuta, firka,* etc.) of Government. Instead of dealing with village leadership jointly, the Government set about trying to deal with the leaders separately and, if possible, to deal directly with every ryot, every family of "gentle" birth in the village.[3]

In the early years of ryotwari administration, revenue collectors were extremely critical of village leaders, *patels* and the like, whose influence was considered to be pernicious. The Collector of South Arcot in 1806 described how village leaders habitually extorted large amounts above the prescribed revenue demand of the Government from "the lesser Ryots."[4] The Collecter of Nellore wrote that two or three "Head Cultivators" in each village usually kept the poorer ryots in a state of vassalage, completely subjugating these persons to their own will.[5] Generally speaking, the collectors in the Madras Presidency took a uniformly unfavorable attitude toward village headmen and leaders, regarding them as little better than pests. They convinced themselves that they should and, in fact, could free the ordinary ryots from the power of their village leaders.

Perhaps, in their zeal, early ryotwari administrators went too far; the point is debatable. They certainly preferred to ignore old institutions such as hereditary *mirasi* privileges and to overlook the fine lines of social distinction, status, and superiority attached to such privileges. In Nellore, a minor social revolution occurred when *payakari* ryots, who were subordinate landholders (subtenants or sharecroppers) were dealt with on equal terms with the *kadim*[6] ryots, who were the village lords.[7] In South Arcot *mirasidari* privileges were simply incorporated into the general ryotwari assessments without any special acknowledgment or compensation being made. One South Arcot collector admitted in 1817 that his predecessors had never deigned to recognize or acknowledge the existence of *mirasi* privilege. In North Arcot, also, all local claims to such special superiorities, together with the special entitlements and revenue exemptions which traditionally accompanied them, were resumed and proceeds accruing therefrom simply absorbed into the Company's revenues.[8] For these reasons there is some substance to the argument that the early Ryotwari Settlement resulted in a lowering of the position of traditional leaders and a consequent elevating of the *payakari* ryots. But we have no reason to suppose that these lower ryots were not also of the high-caste groups in each village.

Nevertheless, remedial measures to correct this comparatively mild social imbalance were felt to be necessary. Accordingly, when the second ryotwari system was put into operation in 1818 and thereafter, collectors were enjoined to guard against infractions of established landholdings in each district. The collectors in Dindigul, Madura, and North and South Arcot, in particular, were instructed to revise earlier ryotwari settlements and to find out how far these settlements had adversely affected the established and ancient privileges of *mirasidars* and how far the restoration of these privileges would be feasible. Collectors in the Tamil districts were ordered to be careful to preserve the ancient positions of *mirasidars, kadims,* and *ulkudis*[9] from infringements made by their subordinates or "tenants." Admission of these lesser ryots to a footing of equality was deemed to have been a just cause for complaint against the earlier, unrevised, ryotwari system.[10]

The Madras Board of Revenue later proposed to the Governor-in-Council that collectors should be forbidden to allow any person who was not by hereditary or prescriptive "right" entitled to pay his taxes directly to the Government to enter into any contracts or engagements with officers of the Government under the revised ryotwari system. The Governor-in-Council agreed that annual ryotwari settlements should in no way be prejudicial to *mirasi* and other similar longstanding land privileges. However, the Government drew a line in such a way as to allow collectors to make agreements with ryots who had never previously paid any revenue directly to the Government.[11]

As a consequence, only a partial restoration of *mirasi* rights and privileges was made under the new ryotwari settlements at the *jamabandis,* the local settlements made with ryots each year. If a *mirasidar* "quitted" his land, the Government policy was to provide for cultivation of such land in order to receive revenue from it. But if grandsons of a *mirasidar* who had abandoned land ninety-nine years previously returned to claim their ancient patrimony and were allowed to oust those ryots who in the meantime had been put in possession or control of the land by the Government and who had regularly paid revenue for so many years, confidence in the Government would have been shaken.[12] This being the case, the Government followed a policy of sympathy toward *mirasidars* and privileged groups, but it would not indiscriminately restore all their old privileges and powers. A comparatively lenient course of action was adopted toward village leadership.

Since one can question whether village leaders ever actually suffered serious damage under the original ryotwari system and since the revised system acted to nullify conditions that may never really have existed, one might well argue that village elite groups became stronger than ever during the second quarter of the nineteenth century. Evidence of the continuous and subtle influence of village leaders abounded. In 1822, the Head Assistant Collector at Cuddapah reported that ryots still stood in respect and scrupulously obeyed their "Chiefs" or Pedda Reddis. The Pedda Reddi was the only person in each locality who had effective control over ryots. The very peace and stability of the area depended upon him. The Reddi had only to express dissatisfaction at his own individual revenue settlement and most other ryots (usually also of the same caste) would follow his example, even if they stood to lose by doing so. Whenever any difficulty arose in coming to an agreement, as in making an annual revenue settlement (*jamabandi*) with village ryots, if the cause could be discovered—and often it could not be—it would be found that the Reddi was responsible. As soon as he was satisfied, troubles would cease. Ryotwari settlements, village settlements, or whatever, his influence persisted. A "good" (or cooperative) Reddi could be an asset to the Government; a "bad" one could be its bane. It was reported that persuasion by the whole staff of the *huzur kachahri,* or collector's office, could not do in two days what a Reddi could do in half an hour.[13]

Along with the influence of the village leaders or headmen, caste was a traditional force with which the Company's ryotwari administrators had to cope. In this, the formulators of the revised system faced a quandary. Was it better to resist or to yield to the claims of caste? That caste status and customs exercised vast influence none could deny. During his rule over Baramahal, Read allowed remissions of revenue to various privileged castes. At the time, Thomas Munro disagreed with him arguing that all should pay the same for the same kind of land. He pointed out that if assessments differed according to one's birthright to idleness the task of regulation would be endless. In fact, such a policy supported, indeed subsidized, idleness rather than enterprise and initiative.[14]

Munro's suggestions were not adopted. Brahmans, in particular, continued to enjoy privileges of remissions and light assessment. John Macleod, another of Read's assistants, feared that succeeding generations of British officers might form the impression that Read and his associates had been "Brahmin-ridden."[15] While it was true that Read's group relied heavily upon Brahmans, especially Maratha Desasthas, for their day-to-day administrative work, the question of how Read came to recognize the hold of Brahmans over what they defined as Sudra cultivators and how, as a consequence, he recognized Brahman claims to light assessment is debatable. Further research is needed to discover the reasoning and motivation behind his apparent favor.

Despite his early criticism of Read's policy, Munro apparently revised his opinion when, as principal collector of the Ceded Districts, he faced the same problem. He found the custom of permitting privileged castes to hold or control land on reduced rates to be general throughout the region. Not only Brahmans and Muslims, but those high and clean castes of husbandmen (and warriors), whose womenfolk had to be kept in seclusion and therefore could not work in the fields, had traditionally enjoyed this indulgence. Of course such privileges and indulgences were liable to abuse. Nevertheless, with certain limitations and careful surveillance, Munro felt that the custom deserved to be continued.[16]

The policy of recognizing caste privileges was continued with the revised revenue settlement. The Collector of Bellary in 1822 wrote that *inaams* or revenue-free lands were, for the most part, held by Brahmans of "religious habits" whose influence over the society was such that it was the policy of the Government to conciliate them.[17]

In Madura District, to cite another example, there were *agraharam* villages. Such villages were inhabited exclusively by Brahmans, and control of village lands annually yielding from twenty to fifty fanams, occasionally even a hundred fanams, was customarily allotted for the enjoyment of each of those who studied the Vedas, Puranas, and other sacred texts. These learned Brahmans were expected to teach, without fees, any pupils of suitable caste who might be brought to them.[18] Such *inaam* allowances were continued everywhere under the ryotwari system. Indeed, in some districts, *agraharam* and other kinds of *inaam* lands constituted a substantial proportion of all land, especially the most fertile. Moreover, it is not surprising that widespread abuse of *inaam* privileges demanded continual vigilance by Government officers.

Clearly, during the formative years of the ryotwari administration, certain caste privileges were recognized. Objections were occasionally raised. But the influence of leaders among these privileged estates, like that of certain Brahman and so-called "Sat-Sudra" castes, was too powerful to be ignored. Collectors increasingly took the view that it would be advisable to conciliate the most influential members from these strata of local society. This could hardly be done without maintaining their traditional perquisites and powers.

Altogether, therefore, it appears that the ryotwari system during its early years, from 1792 to 1827, did not greatly change the social fabric. An individual ryot's legitimate "right" or "privilege" to hold and to cultivate, if not to "own," land was established. But to what extent he was liberated from the immediate influence of the renter, or from the immediate power of the headmen and other local leaders, still remains highly doubtful. The local elite groups continued, although perhaps less directly and openly than before, to set the pace for thought and action in almost every aspect of rural life. Traditional institutions could not be dispensed with by the Company. Indeed, attempts were made to moderate the disruptive aspects of social changes which had been provoked by the initial introduction of the ryotwari system and, with the revised system, to preserve the existing social structure—at least in so far as it did not conflict with the basic assumptions and requirements of the Company.

In an earlier statement we have indicated that the Ryotwari Settlement was an agreement made directly between the Government and the ryots, to the complete exclusion of intermediaries. We have also gone on to show how, even then, one had to distinguish between laborers, lower ryots, and upper ryots, and to identify those of privileged station and caste. But, of course, we must also recognize that the Government was no single person, or even an efficient monolithic institution. It was a bureaucracy, a complex hierarchy with multiple strata of officials who came from many communities and held varied aspirations. Looked at in this sense, especially if inefficient and corrupting influences are taken into account, there were as many intermediaries between the ryot and the Governor-in-Council under the ryotwari as under the zamindari system. Neither their socioeconomic functions nor sociopolitical roles could be dispensed with in either, or under any, system of control.[19]

## NOTES

1　For a full treatment of its growth as a policy, read T. H. Beaglehole, *Thomas Munro and the Development of Administrative Policy in Madras: 1792–1818* (Cambridge, 1966).

2　K. A. N. Sastri, *The Colas* (Madras, 1955), p. 657.

3　We delude ourselves if we see any egalitarian or radical impulses in the motives of Munro and his associates. Jacobinism and the ideals of the French Revolution, one must remember, were viewed as the menace of the day—to be "contained." Gentlemen farmers in England may also perhaps have been "cultivators" in the same sense as some ryots.

4　Madras Board of Revenue Proceedings, 17 July 1806, found in the Madras Record Office and in the India Office Library, London.

5　*Ibid.*, 5 July 1803.

6   *Kadim*: Telugu equivalent of *mirasidar*.
7   Madras Board of Revenue Proceedings, 5 July 1803.
8   *Ibid.*, 5 January 1818.
9   *Ulukudi*: "resident landholder" or "tenant."
10  Madras Board of Revenue Proceedings, 5 January 1818.
11  Madras Revenue Proceedings and Consultations, 11 December 1823.
12  *Ibid.*
13  *Ibid.*, 9 January 1923.
14  Munro to Read, 17 July 1797. Found in A. J. Arbuthnot, *Sir Thomas Munro: Selections from His Minutes and Other Official Writings* (London, 1881), I, 12–22.
15  Macleod to Read, 5 October 1794, in the Baramahal Records, Madras Record Office.
16  Madras Revenue Proceedings and Consultations, 26 September 1805.
17  *Ibid.*, 4 July 1822.
18  *Ibid.*, 13 February 1823.
19  For a fuller treatment of actual operations, see Dharma Kumar, *Land and Caste in South India* (Cambridge, 1965).

# Chapter X

# Village
# Strength in
# South India

*Robert Eric Frykenberg*

An understanding of how local forces could influence government and divert resources from its treasuries can be obtained by looking at the roots from whence such forces sprang. Of course, it would be impossible, and unnecessary, to examine all villages, of the Guntur District for example, to achieve this objective. The Elliot Commission of 1845 investigated the affairs of 547 villages and drew together its findings. The generalizations of the Elliot Report do give us a magnified view of the activities of village leaders within their peculiar local circumstances.[1] A more careful scrutiny of one village, selected at random, together with glimpses of several other villages provides us with ideas about how local influence was exerted and highlights the relationship between social structure and land control.

### The Village of Rudravaram in Kurupad *Thana* (Formerly of Vasireddy Zamindari)

The three dominant, high-caste communities of Rudravaram in the nineteenth century were the Niyogis, the Rajus, and the Kammas. The strong influence of the Niyogi Brahmans can be seen by the village positions they held: The *ijaradar* who rented the village from Vasireddy Ramanadha Babu from 1836–37 to 1841–42 was Chamurthi Venkata Rutnam; the *mirasi karnam* (hereditary village accountant) was Chakkaraya Chatambram; and the *samatdar* (revenue officer) was Ananta Ramiah. The three officials were related to each other. The Rajus of Rudravaram were also numerically strong and a force to be reckoned with, particularly the Conda Raju family. Conda Raju Ranga Raju was the *pettendar* (village official) and also a *dafadar* (police officer). His father, Venkatarama Raju, and his nephew, Chenchu Raju, supported him in his attempts to strengthen the power of the family. The Kammas, mostly illiterate and less wealthy cultivators such as Gunta Shashu and the Guddum Venkata Naidu brothers, ran a poor third, but were strong enough to make loud noises of dissent when their interests were threatened.

Two Niyogis, Chamurthi Venkata Rutnam and Chakkaraya Chatambram, held the whip hand until 1842 when the zamindari was attached by the Government. In cooperation with each other, if not with the other leaders of the village, they had deceived the zamindar about the real productivity of their village, rented the village for 401 rupees, and then defaulted on payments as much as possible. Although large amounts of revenue were outstanding against the village, the exact amounts could not be discovered since no one would say what had happened to the village records for the years prior to 1842.[2]

After the village came under direct management of the *amin,* the Government revenue officer, a good deal of maneuvering went on. Eventually a coalition between the Niyogis, Rajus, and district officers emerged out of the confusion. A rental proposal for a greatly reduced revenue was submitted by Chamurthi Venkata Rutnam and was accepted by the *amin.* Chamurthi Venkata Rutnam and the Conda Raju family then joined in a plan to deceive the new administration. After declaring much of the village land to be vacant and waste, district officers received customary gifts (Table I). The amount of the gifts is

TABLE I
GIFTS RECEIVED BY DISTRICT OFFICERS, 1842–43

|  | Rupees |
|---|---|
| *Amin* (Vetsha Lakshmiah) . . . . . . . . . . . . . . . . . . | 25 |
| *Peshkar* (Ramanujarcharlu) . . . . . . . . . . . . . . . . | 6 |
| *Peshkar*'s son (Appalacharlu) . . . . . . . . . . . . . . | 3 |
| *Samatdar* (Ananta Ramiah) . . . . . . . . . . . . . . . . | 10 |
| *Madadgar* (Shastrulu) . . . . . . . . . . . . . . . . . . . . | 2 |
| *Karnam* (Chakkaraya Chatambram) . . . . . . . . . | 20 |
|  | 66 |

probably below what was actually received and represents only what the *Karnam* would admit.[3]

Details of the settlement for 1842–43 came in two series. When one set of accounts proved false, a second set was produced from the *karnam's* memory. The reliability of this second set cannot be judged.

In the first set, exclusive of *vandra* (special land assessments for high castes), the village was rented for 401 rupees. Total collections for the year were 401–14–00 rupees.[4] Broken down into the fixed revenue payments (*kists*) from individuals, but not into sub-*kists,* the collections are shown in Table II. From these collections, 272–13–03 rupees were dispatched to the Circar treasury. The remaining 129–00–09 rupees were deducted as shown in Table III.

TABLE II
RUDRAVARAM REVENUE PAYMENTS, 1842–43

|  | Rupees |
| --- | --- |
| Conda Raju Venkatarama Raju .............. | 75–04–00 |
| Guddum Venkata Naraina Naidu .............. | 101–00–00 |
| Mukala Ranga Reddy ....................... | 55–00–00 |
| Tuladala Narayana ........................ | 16–02–00 |
| Chakkaraya Cotappah ...................... | 33–00–00 |
| Gunta Shashu Naidu ....................... | 38–00–00 |
| Ambadi Pudailahara Venkiah ................ | 30–00–00 |
| Pushapari Amanah ......................... | 14–00–00 |
| Pushapari Venkiah ......................... | 7–08–00 |
| Vennada Rao ............................. | 3–00–00 |
| Chenchu Raju ............................ | 3–00–00 |
| Chakkaraya Venkiah ....................... | 6–08–00 |
| Mundapalli (a hamlet) .................... | 15–00–00 |
| Gullapalli (a hamlet) ..................... | 4–08–00 |
|  | 401–14–00 |

TABLE III
RUDRAVARAM REVENUE DEDUCTIONS, 1842–43

|  | Rupees |
| --- | --- |
| Extra *vandra* .............................. | 39–09–01 |
| *Inaam* (rent-free land) of *karnam* ............. | 15–00–00 |
| *Kist* of Guddum Venkata Naraina Naidu ....... | 13–12–00 |
| *Kist* of Gunta Shashu Naidu ................ | 6–00–00 |
| *Kists* of Pushapari Amanah and Venkiah ...... | 6–00–00 |
| Waste land cultivated without *kists* ............ | 48–11–08 |
|  | 129–00–09 |

The second set of accounts showed that the village was rented for 359–02–03 rupees of which 272–03–03 rupees were collected and only 248–10–00 were sent to the treasury. The 110–08–03 rupees remaining due were divided as follows: 23–09–03 rupees collected but never sent to the treasury; 27–01–06 rupees unpaid on Raju *kists*; and 59–13–06 rupees collected from other *kists* but not credited.[5]

In short, village leaders (ryots and *rayalu*) drove other ryots from land and declared that land waste during the *jamabandi* in order to gain a light assessment and favorable rent. They then impelled the other villagers to work the land and pocketed the yield which should have gone as revenue. Moreover, after obtaining a greatly reduced rent, the village leaders not only failed to pay their own shares of revenue, but appropriated for themselves the revenue which had been paid by the other villagers. District officers permitted them to do this and shared in the profits.[6]

The undercover operations of the year were so rewarding that a struggle developed over the spoils of the succeeding year, 1843–44. Where the Rajus had previously subrented land from the Niyogi *ijaradar,* Chamurthi Venkata Rutnam, now Ranga Raju secretly sent gifts to the *amin* and his brothers and submitted an *ijara-darkhast* (rental proposal) in the name of his father, Venkatarama Raju. The Kammas, Guddum Venkata Narain and Venkata Narsu Naidu, reacted with alarm and offered a higher bid than the one tendered by Rajus.

In the face of this pressure from the other high-caste communities of Rudravaram, the Niyogis acted very shrewdly. Instead of countering the threat of the more numerous Rajus directly, they apparently gave way gracefully and then resorted to behind-the-scenes maneuvering and intrigue. It is altogether likely that they themselves provoked the alarm of the Kammas. Then, when tension between the Rajus and Kammas was at a high point, they openly worked to mediate the strife while they silently swung the balance of power toward the Rajus. The Niyogi *karnam, samatdar,* and former *ijaradar* acted as intermediaries between the village communities and between the village and the higher authorities. When the *amin,* Vetsha Bashacharlu, informed his *dafadar,* Ranga Raju, that the *samatdar* and the *karnam* were acting under superior orders and should not be hindered, the Conda Raju family exerted further influence so as not to be excluded from any forthcoming arrangement.[7] The *karnam,* Chakkaraya Chatambram, then advised the Kammas not to rock the boat of village affairs, but to reach a good bargain with the Rajus. Village matters, after all, were best kept in the village. The payment of a higher rent or the disclosure of irregularities would only help outsiders to harm the village. The *karnam* then accompanied the Kammas and Rajus to Kurupad to tender the *darkhast* for the village. Under his influence, a written agreement was made in front of both communities and was duly signed.[8]

The outcome of these arrangements was good for both the Niyogis and Rajus. The former Niyogi *ijaradar,* Chamurthi Venkata Rutnam, became a *madadgar* (clerk) in the *thana kachahri,* the local police and revenue station. The *karnam* took four *kuchelas* (about a hundred acres) as his *maniyam*, tax free. Gifts to the district officers are shown in Table IV.[9] In return, the village was rented for 364–10–03 rupees; but

TABLE IV
GIFTS RECEIVED BY DISTRICT OFFICERS, 1843–44

|  | Rupees |
|---|---|
| *Amin* (Vetsha Bashacharlu) | 30 |
| *Peshkar* (Ramanujacharlu) | 6 |
| *Peshkar*'s son (Appalacharlu) | 3 |
| *Samatdar* (Ananta Ramiah) | 12 |
| *Karnam* (Chakkaraya Chatambram) | 20 |
| *Madadgar* (Shastrulu) | 2 |
| *Madadgar* (Chamurthi Venkata Rutnam) | 1 |
| *Huzur gumashta* (Kalyanam Hanumuntha Rao) | 2 |
|  | 76 |

only 256 rupees reached the treasury. The remaining 108–10–03 rupees due to the Government were divided as follows: 69–08–03 rupees paid by but not credited to ryots; 12–00–06 rupees collected but not sent to the treasury; and 27–01–06 rupees not paid by Rajus.[10]

The Kammas did not fare so well. The general agreement which had been made in Kurupad proved to be invalid since the Raju who had signed the *kabuliyat* was not the *ijaradar,* Venkatarama Raju. After agreeing to pay a *kist* of 45 rupees for his small plots of ground, Gunta Shashu Naidu found it necessary to give 54 rupees to the *karnam* and his son-in-law, Subbramaniam, 34 rupees to Ranga Raju, and 35 rupees to the *amin.* Even so, the amount of Gunta Shashu's agreed payment under his contract (*kaul*) was not reduced and, with a warrant from the *amin,* he was driven from his land by Ranga Raju as soon as the sowing was finished. Gunta Shashu attributed his misfortunes to the influence of the *karnam* and the *samatdar*.[11] Similar misfortunes befell the Guddum Naidu brothers. At least 110 rupees were extorted from them; but they were too powerful to be deprived of their land. The Rajus in coalition with the Niyogis, and the village officers in collusion with the district officers, broke the bargain which had been made with the Kammas; moreover, the petitions of the Kammas were simply referred to the *thana kachahri* where they were conveniently filed and forgotten.[12]

If the Kammas fared badly, other villagers fared worse. Other members of the Raju community, such as Timma Raju and Tugadubi Raju, assisted the *ijaradar* in making extra exactions above the *kists* and in trying to alter the *dastu chittha* (journal of actual total collection). An extra levy of twelve annas was taken on every *kunta* (slightly less than half an acre) of land. While the Rajus and other privileged communities rarely paid their full *kists*, much less anything extra, less fortunate ryots not only paid extra but had no way of knowing whether what they had paid was credited to them in the village accounts.[13]

When the next season began, the *amin,* Vetsha Bashacharlu, pressed Rangu Raju to rent Rudravaram for three years from 1844–45 through 1846–47. Reminded by the *dafadar* that it was against the rules for a Government officer to own or to engage in financial transactions over land, the *amin* again advised Ranga Raju to take the village in the name of his father, Venkatarama Raju. Although the *dafadar*'s father was too old for such responsibility, the *amin* promised to help in every way. There was nothing to fear. The village was in good condition and the rent, which would be profitable, would be divided ultimately between the *amin* and the *dafadar.*

On this understanding, Ranga Raju tendered a *darkhast* in the name of the elderly Venkatarama Raju. The rent for three years was to be 291, 321, and 347 rupees progressively. Special remissions (*vandra*) to the high-caste communities were to be increased by as much as 35 per cent, the extra additions in *vandra-bhumi* (remission-land) being registered under the "Rajooloo." A half *kuchela* (more than twelve acres) of land was added to the *maniyam* of the *karnam*. Surpluses of village production remaining after the payment of revenue to the Circar were to be divided equally between the *dafadar* and the *amin*. These terms were "solemnly agreed . . . both in a verbal manner and by [each] striking upon the hands of [the] other."[14] How much was given to district officers by the village leaders is not known. The *darkhast* was accepted by the *amin* on behalf of the Government; and when he came to the village on *jamabandi*, the *naib sarrishtadar*, Nakkalapalli Subha Rao, sanctioned these arrangements and signed the *kabuliyat* (contract).[15] The Kammas, who had also put forward a bid and who had even gone to the *huzur kachahri* in Guntur, were hushed up with generous leases (*kaul-namas*) on their lands and a share in the *vandra* benefits.[16]

An interesting, and indeed revealing, sequel to the story of the affairs of this village is to be found in some of the statements of the *karnam* to the Commissioner, Walter Elliot, at the time of the investigation in 1845. After cross-questioning of witnesses had uncovered much falsehood in his earlier testimony, Chakkaraya Chatambram was repeatedly called upon for more evidence. It behooved him to tell all, that is, as much as Elliot already knew and as much as was necessary to plead mercy, but to tell no more. The following are a series of statements made on successive occasions:

I prepared the accounts as I was directed to do and gave them to the Ameen under the fear that, by disobedience to high functionaries of the Talook, I could not get on at all as Curnum of the village.[17]

I wrote as I was dictated to by both of the parties [Rajus and Kammas]. This I confess; but I have not been guilty of any irregularities in the transaction.[18]

If, on subsequent enquiry, it be proved that I have withheld other accounts from you, I will forego my merassy Curnumship and submit to any punishment that may be inflicted.[19]

I did not commit any frauds of my own will, nor did I appropriate for my own use the money derived from it.[20]

Being apprehensive of the punishment I would have to incur by refusing to [give the truth], I have voluntarily come before your cutcherry and stated what are the facts. I therefore beg you to forgive all my past conduct.[21]

I before refrained from divulging these circumstances being of the opinion that it would be imprudent to bring to light the irregularities of the Circar authorities and so I suffer them to escape the Circar. Notice that I never committed frauds of my own accord and that I did not appropriate the money so derived for my own. I therefore request that I will be kindly pardoned and protected.[22]

As it is the practice in every Talook to prepare false accounts and deliver the same with a view to obtain rents on low terms, I have been following the same example.[23]

Considering that, in Ranga Raju's words, Chatambram was "desirous of obtaining the village on favourable rent in his own name" and that the influence of the Niyogis of Rudravaram was a fundamental element in the operations of the village, these explanations and justifications seem particularly important as reflecting common notions of and attitudes toward Government authority.[24]

Finally, a catalogue of the village records, which were surrendered to the Commissioner and which formed the basis of much of the detailed information in the depositions, is given to show, in some measure, the framework around which the administration of the village was conducted.

CATALOGUE OF VILLAGE RECORDS

1. *Kistu zabitas:* statements of assessment classified by crops, by productivity factors, and by exemptions (e.g., *inaam, agraharam, shrotriam,
   maniyam, vandra, pagoda, choltry,* and other lands).
2. *Dastu zabitas:* statements of actual collections giving aggregates of *kists*
   gathered for each year.
3. *Dastu chitthas:* summary statements of total collections.
4. *Dastu kharchu chittha:* debit and credit account of current collections.
5. *Grama kharchu chittha:* debit and credit account of current village
   expenses.
6. *Wasulbandi:* roll or statement of payments remitted to the district
   treasury.
7. *Kistabandi:* list specifying installments paid on *kaul-namas* issued to
   each cultivator or cultivating community and containing the *karanamas*
   (or *kabuliyats*) signed by the same.[25]

### Operations of Other Villages

Four more cases have been selected to show some of the variety of
ways in which village leaders moved. A glance at these villages serves
to further confirm the conclusion that constant pressure was exerted
from the villages upon the levels of political and administrative authority
immediately above them.

*The Village of Attalur in Kurupad* Thana (*Formerly of Vasireddy
Zamindari*)

Regular records, dating back to the Guntur Famine (1833–34),
showed that until 1843, the village usually paid a rent of 1,080 rupees a
year. Bellamconda Ramiah, the *ijaradar,* prospered exceedingly on this
rent. After Ramiah's death, a controversy developed between his son,
Venkiah, and the village leaders over the disposal of the village revenue.
Venkiah's offer to pay off old balances was not accepted. The *karnam*
of Attalur, Padmaraju Veeriah, was successful in inducing the *samatdar*
and *amin* to manage the village directly.[26]

Polapeddi Nagiah, the *samatdar,* received 39 rupees to lower the
*anchana-kabuliyat* (confirmed estimate of annual produce) for the
1843–44 season. The *amin,* Vetsha Bashacharlu, and the *peshkar,*
Vetsha Venkatacharlu, also received 65 rupees. Extra exactions (*tak-
sim*) amounting to 140 rupees were taken from the poorer ryots in
order to cover these gifts to the district officers; the balance of 36 rupees
was pocketed by the *karnam.* As a result of these arrangements, the

Government demand was lowered to 930 rupees. This figure was reached after the very good harvest had been cut, thrashed, measured, and divided in heaps. A short count went to the Government heap and the conversion rate on the Government share was set below the real market value of the grain. Then, on the grounds that market values on grain were too low, the Government grain was not collected by the district officers but was stored in the village pits until such time as it would bring a better price on the market. In the end, only 680 rupees were paid into the treasury.

The same process was repeated the following year (1844–45). Complicated negotiations over a reduction of the harvest estimates went on between the village leaders and the district officers, with Burriah, the village *shroff,* acting as the mediator. In return for a reduction of nearly 50 per cent in the Circar *berij,* the *amin* received 50 rupees; the *peshkar* received 26 rupees; and the *samatdar* received 13 rupees. The Government grain, which was again stored in the village pits, was reported as spoiled and the revenue declared to be irrecoverable.[27]

### The Village of Bhimavaram in Kurupad Thana (*Formerly of Vasireddy Zamindari*)

Beginning with 1841–42, Damacherla Kotappah rented Bhimavaram from Vasireddy Ramanadha Babu for five years; but when the zamindari came under Government management, district officers demanded security. His friend, a *mirasi karnam* (hereditary village accountant) named Abur Bungaru from the nearby village of Abur, provided the necessary security and took over the village. Despite attempts by the *amin,* Vetsha Bashacharlu, and his district officers to stir up intrigue and to frighten the villagers of Bhimavaram, Bungaru succeeded in conciliating the villagers and in paying off both the current rent and the arrears (765 and 112 rupees respectively), but not without borrowing 60 rupees from Nandigama Akkanappah, a Bhimavaram subrenter.[28]

Whether it was the district officers who aroused the ryots of Bhimavaram against him because he was too strong to bend to their wishes, or whether it was the villagers who aroused the district officers, Bungaru faced more trouble than he wanted. He decided to give up the village as an unprofitable venture. However, when Kotappah came to him with a written assurance that he would cooperate, Bungaru was persuaded to stay on. Still the trouble continued. On his next visit, Bungaru found that Kotappah had neglected his land and had persuaded others to do

the same. A number of subrenters, Guraju Lakshmi Narain, Damacherla Ramanah, and Cherkur Butchannah, sided with Bungaru; but the
*amin* sided with Kotappah. The dissidents were advised to desert the
village, and Bungaru was ordered to pay the whole of the Circar's share,
including that from the untilled fields. Clearly, Vetsha Bashacharlu
wanted the village under his own control.

Damacherla Kotappah feigned the sale of his possessions and crossed
the river into the Nizam's dominions; but he regularly returned to
Bhimavaram, often at night, in order to stir up trouble. Other ryots
also "gave up" their lands and the village deteriorated.

Bungaru went to the *huzur kachahri* and asked the *huzur sarrishtadar*
to cancel his securityship and obligations in Bhimavaram. He wanted
only to manage his two *mirasi* villages in peace. However, N. Shashagiri
Rao turned a deaf ear. Bungaru's two petitions to the British collector
were merely referred back to the *amin*. Bungaru was informed by the
*sarrishtadar* that if he gave up his two *mirasi* villages then the *amin*
would cancel his obligations for Bhimavaram. Later, when it was clear
that Bungaru would not let go of his ancestral villages, Bashacharlu
offered to help him for a hundred rupees. This sum was paid out of the
income of the two *mirasi* villages (Abur and Kalaverlapadu).

Again the Bhimavaram question ascended into the "presence of the
divinity" in Guntur. Janikiram Puntulu, the *jawab-nawis,* took twenty
rupees and Paregai Ramanah, the assistant *sarrishtadar*, took ten rupees
as his "propitiation." Yet, at the next *jamabandi,* Bungaru was ordered
to pay the revenue for all three villages. Another trip was made, this
time to the *thana kasba*, the headquarters of the subdistrict. There,
Bungaru was informed that if he paid one more gift he would need to
care only for his two ancestral villages. The *samatdar* would then deal
directly with the Bhimavaram *karnams,* and with Guraju Lakshmi
Narain, who was the real leader of Bhimavaram.

Abur Bungaru paid another thirty rupees out of the profits of his
home villages and obtained an order of release from his obligation for
the rent of Bhimavaram. Receipts, showing that the current demand of
the village had been discharged and that the security money had been
returned, were given to him. He was told to await the return of the
*jawab-nawis,* Janikiram Puntulu, from Guntur in order to obtain a
document formally cancelling his responsibility for Bhimavaram. Here
was a refractory *ijaradar* who was made to feel his dependence upon the
local authorities, whether they were the village leaders of Bhimavaram,
the district officers, or both.

*The Village of Cherukuru in Chilkalurpad* Thana (*Formerly Manur Rao Zamindari*)

Palapurti Ramachandrulu, Andukur Baviah, and Kora Veerunah were the Daskhat *karnams* of the large village of Cherukuru. Their *dastu chitthas* and other records, dating from the Famine (1833–34), showed not only total collections made under the Manur Rao Zamindar and under the Circar (1840–45) but also extra collections made for village expenses.[29]

Under seemingly innocent listings of expenses, Cherukuru's leaders were remarkably successful in bending the instruments of administration to their own purposes. In the words of the *karnams,* "We have paid Circar servants . . . in order that they may enter favourable Jamabundy accounts without Takesim and that they may use no severity in collecting old balances."[30] Payments were not charged to district officers by name but under necessary items of village expense, village deities, pseudonyms for district officers, mendicant Brahmans, or simply under such words as *padu,* "time" or "occasion," *bhojanam,* "food," *maham,* "cancelled" or "ambiguous," or *mubham kharch,* "sundries" or "general expenses."[31]

During the five years from 1840–41 to 1844–45, no level of the district hierarchy escaped the careful application of Cherukuru influence. Gifts, which were given with proper respect for station and dignity, are shown in Table V. In return for 1,142 rupees in gifts, 18,360 rupees of land revenue was not collected, a more than tenfold return

TABLE V

GIFTS RECEIVED BY DISTRICT OFFICERS, 1840–45

| | Rupees |
|---|---|
| *Huzur sarrishtadar* (Nyapati Shashagiri Rao) . . . . . . . | 400 |
| *Huzur naib* (Sommayyajulu Subbiah) . . . . . . . . . . . . . | 50 |
| *Huzur gumashta* (Pataraju Ramaswami) . . . . . . . . . . . | 31 |
| *Huzur gumashta* (Kalyanam Hanumantha Rao) . . . . . . | 22 |
| *Huzur gumashta* (Ambarkhana Purushottum Rao) . . . | 20 |
| *Thana amin* (Devaraju Dassappa) . . . . . . . . . . . . . . . | 111 |
| *Thana amin* (Devaraju Lakshmi Narainappa) . . . . . . . | 126 |
| *Thana amin* (Akkaraju Buchiah) . . . . . . . . . . . . . . . | 130 |
| *Thana peshkar* (Gotati Kanakaraju) . . . . . . . . . . . . . | 178 |
| *Naib amin* (Mantri Subbiah) . . . . . . . . . . . . . . . . . . | 30 |
| *Naib amin* (Krishniah Puntulu) . . . . . . . . . . . . . . . . | 16 |
| *Thana gumashta* (Pataraju Subbiah) . . . . . . . . . . . . . | 6 |
| *Thana jawab-nawis* (Golamudi Venkataswami) . . . . . . | 12 |
| *Samatdar* (Vydeyam Subha Rao) . . . . . . . . . . . . . . . . | 10 |
| | 1,142 |

on the village investment.[32] Another 32,729 rupees of revenue stood against the village as unpaid for the years between 1833 and 1840.

For one year alone (1843–44), the enormous sum of eight thousand rupees was written off against waste land. The negotiations for this relinquishment of land, which was usually cultivated, were carried on with the *amin,* Akkaraju Buchiah. Petitions with supporting recommendations from the *amin* were sent to the *huzur,* even though the assistant collector, Henry Newill, had already assessed the lands as usual during the *jamabandi.* When no reply came back on these petitions, Buchiah told the village leaders, "As no hookum had been received from the Hoozoor, you may cultivate as much or as little as you like."[33] As a result, land was listed as waste, then cultivated, while the Circar servants simply never collected the revenue due on it.

Thus, by skillful negotiation, deception, evasion, propitious gifts, and by every imaginable device, revenue was kept back, assessments were reduced, rents were obtained on very low terms, and land was thrown out of cultivation, recorded as waste, and quickly recultivated as village influence was thrown against central power. But such encroachment required cooperation from the district hierarchy. Custom demanded a sacrificial offering to divinely instituted authority. Wrath could be averted and favor gained only if the human gods were propitiated. As the Cherukuru *karnams* explained it: "When anything happened that required the interference of the Hoozoor Servants to be settled, the Peishcar used to carry us to the Head Sheristadar and settle our business favourably to us. We therefore continued to pay through the Peishcar."[34] All was done through proper channels, which led inevitably to Shashagiri Rao. As *huzur sarrishtadar,* his influence and power were such after 1842 that he could command a higher payment. Attempts to curb his power or to by-pass his control were difficult since they were bound to meet resistance if not retaliation. The fact that the Madras authorities had supported the *sarrishtadar* against John Goldingham and against Huddleston Stokes, district collectors from 1837 to 1845, on several occasions not only enhanced the prestige of Shashagiri Rao but led to the belief that Stokes could be discredited and removed. It was very well known in Cherukuru that district officers acted "with a view to bring the Collector into the unfavourable opinion of the higher authorities."[35]

### The Village of Punagapad in Rajapet Thana (Part of an Amani Taluk)

The story of this village, as related by Punagapad Appiah who was a member of the hereditary *karnam* family, was a tale of famine, death, desertion, and harsh rents. Ingeniously hidden accounts, however, told of extra collections and of gifts to district officers under fictitious or divine names.[36] When finally deciphered, these records listed payments in the usual ascending order: *samat peon, samatdar, thana peon, thana madadgar, thana shroff, thana peshkar, thanadar* (*amin*), *huzur peon, huzur jamadar, huzur madadgar, huzur naib,* and *huzur sarrishtadar.*

Appiah willingly implicated his cousins and close relatives in these village activities, but most of his blame was reserved for district officers. Between 1837 and 1845, Kotapalli Achiah, the *amin,* deliberately took the village away from its leaders and rented it to the indigent (*nadar*) community led by Krosur Kotappah. The village elite, who could easily pay the full revenue, permitted this artificial arrangement because the *nadar* or poorer people were not difficult to control and because they paid large gifts both to village leaders and to district officers out of the balances of revenue which they withheld from the Government. Achee Raju and Achee Venkiah, who were Appiah's cousins, did the bookwork. Since the *nadar* possessed little property or money which might serve as collateral for the rent, the Government revenue was almost wholly lost.

### Some Examples of *Grama Kharchu* or Village Expenses

The following extracts taken directly from the Guntur District Records are rare and fascinating illustrations of the way in which the agrarian system worked at the lowest recordable level, where elements of social structure and land control are inseparable, if not identical, parts of a whole.

"GRAMA KHARCHU" ITEMS TO BE CONTINUED OR
DISCONTINUED IN PALNAD, 1805[37]

A. *Items to be continued:*
1. Pay to Tahsildars or Peons employed in collecting kists from ryots who must be forced to render what is due.
2. Batta of Kapus and Karnams absent from village for Jamabandi, to the mutual advantage of the whole village.
3. Pay to Pygasti Peons who oversee Mahasuldars (paid by Circar) in seeing that crops and grain are kept safe.
4. Zatra celebrations, including sacrifices to village goddesses, rewards to jugglers . . . a religious institution in which whole village partakes.
5. Charitable gifts to travelers, distressed and needy.
6. Russums or commissions to Village Shroff for trouble of changing money.
7. Batta to tappal runners, treasure carriers, and bearers.

B. *Items to be discontinued:*    ..
1. Supplies for powerful Indian and European travelers—"scandalous abuse!!" [Final two words were scrawled in the margin, presumably by Crawford.]
2. Principal and interest on money loans for kists. Village leaders should not use village funds for this purpose.
3. Batta to village peons sent to summon Ryots to attend Amins or Circar business. Amins have their own peons employed for all government work.
4. Batta to Mohtadus for taking messages, letters and parcels to other villages. Poor ryots should not have to pay for the errands of the rich. Each person should pay for the service he himself requires.
5. Nazaranas and fees to district servants and others.
6. Expenses incurred when troops camp near village. Army officers should see to it that all supplies are paid for on the spot.
7. Returns for bad coin rejected out of the village revenue. The Shroff is paid to see that coin is good. He should not have the opportunity to pass bad coin on the pretense of its being part of the kists, nor should he be reimbursed when such coin are rejected by the Huzur Shroff.
8. Anchanadars, paid entirely or at least in part by the Circar. Their work is for joint benefit of village and government. But no payments should be made until random measurements of grain heaps determine the fidelity of their work.

DONALD CRAWFORD
17 July 1805

ACCOUNTS FOR THREE VILLAGES OF CHILKALURPAD, 1816–1817[38]

|  | Pagodas, fanams, and kasu |
|---|---|
| I. *Accounts of Pedda Cherukuru:* | |
| A. Beriz [demand] | 6,283–28–43 |
| B. Dastu [collections] | 2,543–08–78 |
| C. Kistu [payments to zamindar] | 1,991–22–40 |
| D. Grama Kharchu [village expenses] | 370–06–12 |
|   1. Batta for Bad Coin | 16–11–65 |
|   2. Gumashta Wages: | |
|     *a)* Gopal Rao—6½ months | 65–00–00 |
|     *b)* Mulupu Jenkanah—3 months, 8 days | 24–18–00 |
|     *c)* Peons who collected from Ryots | 119–26–57 |
|     *d)* Mahataudies | 15–28–21 |
|     *e)* Mahasuldars to care for produce | 42–30–50 |
|     *f)* Daily batta to Tahsildar | 1–34–59 |
|     *g)* Anchanadars to appraise crop | 1–17–01 |

| | | |
|---|---|---|
| h) | Zaftidars to take delivery of crop | 10–10 |
| i) | Supplies to Sibandi | 7–27–00 |
| j) | Batta to peon bringing dastak from Chilkalurpet | 1–10 |

3. Sadaravarudu Charges:

| | | |
|---|---|---|
| a) | Paper, pens, sealing wax, thread to tie up cadjan circar accounts | 2–26–80 |
| b) | Making ink | 4–74 |
| c) | Lamp oil for village chawadi | 1–15–37 |
| d) | Repair of cutcherry | 16–36 |
| e) | Gunny bags for holding dubu | 9–00 |
| f) | Loss of dubu | 45 |
| g) | Lamp oil for Sahabang Mamul | 10–77 |
| h) | Cloths for tying up daftarams | 1–55 |
| i) | Vettyman attending Mahasuldars | 34 |
| j) | Batta for tom-tom beaters | 79 |
| k) | Russum to Tadikonda Puttiah, Shroff | 4–00–00 |
| l) | Dak batta for sending money and letters to the Huzur | 2–22–74 |
| m) | Batta for sending Karnams to the Huzur during Jamabandi | 54–00–78 |
| n) | Ceremony for Village Goddess | 1–24–60 |
| o) | Charity to Byragies and Sumasulu | 2–19–55 |
| p) | Charity for god | 1–04–06 |
| q) | Charity for god | 10–32 |
| r) | Annual Mamul for carpenters | 1–00–00 |
| s) | Annual Vuttum to C. Chetty Buchiah | 1–00–00 |
| t) | Cutting crops for poor ryots | 26–35 |

| | | |
|---|---|---|
| E. | Balances of Dastu Remaining | 101–16–58 |

II. *Accounts of Prattipadu:*

| | | |
|---|---|---|
| A. | Beriz [demand] | 9,239–07–36 |
| B. | Dastu [collection] | 7,254–02–40 |
| C. | Kistu [payments to Circar] | 6,763–27–56 |
| D. | Grama Kharchu [village expenses] | 438–16–11 |

1. Batta:

| | | |
|---|---|---|
| a) | Inferior coin | 95–28–10 |
| b) | Performing of god's feast | 14–06–15 |
| c) | Rice to Venkana Purushotum who examined Village Accounts | 6–25–27 |
| d) | Bearers for Puttri Chumiah | 12–06 |
| e) | Rice to Karnams attending Huzur and Chilkalurpet for Jamabandi | 12–29–23 |

2. Gumashta Wages:

| | | |
|---|---|---|
| a) | Sabnavis Appiah, 9½ mo. 3/mo., part | 26–09–00 |
| b) | Nilakanta Subiah, 9½ mo. at 3; part | 13–21–52 |
| c) | Badi Gopal Kistna Rao, 2 mo. 2 at 3 | 6–07–25 |
| d) | Chillara Appiah—Kailudaru | 1–40–10 |

e) Khan Mohamed, Subadar, & 9 peons, 9½ mo. at 10½ mo., in part — 74–30–28
f) Mohamed Khan and 6 peons in part — 20–35–04
g) Mohtadus, in part for 9½ mo. — 15–20–79
3. Russums:
 a) Mamul to Huzur Shroff — 5–00–00
 b) Mamul to Village Shroff — 4–01–32
 c) Mamul to Panchala castes and to Calendar Brahmans — 3–00–22
 d) Mamul to Vetty People — 8–35
 e) Mamul Russums to Karnams — 25–00–00
 f) Gift to Shaik Badda, Tahsildar?
4. Sadaravarudu:
 a) Miscellaneous — 2–03–50
 b) Gumashta to write Regulation — 11–20
 c) Peon of Minor Zamindar — 3–19
 d) Maramat (repair village tank) — 14–29–31
 e) Sending kistu and letters — 20–76
 f) Charity for traveling Brahmans — 26–41
 g) Anchanadars under Bolla Venkatadry — 5–05–50
 h) Mahasuldars — 39–35–58
 i) Ceremony of Village Goddess — 5–00–25
5. Losses to Company Sepoys:
 a) Batta for Coolies — 12–14–50
 b) Articles not paid for — 20–10–32
 c) Batta for peons sent for cattle — 11–06–53
E. Total Disbursements [*kistu* and *kharchu*] — 7,202–07–67
F. Balance Remaining — 51–30–58
III. *Accounts of Gudawada:*
 A. Beriz [demand] — 469–19–55
 B. Dastu [actual collections] — 379–10–09
 C. Kistu [payments to zamindar] — 63–24–15
 D. Kharchu [village expenses] — 314–16–79
 1. Boundary Dispute:
  a) Nazr to Cotty Kistniah, brother of the Zillah Court Nazer — 18–00
  b) Nazr to Amin sent by Court to move boundary stones — 13–04–40
  c) Nazaranulu to Amin's peons — 3–00–00
  d) Nazr to peons bringing Court summons — 19–12–75
  e) Mamul nazrs to Village Panchayat — 34–33–26
  f) Batta for navis; stamp paper — 1–31–40
  g) Batta for Ryots going to Guntur — 103–22–18
  h) Fine levied by Zillah Court — 21–00–00
 2. Sadaravarudu Batta and Russums:
  a) Pindari plunder — 42–04–40

| | | |
|---|---|---:|
| *b*) | Batta for Ijaradar, Manur Ramaswamy | 6–06–43 |
| *c*) | Ceremonies of gods | 1–26–74 |
| *d*) | Bringing of Kistulu to Huzur | 1–07–70 |
| *e*) | Ceremony of Village Goddess | 17–44 |
| *f*) | Batta to peons under Daroga collecting supplies for sepoys | 1–17–35 |
| *g*) | Articles lost to sepoys | |
| *h*) | Mahasuldars | 5–34–59 |
| *i*) | Tappal carriers | 1–21–10 |
| *j*) | Bad coin | 1–11–65 |
| *k*) | Tahsildars of Manur Conda Rao | 11–06–19 |
| *l*) | Mohtadus | 5–03–75 |
| E. | Total Disbursements | 378–05–14 |
| F. | Balance Remaining | 5–05 |

THOMAS OAKES
3 September 1818

The foregoing material has been presented to show, in wearisome detail, how local agrarian forces were able to advance their designs, to combine silently, and to enrich themselves at the expense of a centralizing imperial structure. Partly because he lacked the facilities and "loyal" personnel for obtaining information directly from each of over a thousand villages; partly because he failed to inspire and obtain the cooperation of his high-caste native subordinates (whether Desastha Brahman, Niyogi Brahman, Kamma, or Muslim); partly because he was not able to receive sufficient support and understanding from higher authorities in Madras; but probably because all of these factors worked together against his attempts to exercise administrative control, the British district collector, whether John Goldingham (1837–42) or Huddleston Stokes (1842–45), could never really discover, much less cope with, what was going on beneath him within the agrarian order. In consequence, his words did not carry the weight of authority. He was the chief executive over the district administration on behalf of the imperial power in little more than name. If he was the *huzur*, "the presence of authority" (if not also of divinity), it was only in outward show and ceremony. The reality of central power, if it existed at all, resided elsewhere.

District officers, notably the *huzur* staff, were predominantly Brahmans. These were Maratha Brahmans or Desasthas under the able leadership of the *huzur sarrishtadar*, Nyapati Shashagiri Rao. As the old zamindaris crumbled and disintegrated from the corrosive pressures of village influence beneath them and of family strife, litigation, and dissipation, their establishments were supplanted by district officers. These officers inherited not only the weakened remnants of zamindari organization, but also the perquisites and dignities which the zamindars had long enjoyed. Moreover, in the name of government, they were not only delegates of imperial authority, but they were free from effective supervision, and control. The aura of divinity, the borrowed glow of the *huzur*, fell upon them. A Desastha's daughter being married or a special shrine being erected by a Desastha would be cause enough for an out-flowing of special contributions from the villages, such as those which have been described above. If the Cherukuru *karnams* could openly admit to having given the *sarrishtadar* alone an annual gift of one hundred rupees—and this amount is only what was admitted—one can scarcely begin to imagine what he must have received in aggregate from over a thousand other villages within the district. Certainly his annual income must have been many times that of his European superiors, whether in Guntur or in Madras.

At the same time, however, village leaders probably gained the better part of most bargains with district officers. When a subordinate district officer accepted village money, he became a demon propitiated and disarmed. He became a lower divinity manipulated. He exchanged imperial responsibility (if not authority) for local corruptibility. He also became vulnerable, to discipline from above and to demands from below. Only when he brought his immediate superior into the transaction did he shed blame and shield himself from wrath. As the corrupting influence of village power spread corrosively upward, ever higher into the administrative hierarchy, more and more shields would be raised between the village leaders themselves, along with lower district officers, and the inevitable retribution. Level by level, successively higher and higher levels of district officers became captive to those who were below them, while, at the same time, they risked exposure from still higher authority. Much more like Gulliver than like Leviathan, the district administration became tied down, silently, by one tiny strand after another. A slumbering central authority would be pegged to earth by countless threads of local influence.

Since the *huzur sarrishtadar* was at the top of the native hierarchy, his position was the most vulnerable. For the most part, the gross corruptibility of the Company's European servants had been halted by the policies of Lord Cornwallis a half century before. Hence, blame stopped with the top native revenue officer. When revenues dried up and questions were asked from Madras, he had to supply the answers. He could only plead for consideration for so long. Bad climate, disease epidemics, wretched crops, and poor prices could not be blamed every year. The gullibility, sloth, wrong judgment, and inefficiency of imperial rulers did have limits. Then, the blow would fall. A number of vacancies would appear at the top levels of administration. As a matter of fact, however, most of the district officers in high positions had gone through this process several times before. Their very vulnerability, when combined with uncertainties of tenure, had prompted them to make the most of their moments of power. Simple loyalty to family and to caste interest could demand no less. Meanwhile, those village leaders and lower-level district officers, such as *samatdars*, who were not very vulnerable but who were just as committed to the interests of their own families and castes and villages, would be ever continuing to exert steady pressure from below. Add to this the fact that it was usually possible for dismissed district officers to enter district administration again, if not in Guntur then in some other district, and their behavior is not difficult to explain.

Thus far, the emphasis of this study has been the presentation of detailed samples of village data. Intensive and detailed description of events in just a few villages serves to show how silent combinations of local influence acted to corrode the machinery of district government. I now wish to emphasize that such data is not indicative of occasional, unique, or isolated occurrences. What happened in these villages was no aberration, no departure from normal behavior. Indeed, a careful examination of local records throughout South India for several centuries will show a similar pattern of social and political behavior which was deeply rooted in tradition. Local interest, if not local self-preservation, required continual, energetic, and ingenious efforts to resist the predatory designs of larger aggregations of power. The very existence of a politically centralized system of power, particularly if administratively efficient and territorially expansive, constituted a threat to village leaders. Such systems were dangerous when they were strong and were exploitable when they were weak; but they were "alien" in either case.

In a more comprehensive study of this subject, I gave this traditional process of silent, corrosive, local power a convenient symbolic label. The name applied to this general historical principle of local sociopolitical behavior which was so widespread and so enduring was the "principle of the *white ant*."[39] As a general hypothesis for explaining the influence of social structure on land control in Indian history, the white-ant principle postulates a simplified way of understanding processes operating within the fantastic complexities of the agrarian system. If the characterization of the white ant is an oversimplification, this in no way nullifies the general principle which it proposes. The white ant is a tiny creature of tremendous energy and silence. It joins with its tiny termite brothers. These in silent combination devour the interior of the stoutest wooden structure, leaving it a hollow shell without necessarily destroying its outer form. The white ant typifies what happened in South India when energetic and silent local forces, in combination, made hollow mockery of the stout administrative structures of successive systems of regal and imperial power.[40]

## NOTES

1   Madras Revenue Proceedings and Consultations, 6 December 1847, Elliot Report, Appendix B, Nos. 2 to 5, depositions of Chakkaraya Chatambram, Gunta Shashu Naidu, Guddum Venkata Narusu Naidu, and Conda Raju Ranga Raju before Walter Elliot, 16 April to May 7 1845. Unless otherwise noted, the following references are all to depositions in Appendix B of the Elliot Report.
2   Nos. 2 and 3, Chakkaraya Chatambram and Ranga Raju, 16 April and 6 May 1845.
3   No. 2, Chakkaraya Chatambram, 22 April 1845.
4   The rupee consisted of sixteen annas. Twelve paise comprised one anna. The figures given here are stated in rupees, annas, and paise.
5   No. 2, Chakkaraya Chatambram, 27 April 1845.
6   *Ibid.*, 22 April 1845.
7   No. 3, Ranga Raju, 20 April 1845.
8   No. 4, Gunta Shashu Naidu, 20 April 1845.
9   No. 2, Chakkaraya Chatambram, 22 April 1845.
10  *Ibid.*, 27 April 1845.
11  No. 4, Gunta Shashu Naidu, 20 April 1845.
12  No. 5, Guddum Venkata Narusu Naidu, 20 April 1845; and No. 2 Chakkaraya Chatambram, 21 April 1845.
13  No. 2, Chakkaraya Chatambram, 22 April 1845.
14  No. 3, Ranga Raju, 6 May and 7 May 1845.
15  No. 2, Chakkaraya Chatambram, 21 April 1845.
16  No. 3, Ranga Raju, 7 May 1845.
17  No. 2, Chakkaraya Chatambram, 21 April 1845.
18  *Ibid.*, 22 April 1845.
19  *Ibid.*
20  *Ibid.*

21  *Ibid.*
22  *Ibid.*, 27 April 1845.
23  *Ibid.*
24  No. 3, Ranga Raju, 7 May 1845.
25  No. 2, Chakkaraya Chatambram, 22 April 1845. These terms are defined in John Whish's "Glossary of Revenue Terms," submitted to the Board of Revenue, 10 March 1826, and have been checked against similar entries in H. H. Wilson's *Glossary of Judicial and Revenue Terms* (London, 1855).
26  No. 1, Padmaraju Veeriah, 12 April 1845.
27  *Ibid.*, 17 April 1846.
28  No. 6, Abur Bungaru, 22 April 1845.
29  No. 26, Cherukuru *karnams*, 8, 15, and 20 May 1845.
30  *Ibid.*
31  *Ibid.*, 17 April 1846.
32  *Ibid.*
33  *Ibid.*, 20 May 1845.
34  *Ibid.*
35  *Ibid.*
36  Nos. 7 and 8, Punagapad *karnams*, 27 May and 6 June 1845.
37  Appendix E, "Extract of the Collector's Report with Enclosures."
38  *Ibid.*, "From Mr. Thomas Oakes' Reply, Dated 3rd September 1818 to the Board's Proceedings on his Report of the Settlement of the Minor Estates of Chikaloorpaud and Sattanapully for Fusly 1227. Enclosures: Account Statements for the Same." The pagoda mentioned here was a gold coin named for the Hindu temple or idol displayed on one face. In Madras, there were usually thirty-six fanams to the pagoda. The fanam, no longer used for exchange after 1833 was worth about four Madras rupees. There were eighty kasu to the fanam.
39  R. E. Frykenberg, *Guntur District, 1788–1848: A History of Local Influence and Central Authority in South India* (Oxford, 1965), pp. 231–41.
40  An amazing case of such behavior was that of Casee Chetty of Coimbatore. See R. Rickard, *India; or Facts to Illustrate the Character and Conditions of the Native Inhabitants with Suggestions for Reforming the Present System of Government* (London, 1829–32), II, 79–109.

# Index

Absenteeism: of Bakarganj landowners, 170
Abul Fazl, 57
Act I (1869), 147, 148, 153
Act X (1859), 145
*Agraharam*: defined, 224
Agrarian system: British view of, 176; stable factors in, 178–79; in Pallava-Chola period, 179–88; in Vijayanagar period, 189–96; under British, 196–208; transitions within, 197; within regions, 208–12
Agro-administrative units, 203
*Ain-i-Akbari*: account of revenue settlement in Gujarat, 22; and caste of zamindar, 25; land revenue in, 56–57
Akbar: dismissal of Ilhabad *chaudhuri*, 25; treatment of chieftains, 19; kingdom of, 56
Akkanappah, Nandigama, 235
Alfred Hall: construction of, 86
Alliance systems, 187
*Amaram*: defined, 191
*Amil*: defined, 58, 59; mentioned, 60, 62, 85
*Amin*: defined, 228; mentioned, 232, 234, 235, 236
Amsin pargana: conflict over subsettlement, 131–32
Anand, Mulkraj, 34
*Anchana kabuliyat*: defined, 234
*Andharia kotha*: defined, 173
Appiah, Punagapad, 238
Aristocrats: eighteenth century, 84; descendants of Mughal emperors, 86; traditional, 86; "landed," 159
Aristotle, 5
Arya Samaj, 50

*Arzi*: defined, 170
Asaf-ud-daula: and ceding of Banaras Province, 63
*Asami*: defined, 83, 105; castes of, in Ghazipur taluk, 106
*Asara*: defined, 218
Attalur, 234–35
Aurangzeb: and *mansabdars,* 19; death in 1707, 29; on *chaudhuris,* 25
Ayyavole, 176, 185, 187

Bachgoti Rajputs, 56
Baden-Powell, B. H.: concept of property, 40; mentioned, 13, 14
Badlapur: raja of, 60, 64, 84
*Bahi*: defined, 171
Bahraich District, 134, 135
Bailey, F. G., 10
Bakarganj District: zamindars in, 166, 169–74; land tenure in 1918, 169
Bakhsh, Murad, 25
*Bakhshi*: defined, 170
Ballia: raja of, 64
Balrampur, 135
Banaras: rajas of, 59, 61, 86; revenue collection in, 70; land sales in, 76
Baniyas, 71, 72, 73, 76, 79, 88
*Banth*: defined, 25
Baramahal, 223
Barlow, Robert, 95, 98, 99, 113
"Barons of Oudh": British concept of talukdars, 147, 148, 158
Barton, James, 69, 108
Barwar Rajputs: and Maniar *tappa,* 92–97; and Amsin pargana, 131–32; mentioned, 99, 105
Barwise, James, 109–10
Bashacharlu, Vetsha, 231, 234

Baviah, Andukur, 236
Beg, Kul Ali, 62
*Begar*: defined, 99
*Benami*: defined, 93
Bengal Presidency: land in, 5, 14, 82, 123, 166; Regulations (1793), 59, 69. *See also* Bakarganj District; Permanent Settlement
Bennett, W. C., 159
Bentham, Jeremy, 40
*Berij*: defined, 135
Bernier, François, 22, 42, 43
*Bhadralog*: defined, 143, 172
*Bhaiyachara*: as landholding system, 101, 102, 103
Bhimavaram, 235
Bhuiyas, 164, 166
Bhumihars: description of, 57, 71; in Ghazipur, 67; in Banaras and Jaunpur, 76; in Ballia, 93; mentioned, 68, 72, 73, 88
Bigha: varying size of, 5
Bihar: investment in land, 82
Bijaigrah, 85
Birhar, 135
Bisen Rajputs, 56
Bisipara, 10
Blackstone, William: on property, 40, 41, 48
Board of Agriculture, 10
Board of Revenue, 103, 110, 204
Bohannan, Paul, 3, 4, 6
Boorstin, Daniel, 41
*Brahmadeya*: defined, 177, 180; inscriptions of, 177; assemblies of, 181, 192, 206; mentioned, 186
Brahmans: *agraharam* and *brahmadeya* settlements, 177–86, 192, 206, 224; Deshastha Brahmans, 195; Niyogi Brahmans, 227–33
British Government: agrarian management, 6, 11, 55; and land ownership, 11, 13–14; land policy of, 12, 38, 53, 144, 223; administration, 48, 97, 138; employment of Muslims, 79; talukdari policy, 123–29ff; annexation of Oudh, 124–25; ryotwari policy, 217–24ff; zamindari policy, 218–19
British Indian Association: in Oudh,

148, 151, 152, 155, 157; in Calcutta, 152
British institutions: influence of, in India, 35, 51
Buchiah, Akkaraju, 238
Bundela, Singh-deo, 24
Bundelkhand Land Alienation Act, 12
Bungaru, Abur, 235, 236
Butler, Harcourt, 159
Buxar, Battle of, 86
Buzrugumedpur, 166

Canning, Lord Charles: and talukdars of Oudh, 48, 130, 152, 157; mentioned, 147
Canning College, 149, 150, 160
Capper, W., 135
Carnatic, 219
Carnegy, P., 133
Caste: in *Ain-i-Akbari*, 56; tripartite division of, 179. *See also* Landholding castes
Ceded Districts, 224
*Chak-milan*: defined, 173
Chandel Rajputs, 54, 56, 59
Chatambram, Chakkaraya, 227–28, 230, 232, 233
"Chaudhuri": prestige of title, 165
Cherkur, Butchannah, 235
Cherukuru, 236–39
*Chhappar-band*: defined, 110
*Chitrameli-periyanadu*: description of, 177; inscriptions of, 183, 184
Chola. *See* Pallava-Chola period
Cholamandalam, 184, 186, 203
Churn, Krishna, 80
Colebrooke, Edward, 81
Colebrooke, Henry, 81
Collector: of Dinajpur, 40; of Ghazipur, 76, 89; of Mirzapur, 83; of Banaras, 95; basic objectives of, 204; of Nellore, 221; in Tamil districts, 222; of Bellary, 224; of Guntur, 238, 243
Colvin Taluqdars' School, 149
Commercial families: examples of, in land buyers, 80
Congress Party: in 1930, 160
Coparceners, 101
Cornwallis, Lord Charles: and land ownership, 41–42, 46, 47, 165, 198

*Index* 251

Coromandel, 179
Corporate groups. *See* Pallava-Chola period
Cracroft, W., 69
Cultivators: types of, 90

*Dafadar*: defined, 228; mentioned, 231, 232
*Dastu chittha*: defined, 231; mentioned, 233, 236
*Dastu karchu chittha*: defined, 233
*Dastu zabitas*: defined, 233
Decennial Settlement, 164
Deshastha Brahmans, 195
Dhobi taluk, 64
Dinajpur District, 47
Director of Public Instruction: report on Canning College, 150
*Diwan*: defined, 170
*Dora*: defined, 220
Dube, Sheolal, 70, 79, 108, 110
Dubois, Abbé, 43
Duff, Alexander, 34, 69
Duncan, Jonathan: and land settlement, 63–66, 92; and Sengar Rajputs, 97–98; and Bengal Regulations, 101; mentioned, 58, 91
Duperron, Anquetil, 44
Dyarchy, 164

East India College, 44
East India Company: and land rights, 41; and agrarian integration, 198; revenue collection of, 202, 204, 217; mentioned, 39, 53, 63
Eastern legislation: principles of, 39
Eka agitation, 137
Elliot, Walter, 232
Elliot Report, 227
Elliott, H. E., 13
Encumbered Estates Act (1870), 147
Estate: and mahal, 6; concepts related to, 10–11, 13

Fair shares: meaning of, 5
Faizabad District, 133, 153
Famine: in Guntur, 236; and agricultural prices, 197
Feudalism: and Bakarganj zamindars, 171–73
French, P. C., 89

French Company, 198, 199

Garha Katanga, 21
Ghamar taluk: as case study, 91–92; mentioned, 96, 100, 112
Gir, Mohan Parsram, 83
Goldingham, John, 238, 243
Gonda District, 134, 135
*Grama Chittha*: defined, 233
*Grama kharchu*: defined, 239
*Gramawari* system: defined, 218, 219
Grant, James, 38, 42
*Gumashtah*: defined, 170, 171
Guntur District: *karnams* of, 14; famine in, 234; gifts received by district officers, 237; village accounts of, 239–43

Habib, Irfan: and agrarian system of India, 43, 47, 175–76; meaning of *sarraf*, 81
Haider Ali, 201, 202
Hastings, Warren, 58, 64, 86, 93
*Hawaladar*: defined, 168
Hobbes, Thomas: on land, 39
Home Authorities, 69
Hosein, Karmat, 128

*Idangai*: defined, 186, 187
*Ijaradar*: defined, 219; mentioned, 227, 231, 236
*Ijara-darkhast*: defined, 230
Ikauna estate, 134–35
Ilbert, Courtney, 41
"Improving zamindar": concept of, 11
*Inaam*: defined, 224. *See also Agraharam; Brahmadeya; Muaafi*
India: British views of, 33; British influence in, 33, 36; early European travelers in, 43; local sociopolitical behavior in, 246
Irrigation, 13, 178
Irvine, William, 70
Itinerant guilds, 176

Jack, J. C., 164
Jagir: revenue from, 19
Jagirdari system: crisis of, 26. *See also* Landholding
Jagirdars: defined, 64
*Jagiri-amildari* rights: defined, 62

Jahangir, 20, 24, 26
*Jama*: defined, 69; of Narwar taluk, 100
*Jamabandi*: defined, 93; mentioned, 222,
    229, 232, 236
Jones, Richard, 44, 46

*Kabuliyat*: defined, 65; mentioned, 101,
    231, 232
*Kachahri*: defined, 170
*Kadim*: defined, 220; mentioned, 221
Kahars, 171
*Kailu*: defined, 218
Kammas, 227, 228, 230, 231
Kantit, 61, 83
Kapradih estate, 135
*Kapu*: as caste name used as title, 220
Kapurthala, 134, 154
*Karnams*: defined, 227; in Guntur, 231,
    232, 234, 236, 237, 238; mentioned,
    15
*Kaul-namas*: defined, 232
Kayastha, 62, 76, 99
*Kazis*: defined, 61
*Khalisa*: defined, 18; mentioned, 20
*Kham*: defined, 95
*Kharaj*: defined, 45
*Khasara*: defined, 110
*Khewat*: defined, 105
*Khud-kasht* tenants: defined, 106–7;
    mentioned, 136, 145
Kisan Sabha movement, 146
*Kist*: defined, 229; mentioned, 231
*Kistabandi*: defined, 234
*Kistu zabitas*: defined, 233
Koeris, 105
Kohars, 61
Kolaslahs, 67
Kongumandalam, 184
Kopah, 67
Kosambi, 191
*Kottam*: defined, 184
Kottappah, Damacherla, 235
Kottappah, Krosur, 239
Krishnadevaraya, 191, 207
*Krishnarpan*: defined, 66
Kshatriyas, 151
*Kuchela*: defined, 232
Kunbis, 61
*Kunta*: defined, 231
Kurupad, 230, 231

Laborers: differentiated from ryots, 225
Lakhnessar pargana, 100, 112
Lal, Jassi, 81
*Lambardars*: defined, 102
Land: definitions and perceptions of,
    3–8; as village or mahal, 15; and
    law, 37, 49; "settlements," 38, 48,
    217; revenue from, 63, 217; auc-
    tions in Banaras, 71–78; lords of,
    101–4, 107; price of, 112; tenures,
    144, 167; reform, 176
Landholding: caste distribution of, 87;
    classification of, 144, 167; status of,
    212. *See also Gramawari; Inaam*;
    Jagirdari; *Mirasi; Muaafi*; Talukdari;
    Zamindari
Landholding castes. *See* Bachgoti Raj-
    puts; Baniyas; Barwar Rajputs;
    Bhumihars; Bisen Rajputs; Brahmans;
    Chandel Rajputs; Deshastha Brah-
    mans; Kammas; Kapus; Kayasthas;
    Koeri; Kohars; Kolaslahs; Kshatriyas;
    Kunbis; Majhwas; Mans Rajputs;
    Niyogi Brahmans; Rajputs; Rajus;
    Sat-Sudras
Land revenue: British policy toward,
    53, 144, 223; in *Ain-i-Akbari*, 56;
    difficulty in collecting, 60, 100, 238;
    rate per bigha, 61; districts for col-
    lection, 203, 207, 211
Landlords: types of, 101–4; opposition
    to, 107; fate of, under British, 123
*Lathi*: defined, 171
Lawrence, Sir John: and tenant rights,
    136, 153
Left-hand castes, 187
Lineage territory, 60
Locke, John: concept of property, 39

Macaulay, Thomas Babington, 40, 84
MacKenzie, Holt, 13, 53, 71
Macleod, John, 219, 223
*Madad-maash* grants: defined, 27
*Madadgar*: defined, 230
Madras Presidency: rise of provincial
    capital, 211; government of, 219;
    Nellore District, 221; North Arcot
    District, 221; South Arcot District,
    221; Tamil districts, 222; Bellary
    District, 224; Madura District, 224;
    Guntur District, 227–45; Board of

Revenue, 245. *See also* Ryotwari Settlement
Madura District, 224
Mahajans, 75
Mahal: concepts related to, 6-7; mentioned, 64, 69, 99
*Mahalwari*: defined, 219
*Mahasabha*: defined, 192; mentioned, 202, 206, 208
Maine, Sir Henry: on property, 7–8, 13, 14, 37
Majhwas, 67
Majzi, Mahlvi Abdulla, 79
*Makta*: defined, 218
Malcolm, John, 47
*Malguzar*: defined, 28
*Malikana*: defined, 26; mentioned, 28, 129
Maniar *tappa*: case study of, 92–97
*Maniyam*: defined, 231, 232
Mans Rajputs, 59
*Mansab*: defined, 19; mentioned, 21
*Mansabdars*: under the Mughals, 25; mentioned, 19, 20, 164
Manucci, Niccolo, 43
Manur Rao zamindari, 236
Maratha wars, 84
Marriage expenses: proposed reduction of, in Oudh, 150
Mayne, John D., 49
Measurement: Indian systems of, 5
Mehdona estate, 125, 131, 137
*Meli*: defined, 177
Merchants. *See Nanadesi*
Metcalfe, Charles, 47, 54
Mill, James, 42, 43, 44, 46
*Mirasi* privileges, 221, 222, 227, 235
*Mirasidari*, 209, 220, 222
Mirzapur, 55
Misra, B. B., 81
Mitter, Rajendra, 81
Mongra pargana, 67
Moreland, W. H., 13
Morrison, D. B., 59
*Mricchakatika*, 49
*Mridhas*: defined, 171
*Muaafi*: defined, 61, 107
Mughals: zamindars under, 18, 27; chieftains under, 19–24; emperors, 19, 25, 54, 56; in *Ain-i-Akbari*, 22,

25, 56–57; jagirdars in, 43; armies of, 56
*Muhuris*: defined, 176
Mukherjee, Babu Dakshinaranjun, 152, 153
Munro, Thomas, 198, 202, 205, 219, 223, 224
Muslims: Haveli Ghazipur, 67; jagirdars, 56; land to fakirs, 61; landlords, 67; *mridhas*, 171; power, 189
*Mutthadar*: defined, 218–19
Muzaffarnagar Association, 158

*Nadar*: defined, 239
*Nadu*: defined, 184
Nagiah, Polapeddi, 234
Naidu, Guddum Venkata, 228, 231
Naidu, Gunta Shashu, 231
Naidu, Venkata Narasu, 230
Naik, Sataram, 80
*Nanadesi*: defined, 176; activities of, 176–77
*Nankar*: defined, 25
Narain, Guraju Lakshmi, 235
Narain, V. A., 62
Narwar taluk: case study of, 99–102
*Nayaka*: defined, 192–93
*Nazrana*: defined, 172
Neave, John, 61
Nehru, Jawaharlal, 146
Nellore District, 221
Nelson, J. H., 45
"New men": as large revenue payers in Banaras (1885), 78; origins of, 79–80
Newill, Henry, 238
Niyogi Brahmans: as leaders of Rudravaram, 227, 228, 230, 233
Nizam of Allahabad, 85
Noniyas, 95
Norman Conquest, 37
North Arcot District, 221
North-Western Provinces, 84, 114
Noyes, C. Reinhold, 37
Nuclear areas: institutions of, 180, 184; as autonomous units, 186; as centers of Hindu civilization, 187; general characteristics of, 188

Oakes, Thomas, 243
Oldham, Wilton, 69, 86, 94

Orissa Campaign, 21
Oudh: Talukdari Settlement of, 12, 14, 38, 48, 50; mutiny in, 14, 48, 126–28; description of talukdars, 123, 124, 137; Sub-Settlement Act, 130; Rent Act, 136; marriage expenses in, 151; British Indian Association in, 148, 151, 152, 155, 157

*Paikasht*: defined, 105
Pallava-Chola period: agrarian integration during, 178–88; territorial units in, 184; political system of, 185
Pandit, Beni Ram, 64, 67
Pandyamandalam, 184
Pandyans, 189
Paramountcy: meaning of, 20
*Patel*: defined, 220, 221
*Patta*: defined, 63
*Patti*: defined, 65, 101
*Pattidar*: defined, 65; as agnate of zamindar, 91, 101
*Pattidari*: British view of, 101
*Periyanadu*: defined, 180
*Periyanadu* assemblies: characteristics of, 177; functions of, 181, 183; inscriptions of, 182–83; composition of, 206
Permanent Settlement: rationale for, 13–14, 35, 41; in Bengal, 14, 170; in Banaras, 82, 94; and land ownership, 163, 165–66, 170; in Bakarganj, 166, 167, 170; in Madras, 218–19
*Peshkash*: defined, 22; mentioned, 164, 200
*Pettendar*: defined, 228
*Poligar*: defined, 210
Poligar War, 201
*Praja*: defined, 172
Property: British concept of, 37–42; European view of, in India, 42–44; in Islamic law, 45. *See also* Land
Proprietary rights, 166, 218
Pungapad, 238
Punjab, 10
Puntulu, Janakiram, 236

*Rabia*: defined, 100
Rae, Abdhut, 91
Rai, Ganesh, 64
*Raiyat. See* Ryot; Ryotwari

Rajballabh, Raja, 164
Rajkumar Rajputs, 108
Rajputs: land control by, 57, 58; in Jaunpur District, 59, 60, 61, 99; in Katihar, 67; as landlords, 67; and land auctions, 76; in Monas, 85; in Kopachit and Saidpur Bhitri, 87
Raju, Achee, 239
Raju, Conda, 227, 228, 230
Rajus, 227–34
Ram, Mansa, 58, 59, 85
Ramachandrulu, Palarpurti, 236
Ramiah, Ananta, 227
Ramiah, Bellamconda, 234
Ramanah, Damacherla, 235
Ramannah, Paregai, 236
Rao, Nakkalapalli Subha, 232
Rao, Shashagiri Nyapati, 243
Rathkara, 185
*Rayalu*: defined, and compared with *rayatulu*, 220
*Razinama*: defined, 133
Read, Captain Alexander, 202, 219, 223, 224
Reade, E. A., 83
*Reddi*: caste name applied as title, 220, 223
Revenue. *See* Land revenue
Right-hand castes, 187
*Risaldar*: defined, 134
Roe, Thomas, 43, 200
Rozfzum, Raja, 20
Rudravaram, 227–33
Rutnam, Chamurthi Venkata, 227, 228, 230
Ryot: four grades of tenure of, 165; rights or privileges of, 220; upper and lower ryots, 225
Ryotwari Settlement: definition of, 218; disagreement about intent of, 220; and position of traditional leaders, 221; mentioned, 197, 219, 223, 225
Ryotwari System: land tenure under, 50; distinguished from zamindari and village lease systems, 218; origin of, 219; in operation, 224; revision of, 222, 225; under zamindari system, 225

*Sadar amins*: defined, 79
Sadar Divani Adalat, 93, 94

Saidpur Bhitri, 109, 112
*Sair*: defined, 109; mentioned, 65
*Samatdar*: defined, 227; mentioned, 230, 234, 235, 236, 245
*Sanad*: defined, 58; awarded talukdars of Oudh, 129, 147
Sangaram, Raja, 20
*Sarai*: defined, 25
*Sarkar*: defined, 81
*Sarraf*: defined, 81
*Sarrishtadar*: defined, 79; mentioned, 236
Sastri, K. A. Nilakanta, 180
Sat-Sudras, 194, 198
Sawai, Jai Singh, 24
*Sawar*: defined, 21
*Sazawal*: defined, 67; mentioned, 95, 96
Schumpeter, Joseph, 11
Sengar Rajputs, 60, 97, 99, 105
Sepoy Mutiny, 14, 48, 126–28
Settlement. *See* Decennial Settlement; *Jamabandi*; Permanent Settlement; Ryotwari Settlement; Talukdari Settlement
Shah, Firoz, 134
Shah, Mohammed, 24
*Shikami*: defined, 105–6
Singh, Ausan, 62, 86
Singh, Balwant, 60, 85
Singh, Bhao, 20
Singh, Bukhlawa, 125
Singh, Chait, 53, 62, 64, 86, 93
Singh, Darshan, 125
Singh, Devikanundan, 70, 79
Singh, Dip Narain, 81
Singh, Hanwant, 126
Singh, Jag Deo, 92
Singh, Jaswant, 20
Singh, Mahip Narayan, 58, 59, 62, 86
Singh, Man, 20, 21, 125, 133, 153, 154
Singh, Oudit Narayan, 98, 99
Singh, Rai Rai, 20
Singh, Rupan, 95
Singh, Saltanant, 110
Singh, Shivanaryan, 93, 94
Singh, Suraj, 22
*Sir* land: defined, 58, 90; mentioned, 92, 93, 94, 106, 109
Smith, E. P., 95
Soho and Company, 83

South Arcot District, 221
Southeast Asia: expeditions to 186, 221
Spear, Percival: and introduction of village police, 51
Stokes, Eric, 42, 197
Stokes, Huddleston, 238, 243
Subrenter, 235
Subsettlement: defined, 130; Oudh Sub-Settlement Act (1866), 130; problems of, 132, 133
Sudra cultivators: described, 223. *See also* Sat-Sudra
Sultanpur District, 136
Surs, 19

*Tahsildar*: defined, 70, 171
*Tahsildari* system: described, 71, 79, 84
*Takesim*: defined, 234, 237
Talukdar: mutiny in Oudh, 14, 48, 134; challenge to, 125; role of, 138; and community concern, 155; social ties of, 156; as "improving" landlords, 158; response to new order, 159. *See also* British Indian Association
Talukdari Settlement: compromise of, 12, 14; opposition to, 60, 126; subsettlement, 130; and succession law, 147; mentioned, 149, 150
Tamil literature, 173
Tanjore, 186
Tax farming, 202
Tenants: *asami* or permanent tenants, 85; tenants-at-will, 90; definitions of, 105–6; rights of, 110, 136, 145; passivity of, 137
Tenure: meaning of, 3–6. *See also* Landholding
Thevenot, Jean de, 43
Third Mysore War, 196, 202, 219
Thomson, James, 13
Thorner, Daniel: on agrarian structure, 175, 176
Tipu Sultan, 201, 202
Todar Mal, 22
Tondaimandalam, 179, 184, 186, 206
Townsend, Meredith, 33
Trevelyan, George, 13

Ungli taluk, 108

United Provinces, 10. *See also* Uttar Pradesh
Units of thought: definition of, 6
Utilitarians, 43
Uttar Pradesh, 75, 95, 97, 105. *See also* United Provinces

*Vakil*: defined, 85
*Valanadu*: defined, 184
*Valangai*: defined, 186
*Vandra*: defined, 229, 232
Vasireddy zamindari, 234, 235
Vedas, 224
Veeriah, Padmaraja, 234
Veerunah, Kora, 236
Vellalas, 179, 180
Venkayya, V., 180
Venkiah, Achee, 239
Vijayanagar period: and agrarian integration, 188–89; warrior rule during, 192–93; inscriptions of, 193; social organization in, 195
Villages: as organizing concept, 8; managers of, 13; leaders in, 13, 229, 234, 239; role of zamindars in, 64, 129; accounts of, in Guntur, 238–43. *See also* Landholding

Warriors: in nuclear areas, 186; in Vijayanagar period, 188–90; under British, 201–2
*Wasulbandi*: defined, 233
"White ant principle": described, 246
William the Conqueror, 37
Wilmot, E., 98
Wilson, H. H., 105
Wingfield, Charles, 127, 128, 130, 136, 153
Wyne, R. O., 70

Young, Arthur, 11

Zamania pargana, 102
Zamindar: Indian vs. European idea of, 11–12; role of, 14, 17, 20; functions of, 18, 24, 27, 28, 29; categories under Mughals, 18; rights of, 42, 63, 66, 90, 96, 164; abolition of, 53, 160; and revenue collection, 101, 109; associations of, 157; relationship to subordinates, 170–72; life style of, 173–74
Zamindari: as landholding system, 14, 218; differed from ryotwari and *gramawari*, 218–19
*Zimbadari* system: described, 172–73